"十二五"普通高等教育本科国家级规划教材

WORKBOOK FOR
LINGUISTICS:
A COURSE BOOK (FIFTH EDITION)

语言学教程(第五版)练习册

胡壮麟 ◎ 主　编
姜望琪　钱军 ◎ 副主编

北京大学出版社
PEKING UNIVERSITY PRESS

图书在版编目（CIP）数据

语言学教程（第五版）练习册 / 胡壮麟主编 . —北京：北京大学出版社，2017.7
（21 世纪英语专业系列教材）
ISBN 978-7-301-28545-9

Ⅰ.①语… Ⅱ.①胡… Ⅲ.①英语—语言学—高等学校—习题集 Ⅳ.① H31-44

中国版本图书馆 CIP 数据核字（2017）第 158926 号

书　　名	语言学教程（第五版）练习册 YUYANXUE JIAOCHENG（DIWUBAN）LIANXICE
著作责任者	胡壮麟　主编　姜望琪　钱　军　副主编
责 任 编 辑	刘文静
标 准 书 号	ISBN 978-7-301-28545-9
出 版 发 行	北京大学出版社
地　　址	北京市海淀区成府路 205 号　100871
网　　址	http://www.pup.cn　　新浪微博：@北京大学出版社
电 子 信 箱	liuwenjing008@163.com
电　　话	邮购部 62752015　发行部 62750672　编辑部 62754382
印 刷 者	三河市博文印刷有限公司
经 销 者	新华书店
	650 毫米 ×980 毫米　16 开本　12 印张　200 千字 2017 年 7 月第 1 版　2022 年 7 月第 7 次印刷
定　　价	30.00 元

未经许可，不得以任何方式复制或抄袭本书之部分或全部内容。
版权所有，侵权必究
举报电话：010-62752024　电子信箱：fd@pup.pku.edu.cn
图书如有印装质量问题，请与出版部联系，电话：010-62756370

前　言

今年年初，由姜望琪教授和钱军教授牵头完成了北大版《语言学教程》第五版的修订工作，我写了前言。转眼之间，配合《教程》第五版的练习册修订稿又呈现案头。我对两位教授和北京大学出版社刘文静女士等编辑人员的辛勤劳动深表敬意。

在《教程》第五版的前言中我曾经提到习主席有关"一带一路"的创议和对外语人才的需求；科学技术，特别是信息技术的迅猛发展；机器翻译正确率和普及率的提高；教育系统各个层次的改革，等等，所有这些都表明修订《语言学教程》的重要性和紧迫性。一本教材的生命在于它能与时共生、与时俱进，为教师和同学更好地服务。

显然，上述这个认识，也适用于《语言学教程（第五版）练习册》的修订，受到各章作者和出版社的重视。正是由于他们的相互督促、相互配合，使本项任务胜利完成。

第五版练习册修订的内容包括以下各个方面：

——做重大改动，重新排版或部分改版：第 2,6 章。
——部分改动：第 7,8,9 章。
——增加习题及答案：第 3,4,7,11,12 章。
——删除部分习题及答案：第 3,10 章。
——改动答案：第 5 章。
——增加术语解释：第 10 章。
——增加文献：第 4,5,7,8 章。
——纠正打印和文字错误：第 5,9,10 章。

由于时间紧迫和水平有限，教师和同学在使用中可能会有这样那样的意见，或发现某个方面的错误，希望能及时向我们反馈。我们会认真听取大家的意见，继续完成《练习册》的修订工作。

胡壮麟
2017 年 7 月 1 日

CONTENTS

Questions and Exercises ··· (1)

Part I 英文练习及参考答案 ··· (1)

Chapter 1　Invitations to Linguistics ······················· (1)
Chapter 2　Speech Sounds ································· (7)
Chapter 3　Words and Morphology ·························· (15)
Chapter 4　From Word to Text ····························· (24)
Chapter 5　Meaning ·· (30)
Chapter 6　Language and Cognition ························ (36)
Chapter 7　Language, Culture, and Society ················ (53)
Chapter 8　Language in Use ································ (60)
Chapter 9　Language and Literature ······················· (65)
Chapter 10　Language and Computer ······················· (69)
Chapter 11　Second and Foreign Language Teaching ········ (74)
Chapter 12　Theories and Schools of Modern
　　　　　　Linguistics ·································· (78)

Part II 中文练习及参考答案 ··· (93)

第一章　语言学导论 ·· (93)
第二章　语音 ·· (98)
第三章　单词与形态学 ····································· (105)
第四章　句法:从语词到篇章 ································ (112)
第五章　意义 ··· (119)
第六章　语言与认知 ······································· (124)
第七章　语言 文化 社会 ··································· (136)
第八章　语言的使用 ······································· (140)
第九章　语言与文学 ······································· (145)
第十章　语言和计算机 ····································· (148)
第十一章　二语教学与外语教学 ····························· (151)
第十二章　现代语言学理论与流派 ··························· (154)

Questions and Exercises

Chapter 1 Invitations to Linguistics

1. Define the following terms.

design features	function	synchronic
diachronic	prescriptive	descriptive
arbitrariness	duality	displacement
phatic communion	metalanguage	macrolinguistics
competence	performance	*langue*
parole		

2. Consult at least four introductory linguistics textbooks (not dictionaries), and copy the definitions of "language" that each gives. After carefully comparing the definitions, write a paper discussing which points recur and explaining the significance of the similarities and differences among the definitions.

3. Can you think of some words in English which are onomatopoeic?

4. Do you think that onomatopoeia indicates a non-arbitrary relationship between form and meaning?

5. A story by Robert Louis Stevenson contains the sentence "As the night fell, the wind rose." Could this be expressed as "As the wind rose, the night fell?" If not, why? Does this indicate a degree of non-arbitrariness about word order? (Bolinger, 1981:15)[1]

6. Does the traffic light system have duality? Can you explain by drawing a simple graph?

7. The recursive nature of language provides a theoretical basis for the creativity of language. Can you write a recursive sentence following the example in section 1.3.3?

8. Communication can take many forms, such as sign, speech, body language and facial expression. Do body language and facial expression share or lack the distinctive properties of human language?

9. Do you agree with the view that no language is especially simple?

10. What do you think of Bertrand Russell's observation of the dog language: "No matter how eloquently a dog may bark, he cannot tell you that his parents were poor but honest"? Are you familiar with any type of ways animals communicate among themselves and with human beings?

---

[1] 本书为《语言学教程》(第五版)的配套练习册,书中涉及文献请参照《语言学教程》(第五版)的参考文献部分。

11. Can you mention some typical expressions of phatic communion in Chinese? There is a dialogue between Mrs. P and Mrs. Q on p. 12. When someone sneezes violently, do you say anything of the nature of phatic communion? Have you noticed your parents or grand-parents say something special on such an occasion?
12. There are many expressions in language which are metalingual or self-reflexives, namely, talking about talk and think about thinking, for instance, *to be honest*, *to make a long story short*, *come to think of it*, *on second thought*, can you collect a few more to make a list of these expressions? When do we use them most often?
13. Comment on the following prescriptive rules. Do you think they are acceptable?
    (A) It is I.
    (B) It is me.
    You should say A instead of B because "be" should be followed by the nominative case, not the accusative according to the rules in Latin.
    (A) Who did you speak to?
    (B) Whom did you speak to?
    You should say B instead of A.
    (A) I haven't done anything.
    (B) I haven't done nothing.
    B is wrong because two negatives make a positive.
14. The prescriptivism in grammar rules has now shifted to prescriptions in choice of words. In the "guidelines on anti-sexist language" issued by the British sociological association, some guidelines are listed below. Do you think they are descriptive and prescriptive? What's your comment on them?
    (1) Do not use *man* to mean humanity in general. Use *person*, *people*, *human beings*, *men and women*, *humanity* and *humankind*.
    (2) colored: This term is regarded as outdated in the UK and should be avoided as it is generally viewed as offensive to many black people.
    (3) civilized: This term can still carry racist overtones which derive from a colonialist perception of the world. It is often associated with social Darwinist thought and is full of implicit value judgments and ignorance of the history of the non-industrialized world.
15. Why is the distinction between competence and performance important in linguistics? Do you think the line can be neatly drawn between them? How do you like the concept communicative competence?
16. Which branch of linguistics do you think will develop rapidly in China and why?
17. The following are some well-known ambiguous sentences in syntactic studies of language. Can you disambiguate them?
    (1) *The chicken is too hot to eat.*
    (2) *Flying planes can be dangerous.*
18. There are many reasons for the discrepancy between competence and performance in normal language users. Can you think of some of them?
19. What do these two quotes reveal about the different emphasis or perspectives

of language studies?

> A human language is a system of remarkable complexity. To come to know a human language would be an extraordinary intellectual achievement for a creature not specifically designed to accomplish this task. A normal child acquires this knowledge on relatively slight exposure and without specific training. He can then quite effortlessly make use of an intricate structure of specific rules and guiding principles to convey his thoughts and feelings to others,... Thus language is a mirror of mind in a deep and significant sense. It is a product of human intelligence, created anew in each individual by operations that lie far beyond the reach of will or consciousness. (Noam Chomsky: *Reflections on Language*. 1975: 4)
>
> It is fairly obvious that language is used to serve a variety of different needs, but until we examine its grammar there is no clear reason for classifying its uses in any particular way. However, when we examine the meaning potential of language itself, we find that the vast numbers of options embodied in it combine into a very few relatively independent "networks"; and these networks of options correspond to certain basic functions of language. This enables us to give an account of the different functions of language that is relevant to the general understanding of linguistic structure rather than to any particular psychological or sociological investigation. (M. A. K. Halliday: 1970: 142)

20. You may be familiar with the following proverbs. How do you perceive them according to the arbitrariness and conventionality of language:
    The proof of the pudding is in the eating.
    Let sleeping dogs lie.
    You can't make a silk purse out of a sow's ear.
    Rome was not built in a day.
    When in Rome, do as the Romans do.
    All roads lead to Rome.
21. Give examples of situations in which a usage generally considered non-standard (e. g. ain't) would be acceptable, even appropriate.
22. The following are some book titles of linguistics. Can you judge the synchronic or diachronic orientation just from the titles?
    (1) *English Examined: Two Centuries of Comment on the Mother-Tongue*
    (2) *Protean Shape: A Study in Eighteenth-century Vocabulary and Usage.*
    (3) *Pejorative Sense Development in English.*
    (4) *The Categories and Types of Present-Day English Word-Formation.*
    (5) *Language in the Inner City: Studies in the Black English Vernacular.*

Chapter 2 Speech Sounds

1. Define the following terms:

phonetics	articulatory phonetics	phonology
gesture	speech organs	voicing
International Phonetic Alphabet	consonant	vowel
manner of articulation	place of articulation	Cardinal Vowels
semi-vowel	vowel glide	phoneme
allophone	complementary distribution	assimilation

Elsewhere Condition	syllable	Maximal Onset Principle
sonority scale	stress	intonation
tone	tone sandhi	OCP

2. Give the description of the following sound segments in English.
   1) [ð]   2) [ʃ]   3) [ŋ]   4) [d]   5) [p]
   6) [k]   7) [l]   8) [ɪ]   9) [uː]   10) [ɒ]

3. Give the IPA symbols for the sounds that correspond to the descriptions below.
   1) voiceless labiodental fricative   2) voiced postalveolar fricative
   3) palatal approximant   4) voiceless glottal fricative
   5) voiceless alveolar stop   6) high-mid front unrounded vowel
   7) high central rounded vowel   8) low front rounded vowel
   9) low-mid back rounded vowel   10) high back rounded tense vowel

4. Transcribe the following sentences into normal orthography.
   1) ɒn ə klɪə deɪ jʊ kn siː fə maɪlz
   2) səm piːpl θɪŋk ðət fɜːst ɪmpɹɛʃnz kaʊnt fə ə lɒt

5. Here is the official IPA website. See what you can find there and then report to your class.
   https://www.internationalphoneticassociation.org/

6. Discuss the following questions.
   1) What organs are involved in speech production?
   2) Why did George Bernard Shaw say he could spell the word *fish* as *ghoti*?
   3) How is the description of consonants different from that of vowels?
   4) To what extent is phonology related to phonetics and how do they differ?
   5) The pronunciation of *tell* is [teɫ], but that of *teller* is [telə]. Discuss why the phoneme /l/ is realized as [ɫ] and [l] respectively in this situation.

7. The relationship between the spelling and pronunciation of English words is not always simple. Examine the following words and discuss in what ways the relationship is complex (irregular) and if there are any regularities. Use other examples to illustrate your discussion if necessary.

   > although, beauty, bomb, ceiling, charisma, choice, cough, exercise, hour, light, phase, quiche, quake, sixteen, thigh, tongue, whose, writhe

8. In some dialects of English the following words have different vowels, as shown by the phonetic transcription. Based on these data, answer the questions that follow.

A		B		C	
bite	[bʌɪt]	bide	[baɪd]	tie	[taɪ]
rice	[rʌɪs]	rise	[ɹaɪz]	by	[baɪ]
type	[tʌɪp]	bribe	[bɹaɪb]	sigh	[saɪ]
wife	[wʌɪf]	wives	[waɪvz]	die	[daɪ]
tyke	[tʌɪk]	time	[taɪm]	why	[waɪ]

   1) How may the classes of sounds that end the words in columns A and B be characterized?
   2) How do the words in column C differ from those in columns A and B?

3) Are [ʌɪ] and [aɪ] in complementary distribution? Give your reasons.
4) What are the phonetic transcriptions of (a) *life* and (b) *lives*?
5) What would the phonetic transcriptions of the following words be?
   (a) trial   (b) bike   (c) lice   (d) fly   (e) mine
6) State the rule that will relate the phonemic representations to the phonetic transcriptions of the words given above.
(Based on Fromkin, et al. 2014: 268—269)

9. The following words contain different forms of the negative prefix *in-*. Group the data according to the variants and try to determine which kinds of base word take which kinds of prefix variant and what kind of mechanism is responsible for the variation. Formulate a rule and then test it against words that are formed in this way but are not mentioned here.

irregular	incomprehensible	illiterate
ingenious	inoffensive	inharmonic
impenetrable	illegal	incompetent
irresistible	impossible	irresponsible
immobile	illogical	indifferent
inconsistent	innumerable	inevitable

(Based on Plag, 2003: 42)

10. In Old English, the fricatives /f/, /þ, ð/, and /s/ each represented two separate sounds:

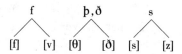

Voicing is predictable by context. Study the words below and state the rule.

sæt	[sæt]	'sat'
hūs	[huːs]	'house'
ēast	[æːəst]	'east'
cyssan	[kyssɑn]	'to kiss'
hlāf	[hlɑːf]	'loaf'
cēosan	[tʃeːozɑn]	'choose'
heofon	[hɛovɔn]	'heaven'
Wuldorfæder	[wʊldɔrvædɛr]	'Father of Glory, God'
onstal	[ɔnstɑl]	'supply'
hrōfe	[hroːvɛ]	'roof'
eorðan	[ɛorðɑn]	'earth'
æfter	[æftɛr]	'after'
ēðel	[eːðɛl]	'native lord'
nīþ	[niːθ]	'hatred'
niþer	[nɪðɛr]	'downward'
nīeheard	[niːθhæərd]	'daring'

(Based on Fennell, 2001: 60-64 and Mitchell & Robinson, 2002: § 9)

11. Project Topics
    1) Estuary English (EE) is a name given to the form(s) of English widely spoken in and around London and, more generally, in the southeast

of England-along the river Thames and its estuary. The websites below contain much information about this variety of English. Find out what EE is like.

http://www.phon.ucl.ac.uk/home/estuary
http://www.ic.arizona.edu/~lsp/EstuaryEnglish.html

See also Cruttenden (2014: Chapter 7) for some discussion on the changes of British English pronunciation.

2) Based on your observation of Chinese students learning to speak English, discuss some of the typical phonetic and phonological difficulties they may encounter and make suggestions as to how you may help them tackle the problems. Make use of, as far as possible, what you have learned in this chapter.

3) The discussion of phonological processes and phonological rules in this chapter are all illustrated with examples from English. Consider relevant facts in Chinese (Mandarin or a local dialect/accent) and see if they work in the same way.

Chapter 3 Words and Morphology

1. Define the following terms.

morpheme	compound	inflection
affix	derivation	root
allomorph	stem	bound morpheme
free morpheme	grammatical word	lexical word
closed-class	open-class	blending
acronym	back-formation	

2. Complete the words with suitable negative prefixes.

    a. removable   b. formal   c. practicable   d. sensible
    e. tangible   f. logical   g. regular   h. proportionate
    i. effective   j. elastic   k. ductive   l. rational
    m. syllabic   n. normal   o. workable   p. written
    q. usual   r. thinkable   s. human   t. relevant
    u. editable   v. mobile   w. legal   x. discreet

3. Read the following paragraph and list all the function words you can find. (Include all forms of *be* as function words.) Give the percentage of function words in this paragraph.

    > She was a small woman, old and wrinkled. When she started washing for us, she was already past seventy. Most Jewish women of her age were sickly, weak, broken in body. But this washwoman, small and thin as she was, possessed a strength that came from generations of peasant ancestors. Mother would count out to her a bag of laundry that had accumulated over several weeks. She would lift the heavy bag, load it on her narrow shoulders, and carry it the long way home.

4. "A free form which consists entirely of two or more lesser free forms...is a phrase. A free form which is not a phrase is a word. A word, then,...is a minimum free form" (Bloomfield, 1935: 178). Answer the following questions:

(a) The term "word" is ambiguous. What kind of words is Bloomfield's definition intended to cover?
(b) Are there any traditionally recognized words of English (in the appropriate sense of "word") that fail to satisfy Bloomfield's definition?
(c) What other criteria have been involved in the definition of the word?
5. Find the sources of the following blends. In cases where the dictionary does not provide the answer, your own ingenuity will be your guide.
(a) bash (b) smash (c) glimmer
(d) flimmer (e) clash (f) flare
(g) brunch (h) motel (i) transistor
(j) medicare (k) workaholic (l) spam
(m) telethon (n) aerobicise (o) chunnel
(p) chortle (q) bit (r) modem
(s) guestimate (t) threepeat
6. Determine the historically accurate etymology of the words in the first column, and underline the correct one in the second or in the third column.

Column 1	Column 2	Column 3
(a) hangnail	aching nail	hanging nail
(b) female	a male's companion	little woman
(c) crayfish	crawling fish	crab
(d) shamefaced	face reflecting shame	bound by shame
(e) Jordan almond	imported almond	garden almond
(f) sparrowgrass	a genus of herbs	bird nesting in grass
(g) belfre	bell tower	bell
(h) bridegroom	a woman is just or about to be married	a man is just, or about to be married
(i) muskrat (Algonquian: musquash)	a large rat-like animal	a large musk deer
(j) woodchuck (Algonquian: otchek)	a north American goat	a north American marmot

7. Determine the original term from which the following words were back-formed.
(a) asset (b) burgle (c) enthuse
(d) greed (e) hush (f) automate
(g) donate (h) escalate (i) homesick
(j) peddle (k) diagnose (l) tuit
(m) amusing (n) loaf (o) self-destruct
(p) attrit (q) hairdress (r) emote
(s) drowse (t) frivol
8. Identify the immediate etymological source of the following words. (For example, the immediate source of "meaning" is French, although the more remote source is Latin.)
(a) air (b) barbecue (c) bungalow
(d) cola (e) gusto (f) babel
(g) buffalo (h) cocoa (i) costume
(j) ill (k) mule (l) decreed

(m) revolution   (n) benevolent   (o) lie
(p) topic   (q) subject   (r) theme
(s) wind   (t) datum

9. If there are two affixes -*ly*, one producing adjectives and the other attaching to adjectives to produce adverbs, can we find words with both of these affixes?
10. Make a list of nouns from the following words that -*s* can attach to.
    Epiphany   foot   hat   house
    kitchen   ox   phenomenon   region
    sheep   tomato
11. Are there any affixes that attach (relatively) productively to verbs, contribute no or very specific meaning, and do not change category?
12. Some people claim that Chinese is a language with no morphology. Do you agree with this claim and why?
13. A compound like blackbird can consist of an adjective and a noun, while a nominal phrase can have the same components, for example, black tie. Now ignore the lack of space between the two words in English compounds, what distinguishes a compound like blackbird from nominal phrases like black tie?

Chapter 4　From Word to Text

1. Define the following terms.
   syntax   co-occurrence   construction
   constituent   endocentric   exocentric
   subordination   category   coordinate
   agreement   embedding   recursiveness
   grammatical subject & logical subject   cohesion   coherence
2. Indicate the category of each word in the following sentences (Hint: It may help to refer back to section 4.2.2)
   (1) The instructor told the students to study.
   (2) The customer requested for a cold beer.
   (3) The pilot landed the jet.
   (4) These dead trees must be removed.
   (5) That glass suddenly broke.
3. Put brackets around the immediate constituents in each sentence.
   Ex. ((I) ((rode) (back))) ((when) ((it) ((was) (dark)))).
   (a) The boy was crying.
   (b) Shut the door.
   (c) Open the door quickly.
   (d) The happy teacher in that class was beaming away.
   (e) He bought an old car with his first pay cheque.
4. For each of the underlined constructions or word groups, do the following.
   —State whether it is headed or non-headed.
   —If headed, state its headword.
   —Name the type of constructions.

Ex. His son <u>will be keenly competing</u>.
Answer: headed, headword—competing; verbal group
(a) <u>Ducks quack</u>.
(b) The ladder <u>in the shed</u> is long enough.
(c) I saw a bridge <u>damaged beyond repair</u>.
(d) <u>Singing hymns</u> is forbidden in some countries.
(e) <u>His handsome face</u> appeared in the magazine.
(f) A lady <u>of great beauty</u> came out.
(g) He enjoys <u>climbing high mountains</u>.
(h) <u>The man nodded patiently</u>.
(i) A man <u>roused by the insult</u> drew his sword.

5. In the pairs of sentences that follow, indicate with "N" those that need not follow a particular order when they are joined by "and". Indicate with "Y" those that need to be ordered. Aside from the examples below, in your opinion, which type is more relevant.

　　　＿＿＿＿＿(a) The sun is shining.
　　　　　　　　　The wind is blowing.
　　　＿＿＿＿＿(b) Susie went to sleep.
　　　　　　　　　She had a dream.
　　　＿＿＿＿＿(c) John came in.
　　　　　　　　　He closed the door.
　　　＿＿＿＿＿(d) He came in.
　　　　　　　　　John closed the door.
　　　＿＿＿＿＿(e) She felt embarrassed.
　　　　　　　　　She blushed.
　　　＿＿＿＿＿(f) The sky is blue.
　　　　　　　　　The grass is green.
　　　＿＿＿＿＿(g) He walked away.
　　　　　　　　　He got up.
　　　＿＿＿＿＿(h) He enjoyed the meal.
　　　　　　　　　He loved the pickles.

6. Combine the following pairs of sentences. Make the second sentence of each pair into a relative clause, and then embed it into the first.
   (a) The comet appears every twenty years. Dr. Okada discovered the comet.
   (b) Everyone respected the quarterback. The quarterback refused to give up.
   (c) The most valuable experiences were small ones. I had the experiences on my trip to Europe.
   (d) Children will probably become abusers of drugs or alcohol. Children's parents abuse alcohol.
   (e) Many nations are restricting emissions of noxious gases. The noxious gases threaten the atmosphere.

7. Use examples to illustrate different ways to extend syntactic constituents.

8. Mark the underlined parts of the sentences in Ex. 4—37 with the terms such as participial phrase, gerundial phrase, and so on.
   (a) The best thing would be <u>to leave early</u>.
   (b) It's great <u>for a man to be free</u>.

(c) Having finished their task, they came to help us.
   (d) Xiao Li being away, Xiao Wang had to do the work.
   (e) Filled with shame, he left the house.
   (f) All our savings gone, we started looking for jobs.
   (g) It's no use crying over spilt milk.
   (h) Do you mind my opening the window?
9. Explain the main characteristics of subjects in English.

Chapter 5   Meaning

1. Define the following terms.

conceptual meaning	denotation
connotation	reference
sense	synonymy
gradable antonymy	complementary antonymy
converse antonymy	relational opposites
hyponymy	superordinate
semantic component	compositionality
propositional logic	proposition
predicate logic	logical connective

2. Read the following passage from *Through the Looking Glass* by Lewis Carroll, and discuss the meaning of *mean* in it.

   > "Don't stand chattering to yourself like that," Humpty Dumpty said, looking at her for the first time, "but tell me your name and your business."
   > "My name is Alice, but—"
   > "It's a stupid name enough!" Humpty Dumpty interrupted impatiently. "What does it *mean*?"
   > "Must a name *mean* something?" Alice asked doubtfully.
   > "Of course it must," Humpty Dumpty said with a short laugh: "my name *means* the shape I am—and a handsome shape it is, too. With a name like yours, you might be any shape, almost."

3. Analyse the poem below from the semantic point of view, taking a special account of sense relations.

	Coloured
Dear White Fella	You White Fella
Couple things you should know—	When you born, you pink
When I born, I black	When you grow up, you white
When I grow up, I black	When you go in sun, you red
When I go in sun, I black	When you cold, you blue
When I cold, I black	When you scared, you yellow
When I scared, I black	When you sick, you green
When I sick, I black	And when you die you grey
And when I die, I still black	And you have the cheek
	To call me coloured?

4. Do the following according to the requirements.
   (a) Write out the synonyms of the following words:
       youth; automobile; remember; purchase; vacation; big

(b) Give the antonyms of the following words, and point out in which aspect the two of each pair are opposite:
dark, boy, hot, go
(c) Provide two or more related meanings for the following:
bright, to glare, a deposit, plane
5. Some people maintain that there are no true synonyms. If two words mean really the same, one of them will definitely die out. An example often quoted is the disuse of the word *wireless*, which has been replaced by *radio*. Do you agree? In general what type of meaning we are talking about when we say two words are synonymous with each other?
6. In the text, we did not mention antonyms like "friendly: unfriendly", "honest: dishonest", "normal: abnormal", "frequent: infrequent", "logical: illogical" and "responsible: irresponsible". Which type of antonymy do they belong to?
7. The British linguist F. R. Palmer argues in his Semantics (p. 97) that "there is no absolute distinction between [gradable antonyms and complementary antonyms]. We can treat *male/female*, *married/single*, *alive/dead* as gradable antonyms on occasions. Someone can be *very male or more married and certainly more dead than alive*." Comment on it.
8. 姜望琪 (1991: 79) claims that "To some extent, we can say that any two words of the same part of speech may become antonyms, as long as the meaning difference between them is what needs to be emphasized in the particular context." He uses the two sentences below as examples. What do you think of the claim?
You have to *peel* a raw potato but you can *skin* a boiled one.
He's no *statesman*, but a mere *politician*.
9. What is the superordinate term in the following list?
man, stallion, male, boy, bull, boar
10. Basing yourself on the model of componential analysis, analyze the following words:
teacher, typewriter, chopsticks
11. Circle the two-place predicates in the list below:
attack (verb), die (verb), between, put, love (verb), in, cat, elephant, forget
12. Translate the following logical forms into English, where a=Ann, b=Bill, c=Carol, L=like, M=mother, and x and y are variables which may be translated as "someone", "anyone" or "everyone" depending on the quantifier:
(a) M (a, b)
(b) L (b, c) & L (c, b)
(c) L (a, b) & ~ L (a, c)
(d) ∃x (L (x, b))
(e) ~ ∀x (L (x, c))
(f) ~ ∃x (∀y (L (y, x)))

Chapter 6 Language and Cognition

1. Define the following terms.
   - cognition
   - cognitive linguistics
   - holophrastic stage
   - three-word utterances
   - cohort model
   - race model
   - parallel model
   - construal
   - figure-ground alignment
   - landmark
   - subordinate level category
   - metaphor
   - ontological metaphors
   - generic space
   - ICMs
   - psycholinguistics
   - language acquisition
   - two-word stage
   - connectionism
   - interactive model
   - serial model
   - resonance model
   - construal operations
   - trajectory
   - basic level category
   - image schema
   - metonymy
   - structural metaphors
   - blend space

2. What does psycholinguistics study and what are the subjects of it?
3. Describe the stages of first language acquisition.
4. Illustrate the models explaining the process of word recognition.
5. What are the factors influencing sentence comprehension?
6. Explain the various aspects of process of language production.
7. What is the definition of cognitive linguistics?
8. Describe the three categories of conceptual metaphors.
9. Illustrate the model of blending theory.
10. Analyze the following paragraph by image schemas.

    You wake out of a deep sleep and peer out from beneath the covers into your room. You gradually emerge out of your stupor, pull yourself out from under the covers, climb into your robe, stretch out your limbs, and walk in a daze out of the bedroom and into the bathroom. You look in the mirror and see your face staring out at you. You reach into the medicine cabinet, take out the toothpaste, squeeze out some toothpaste, put the toothbrush into your mouth, brush your teeth in a hurry, and rinse out your mouth. At breakfast you perform a host of further in-out moves— pouring out the coffee, setting out the dishes, putting the toast in the toaster, spreading out the jam on the toast, and on and on. Once you are more awake you might even get lost in the newspaper, might enter into a conversation, which leads to your speaking out on some topic.

Chapter 7 Language, Culture, and Society

1. Define the following terms.
   - Anthropological Study of Linguistics
   - Communicative Competence
   - Nida's Classification of Culture
   - Communication
   - Context of Situation
   - Ethnography of Communication

FLB	FLN
Gender Difference	Linguistic Determinism
Linguistic Relativity	Linguistic Sexism
Six-Person System	Speech Community
SPEAKING	Sapir-Whorf Hypothesis
Sociolinguistics of Language	Sociolinguistics of Society
Tripartite Model for Successful Communication	
Variationist Linguistics	Women Register

2. What are some important contributions that sociolinguistics has made to linguistic studies?
3. Why do we need to teach culture in our language classroom?
4. As students of linguistics, how should we understand the relationships between functionalism and formalism?
5. Over the past two decades, hundreds of new words have rushed into the daily life of Chinese people. Try to collect a bunch of these words, examine the context of their usage, and provide a feasible explanation to their booming.
6. It has been widely recognized that the so-called "magic words" like "thank you" and "please" are more frequently used in English speaking society than they will in Chinese speaking society. One of explanations for this phenomenon may go like this: Look, these foreigners are really more polite than our countrymen. Try to use your knowledge in sociolinguistics and make some comments on this understanding of cultural differences.
7. What will you say to a statement like "one culture's meat is another culture's poison"?
8. Why should language instructors look to sociolinguistics?
9. For linguistic studies of the new century, what is the significance of the division made between the faculty of language in the broad sense (FLB) and in the narrow sense (FLN)?
10. As we all know, compared with the rapid change in vocabulary, address forms in a language usually keep constant and stable. However, a dramatic change did take place in the address system of Chinese recently. A typical case in this respect is the use of *qin* (亲) and its plural form *qinmen* (亲们) as address forms. As a student of sociolinguistics, how are you going to explain this phenomenon?

Chapter 8 Language in Use

1. Define the following terms.

performative	constative
locutionary act	illocutionary act
perlocutionary act	cooperative principle
conversational implicature	entailment
ostensive communication	communicative principle of relevance
relevance (as a comparative notion)	(Horn's) Q-principle
R-principle	division of pragmatic labor
Levinson's three heuristics	

2. Consider the following dialogue between a man and his daughter. Try to explain the illocutionary force in each of the utterances.

   [The daughter walks into the kitchen and takes some popcorn.]
   Father: I thought you were practicing your violin.
   Daughter: I need to get the [violin] stand.
   Father: Is it under the popcorn?

3. If you ask somebody "Can you open the door?" he answers "Yes" but does not actually do it, what would be your reaction? Why? Try to see it in the light of speech act theory.

4. On 14 January, 1993, US President-elect Bill Clinton spoke to journalists in the wake of rumours that he might go back on some of his promises made during the electoral campaign. When cornered by some insistent journalists, he came up with the following statement.

    I think it would be foolish for the President of the United States, for any President of the United States, not to respond to changing circumstances. Every President of the United States, as far as I know, and particularly those who have done a good job, have known how to respond to changing circumstances. It would clearly be foolish for a President of the United States to do otherwise.

    Some linguists argue that campaign speeches, like all political speeches, are one of the occasions on which the CP and its maxims are suspended, do you agree? Can you think of any other similar occasion?

5. "The Club" is a device for blocking an automobile's steering wheel, thus protecting the car from being stolen. And one of its ads reads:

   THE CLUB!
   Anti-theft device for cars
   POLICE SAY:
   'USE IT'
   OR LOSE IT

    In terms of the Gricean theory, what maxim is exploited here? Find two Chinese ads of the same type.

6. A is reading the newspaper. When B asks "What's on television tonight?" he answers "Nothing." What does A mean in normal situations? Think of two situations in which this interpretation of "Nothing" will be cancelled.

7. Of the following pairs of sentences, say whether A entails B in each case.
   (1) A. John is a bachelor.
       B. John is a man.
   (2) A. Janet plays the fiddle.
       B. Someone plays a musical instrument.
   (3) A. I've done my homework.
       B. I haven't brushed my teeth.
   (4) A. Some of the students came to my party.
       B. Not all of the students came to my party.
   (5) A. Mary owns three canaries.
       B. Mary owns a canary.

(6) A. John picked a tulip.
B. John didn't pick a rose.
8. Each of the following conversational fragments is to some degree odd. To what extent can the oddness be explained by reference to Grice's CP and maxims?
(1) A: Have you seen Peter today?
B: Well, if I didn't deny seeing him I wouldn't be telling a lie.
(2) A: Are you there?
B: No, I'm here.
(3) A: Thank you for your help, you've been most kind.
B: Yes, I have.
(4) A: Can you tell me where Mr Smith's office is?
B: Yes, not here.
(5) A: Would you like some coffee?
B: Mary's a beautiful dancer.
(6) A: Has the postman been?
B: He leant his bicycle against the fence, opened the gate, strode briskly down the path, stopped to stroke the cat, reached into his bag, pulled out a bundle of letters and pushed them through our letter box.

Chapter 9 Language and Literature

1. Define the following terms.
   third-person narrator   I-narrator
   free indirect speech   direct thought
   stream of consciousness writing   text style
2. What different forms of sound patterning can you find in the first stanza of the poem, "Easter Wings", by George Herbert (1593—1663)?

    Lord, who createdst man in wealth and store,
     Though foolishly he lost the same,
      Decaying more and more,
       Till he became
        Most poore:
       With thee
      O let me rise
     As larks, harmoniously,
    And sing this day thy victories:
   Then shall the fall further the flight in me.

3. Identify the type of trope employed in the following examples.
   1) The boy was as cunning as a fox.
   2) ...the innocent sleep,...the death of each day's life,... (Shakespeare)
   3) Buckingham Palace has already been told the train may be axed when the rail network has been privatised. (*Daily Mirror*, 2 February 1993)
   4) Ted Dexter confessed last night that England are in a right old spin as to how they can beat India this winter. (*Daily Mirror*, 2 February 1993)
4. Choose a scene from a play, one you have seen or read, one you have heard

on the radio(there are published collections of radio plays available), or one you are studying.
  1) Write a *paraphrase* of it, as described in Stage One in this course;
  2) Write a *commentary* on the same scene, as described Stage Two in this course;
  3) Choose one of the discourse features discussed above, and *analyse* the same scene to see how that feature is made use of in the scene, and the effect this has on your interpretation of it.
5. Discuss questions related to Exercise 4. Does your analysis change your attitude to anything you wrote in your paraphrase or commentary of the play? If so, what, and how?
6. Do you know anything about the British poet Philip Larkin?
7. What do you think of the cognitive approach to literature?

Chapter 10   Language and Computer

1. Define the following terms.
computational linguistics	computer literacy
speech synthesis	CALL
programmed instruction	LAN
CD-ROM	MT
concordance	e-mail
blog	chatroom
IE	FYI
corpus	CMC
drill and practice	MOOC

2. What is the basic difference between CAI and CAL in educational philosophy?
3. What are the 4 phases in the course of CALL development?
4. Is the linguist approach in MT research successful? Why?
5. What do you think about the knowledge-based approach?
6. What's your view about the relation between MT and human translation?
7. Choose the correct answer from each of the following set of options.
   a. Qualitative analysis is not useful in recognizing ambiguities in data. True/False
   b. Corpus A has 350,000 words in it and 615 examples of "get". Corpus B has 20,000 words in it and 35 examples of "get". Which corpus has the greatest proportion of the word "get"?
      Corpus A/Corpus B
   c. A word frequency lexeme analysis is carried out on the data below. Which lexeme has the highest frequency?
bat 16	bats 2	batting 1	batty 4
can 22	clock 16	clocked 4	dark 7
darkening 11	gave 11	give 6	given 3
gives 1			
8. What do you think about Chomsky's criticism and the revival of corpus

linguistics?
9. What is the difference between blog and chatroom?
10. Why should chatroom sometimes be monitored?
11. What is the difference between cMOOCs and xMOOCs?
12. In what sense WeChat is more advanced than Chatroom and Facebook?
13. What does each of the following acronyms and numbers stand for?

ADN	AISI	B4	CU
DIY	EOD	F/FF	YA
G2G	GA	HAGD	HLM
IDC	IHU	JAM	JK
KIT	LHM	LMA	NM
PM	Q4Y	SYS	TA
TTUL	U2	VBS	W8
WB	Y	YATB	WW4U

14. Can you guess the meaning of the following Emoticons or Smiley?

:-*	:{ }:	:<	(-:
:-()	:OI	XD	:)
:-D	|-I		

Chapter 11 Second and Foreign Language Teaching

1. Why should language teachers learn some knowledge of linguistics?
2. What is FOCUS ON FORM?
3. What is the INPUT HYPOTHESIS?
4. What is INTERLANGUAGE? Can you give some examples of interlanguage?
5. What is the discourse-based view of language teaching?
6. What are real-world tasks and pedagogical tasks? Can you give some examples?
7. What are the most important tasks for a syllabus designer?
8. What is a structural syllabus?
9. The structural syllabus is often criticised. Do you think it has some merits as well?
10. What are the important features of a task as defined in a task-based syllabus?
11. What are non-language outcomes?
12. What is Contrastive Analysis?
13. What are the differences between errors and mistakes? Can you identify the errors and mistakes in the sentences below?
    (1) I bought in Japan.
    (2) These dog are big.
    (3) He was arrived early.
    (4) Joe doesn't likes it.
    (5) Why didn't you came to school.
    (6) I doesn't know how.
    (7) She has been smoking less, isn't it?
    (8) I falled from the bike.
    (9) I no have it.

(10) Why they look at each other?
(11) I know what is that.
(12) Although he was ill, but he still came.
(13) I go to the university yesterday.
(14) Teacher said he is right.

14. What is a corpus? Can you give some examples of how the use of a corpus contributes to language teaching?

Chapter 12 Theories and Schools of Modern Linguistics

1. Why is Saussure hailed as the father of modern linguistics?
2. What are the three important points of the Prague School?
3. What is the Prague School best known for?
4. What is the essence of Functional Sentence Perspective (FSP)?
5. What is the tradition of the London School?
6. What is the difference between Malinowski and Firth on context of situation?
7. What is important about Firth's prosodic analysis?
8. What is the relation between Systemic Grammar and Functional Grammar?
9. What is special about Systemic-Functional linguistics?
10. Analyze the following sentences by identifying the Subject and Predicate on the first level and Theme and Rheme on the second level.
    (1) Mary gave her daughter a birthday present.
    (2) A birthday gift was given to Jenny.
    (3) The play was written by William Shakespeare.
    (4) Do have another drink.
11. Please put the following items in a diagram according to Halliday's notion of system and scale of delicacy.
    (1) she (2) we (3) always (4) a perception process
    (5) an action process
12. Analyze the following Relational-process sentences according to their mode and type.
    (1) Linguistics is a difficult course.
    (2) This laptop is Professor Huang's.
13. Analyze the following sentences on two levels. First, identify the Subject, Finite, Predicator, and Adjunct. Second, identify Mood and Residue. Explain the difference, if any, between the two levels of analysis.
    (1) Mr Hu made a speech at a conference yesterday.
    (2) The university president has been awarded an international prize.
    (3) Three days ago, an honorary title was given to a professor from Yale.
14. Analyze the following sentences on three levels of metafunctions.
    (1) John likes linguistics.
    (2) The paper was handed in three days later.
15. What is "appliable linguistics"?
16. What are the special features of American structuralism?

17. How is behaviourist psychology related to linguistics?
18. What is Harris's most important contribution to linguistics?
19. What is the theoretical importance of Tagmemics?
20. What are the main features of Stratificational Grammar?
21. How many stages of development has Chomsky's TG Grammar undergone?
22. What does Chomsky mean by Language Acquisition Device?
23. Draw a tree diagram for each of the following sentences.
    (1) The police attacked the suspect.
    (2) These children cannot understand her painting.
24. Explain why Generative Grammar can produce well-formed sentences (e.g. *Mary reads a book*) but not ill-formed ones (e.g. * *A book reads Mary*).
25. Why can a sentence like *John kills John* be transformed into *John kills himself*?
26. What is special about TG Grammar?
27. What are the latest developments of Chomsky's linguistic theory?
28. What is Case Grammar?
29. What is Generative Semantics?
30. What should we study theories and schools of linguistics?

Part I 英文练习及参考答案

Chapter 1 Invitations to Linguistics

1. Define the following terms.

    design features: the distinctive features of human language that essentially make human language distinguishable from languages of animals.
    function: the role language plays in communication (e. g. to express ideas, attitudes) or in particular social situations (e. g. religious, legal).
    synchronic: said of an approach that studies language at a theoretical "point" in time.
    diachronic: said of the study of development of language and languages over time.
    prescriptive: to make authoritarian statement about the correctness of a particular use of language.
    descriptive: to make an objective and systematic account of the patterns and use of a language or variety.
    arbitrariness: the absence of any physical correspondence between linguistic signals and the entities to which they refer.
    duality: the structural organization of language into two abstract levels: meaningful units (e. g. words) and meaningless segments (e. g. sounds, letters).
    displacement: the ability of language to refer to contexts removed from the speaker's immediate situation.
    phatic communion: said of talk used to establish atmosphere or maintain social contact.
    metalanguage: a language used for talking about language.
    macrolinguistics: a broad conception of linguistic enquiry, including psychological, cultural, etc.
    competence: unconscious knowledge of the system of grammatical rules in a language.
    performance: the language actually used by people in speaking or writing.
    langue: the language system shared by a "speech community".
    parole: the concrete utterances of a speaker.

2. Consult at least four introductory linguistics textbooks (not dictionaries), and copy the definitions of "language" that each gives. After carefully comparing the definitions, write a paper discussing which points recur and explaining the significance of the similarities and differences among the definitions.

    All the definitions should not exclude the description of design features that have been mentioned in this course book. Also it will be better if other design features, say, interchangeability or cultural transmission is included. But it seems impossible to give an unimpeachable definition on language, because the facets people want to emphasize are seldom unanimous. To compare several definitions can make you realize where the argument is.

3. Can you think of some words in English which are onomatopoeic?

   Creak: the sound made by a badly oiled door when it opens.
   Cuckoo: the call of cuckoo.
   Bang: a sudden loud noise.
   Roar: a deep loud continuing sound.
   Buzz: a noise of buzzing.
   Hiss: a hissing sound.
   Neigh: the long and loud cry that a horse makes.
   Mew: the noise that a gull makes.
   Bleat: the sound made by a sheep, goat or calf.

4. Do you think that onomatopoeia indicates a non-arbitrary relationship between form and meaning?

   No matter whether you say "Yes" or "No", you cannot deny that onomatopoeia needs arbitrariness. Before we feel a word is onomatopoeic we should first know which sound the word imitates. Just as what is said in Chapter One, in order to imitate the noise of flying mosquitoes, there are many choices like "murmurous" and "murderous". They both bear more or less resemblance to the genuine natural sound, but "murmurous" is fortunately chosen to mean the noise while "murderous" is chosen to mean something quite different. They are arbitrary as signifiers.

5. A story by Robert Louis Stevenson contains the sentence "As the night fell, the wind rose." Could this be expressed as "As the wind rose, the night fell?" If not, why? Does this indicate a degree of non-arbitrariness about word order? (Bolinger, 1981:15)

   No, these two parts cannot interchange. Yes, it is a case in point to illustrate non-arbitrariness about word order. When the two parts interchange, the focus and the meaning of the sentence is forced to change, because clauses occurring in linear sequence without time indicators will be taken as matching the actual sequence of happening. The writer's original intention is distorted, and we can feel it effortlessly by reading. That is why systemic-functionalists and American functionalists think language is not arbitrary at the syntactic level.

6. Does the traffic light system have duality? Can you explain by drawing a simple graph?

   Traffic light does not have duality. Obviously, it is not a double-level system. There is only one-to-one relationship between signs and meaning but the meaning units cannot be divided into smaller meaningless elements further. So the traffic light only has the primary level and lacks the secondary level like animals' calls.

Red	→ stop
Green	→ go
Yellow	→ get ready to go or stop

7. The recursive nature of language provides a theoretical basis for the creativity of language. Can you write a recursive sentence following the example in section 1.3.3?

    Today I encountered an old friend who was my classmate when I was in elementary school where there was an apple orchard in which we slid to select ripe apples that...

8. Communication can take many forms, such as sign, speech, body language and facial expression. Do body language and facial expression share or lack the distinctive properties of human language?

    On the whole, body language and facial expression lack most of the distinctive properties of human language such as duality, displacement, creativity and so on. Body language exhibits arbitrariness a little bit. For instance, *nod* means "OK/YES" for us but in Arabian world it is equal to saying "NO". Some facial expressions have non-arbitrariness because they are instinctive such as the cry and laugh of a newborn infant.

9. Do you agree with the view that no language is especially simple?

    Yes. All human languages are complicated systems of communication. It is decided by their shared design features.

10. What do you think of Bertrand Russell's observation of the dog language: "No matter how eloquently a dog may bark, he cannot tell you that his parents were poor but honest"? Are you familiar with any type of ways animals communicate among themselves and with human beings?

    When gazelles sense potential danger, for example, they flee and thereby signal to other gazelles in the vicinity that danger is lurking. A dog signals its wish to be let inside the house by barking and signals the possibility that it might bite momentarily by displaying its fangs.

11. Can you mention some typical expressions of phatic communion in Chinese? There is a dialogue between Mrs P and Mrs. Q. on p. 12. When someone sneezes violently, do you say anything of the nature of phatic communion? Have you noticed your parents or grand-parents say something special on such an occasion?

    Some of the typical phatic expressions in Chinese are: 吃了吗？家里都好吧？这是去哪里啊？最近都挺好的？

    If someone is sneezing violently, maybe your parents and grandparents may say: "Are you ok?", "Do you need to see a doctor?", "Do you need some water?", "Do you need a handkerchief?", "Do you have a cold?" or something like these to show their concerns.

12. There are many expressions in language which are metalingual or self-reflexives, namely, talking about talk and think about thinking, for instance, *to be honest*, *to make a long story short*, *come to think of it*, *on second thought*, can you collect a few more to make a list of these expressions? When do we use them

most often?

> There are many expressions such as *To tell the truth*, *frankly speaking*, *as a matter of fact*, *to be precise*, *in other words*, *that is to say*.

Such expressions are used most frequently when we want to expatiate the meaning of former clauses in anther way in argumentation.

13. Comment on the following prescriptive rules. Do you think they are acceptable?

    (A) It is I.
    (B) It is me.

    You should say A instead of B because "be" should be followed by the nominative case, not the accusative according to the rules in Latin.

    (A) Who did you speak to?
    (B) Whom did you speak to?

    You should say B instead of A.

    (A) I haven't done anything.
    (B) I haven't done nothing.

    B is wrong because two negatives make a positive.

    (1) the Latin rule is not universal. In English, *me* is informal and *I* is felt to be very formal.
    (2) *Whom* is used in formal speech and in writing; *who* is more acceptable in informal speech.
    (3) Language does not have to follow logic reasoning. Here two negatives only make a more emphatic negative. This sentence is not acceptable in Standard English not because it is illogical, but because language changes and rejects this usage now.

14. The prescriptivism in grammar rules has now shifted to prescriptions in choice of words. In the "guidelines on anti-sexist language" issued by the British sociological association, some guidelines are listed below. Do you think they are descriptive and prescriptive? What's your comment on them?

    (1) Do not use *man* to mean humanity in general. Use *person*, *people*, *human beings*, *men* and *women*, *humanity* and *humankind*.
    (2) colored: This term is regarded as outdated in the UK and should be avoided as it is generally viewed as offensive to many black people.
    (3) civilized: This term can still carry racist overtones which derive from a colonialist perception of the world. It is often associated with social Darwinist thought and is full of implicit value judgments and ignorance of the history of the non-industrialized world.

    They are undoubtedly descriptive. Guidelines are not rules that can determine whether a sentence is right or not. The guidelines advise you to avoid the use of particular words that are grammatically correct but offensive to some certain groups. Actually, they describe the way anti-sexist advocators speak and write.

15. Why is the distinction between competence and performance important in linguistics? Do you think the line can be neatly drawn between them? How do you like the concept communicative competence?

This is proposed by Chomsky in his formalist linguistic theories. It is sometimes hard to draw a strict line. Some researchers in applied linguistics think communicative competence may be a more revealing concept in language teaching than the purely theoretical pair—competence and performance.

16. **Which branch of linguistics do you think will develop rapidly in China and why?**

    It is up to you to decide after you have gone through the whole book. At this stage, we suggest all branches of linguistics have the potential to flourish.

17. **The following are some well-known ambiguous sentences in syntactic studies of language. Can you disambiguate them?**
    (1) *The chicken is too hot to eat.*
    (2) *Flying planes can be dangerous.*

    There are two meanings to ex. (1): (a) The chicken meat is too hot, so it cannot be eaten at the moment; (b) The chicken feels so hot (maybe after some intense aerobic exercises) that it cannot start eating and needs to calm down first.

    The ambiguity of ex. (2) comes from "flying planes". It can be deciphered as "the planes that is flying" or "to fly planes".

18. **There are many reasons for the discrepancy between competence and performance in normal language users. Can you think of some of them?**

    Ethnic background, socioeconomic status, region of the country, and physical state (such as intoxication, fatigue, distraction, illness) vary from individual to individual.

19. **What do these two quotes reveal about the different emphasis or perspectives of language studies?**

    > A human language is a system of remarkable complexity. To come to know a human language would be an extraordinary intellectual achievement for a creature not specifically designed to accomplish this task. A normal child acquires this knowledge on relatively slight exposure and without specific training. He can then quite effortlessly make use of an intricate structure of specific rules and guiding principles to convey his thoughts and feelings to others,... Thus language is a mirror of mind in a deep and significant sense. It is a product of human intelligence, created anew in each individual by operations that lie far beyond the reach of will or consciousness. (Noam Chomsky: *Reflections on Language.* 1975: 4)

    > It is fairly obvious that language is used to serve a variety of different needs, but until we examine its grammar there is no clear reason for classifying its uses in any particular way. However, when we examine the meaning potential of language itself, we find that the vast numbers of options embodied in it combine into a very few relatively independent "networks"; and these networks of options correspond to certain basic functions of language. This enables us to give an account of the different functions of language that is relevant to the general understanding of linguistic structure rather than to any particular psychological or sociological investigation. (M. A. K. Halliday: 1970: 142)

    The first quote shows children's inborn ability of acquiring the knowledge of intricate structure of specific rules. It implies that the language user's underlying knowledge about the system of rules is the valuable object of study for linguists. The second attaches great importance to the functions of language. It regards the use of language as the choice of needed function. The meaning of language can be completely included by a few "networks" which is directly related to basic functions of language. It indicates the necessity to study the functions of language.

20. You may be familiar with the following proverbs. How do you perceive them according to the arbitrariness and conventionality of language:
    The proof of the pudding is in the eating.
    Let sleeping dogs lie.
    You can't make a silk purse out of a sow's ear.
    Rome was not built in a day.
    When in Rome, do as the Romans do.
    All roads lead to Rome.

    Arbitrariness and conventionality derive from the choice of the subject matter. For example, in the "*The proof of the pudding is in the eating.*" The word "pudding" is selected arbitrarily, for we can use another word such as cheese instead of pudding without changing the associative meaning of the proverb. On the other hand, once such links between particular words and associative meaning are fixed, it becomes a matter of conventionality.

21. Give examples of situations in which a usage generally considered nonstandard (e.g. ain't) would be acceptable, even appropriate.

    In the talks between intimate friends, one may say "gimme that!" instead of "give me that!" and "wachya doin'?" instead of "what are you doing?" and this list may go on.

22. The following are some book titles of linguistics. Can you judge the synchronic or diachronic orientation just from the titles?
    (1) *English Examined: Two Centuries of Comment on the Mother-Tongue.*
    (2) *Protean Shape: A Study in Eighteenth-century Vocabulary and Usage.*
    (3) *Pejorative Sense Development in English.*
    (4) *The Categories and Types of Present-Day English Word-Formation.*
    (5) *Language in the Inner City: Studies in the Black English Vernacular.*

    Synchronic: (2), (4), (5).
    Diachronic: (1), (3).

Further Reading

Atkinson, Martin, David Kilby & Iggy Roca. 1982. *Foundations of General Linguistics*. London: George Allen & Unwin.

Bolinger, Dwight & Sears, Donald A. 1981. *Aspects of Language*. New York: Harcourt Brace Javanovich.

Clark, Virginia P. (et al. eds.) 1985. *Language. Introductory Readings*. New York: St. Martin's Press.

David, Crystal. 1992. *The Cambridge Encyclopedia of Language*. Cambridge: Cambridge University Press.

Gee, James Paul. 1993. *An Introduction to Human Language—Fundamental Concepts in Linguistics*. New Jersey: Prentice Hall.
Harris, Roy & George Wolf. 1998. *Integrational Linguistics: A First Reader*. Oxford: Pergamon.
Hartley, Anthony F. 1982. *Linguistics for Language Learners*. Kent: Multiplex Techniques Ltd.
Lyons, John. 1981. *Language and Linguistics*. Cambridge: Cambridge University Press.
Napoli, Donna Jo. 1996. *Linguistics*. New York: Oxford University Press.
Thomas, Linda & Shan Wareing. 2004. *Language, Society and Power: An Introduction*. London: Routledge.
Wardhaugh, Ronald. 1993. *Investigating Language—Central Problems in Linguistics*. Oxford: Oxford University Press & Cambridge USA: Blackwell.
Widdowson, H. G. 1996. *Linguistics*. Oxford: Oxford University Press.

Chapter 2   Speech Sounds

1. Define the following terms.

    phonetics: the study of how speech sounds are produced, transmitted, and perceived. It can be divided into three main areas of study—articulatory phonetics, acoustic phonetics, and perceptual or auditory phonetics.

    articulatory phonetics: the study of the production of speech sounds, or the study of how speech sounds are produced/made.

    phonology: the study of the sound patterns and sound systems of languages. It aims to discover the principles that govern the way sounds are organized in languages, and to explain the variations that occur.

    gesture: movements of the tongue and the lips for the production of speech sounds, as compared to gestures made by hands.

    speech organs: those parts of the human body involved in the production of speech, also known as "vocal organs".

    voicing: the vibration of the vocal folds. When the vocal folds are close together, the airstream causes them to vibrate against each other and the resultant sound is said to be "voiced". When the vocal folds are apart and the air can pass through easily, the sound produced is said to be "voiceless".

    International Phonetic Alphabet: a set of standard phonetic symbols in the form of a chart (the IPA chart), designed by the International Phonetic Association since 1888. It has been revised from time to time to include new discoveries and changes in phonetic theory and practice. The latest version was revised in 2015.

    consonant: a major category of sound segments, produced by a closure in the vocal tract, or by a narrowing which is so marked that air cannot escape without producing audible friction.

    vowel: a major category of sound segments, produced without obstruction of the vocal tract so that air escapes in a relatively unimpeded way through the mouth or the nose.

manner of articulation: ways in which articulation of consonants can be accomplished—(a) the articulators may close off the oral tract for an instant or a relatively long period; (b) they may narrow the space considerably; or (c) they may simply modify the shape of the tract by approaching each other.

place of articulation: the point where an obstruction to the flow of air is made in producing a consonant.

Cardinal Vowels: a set of vowel qualities arbitrarily defined, fixed and unchanging, intended to provide a frame of reference for the description of the actual vowels of existing languages.

semi-vowel: segments that are neither consonants nor vowels, e. g. /j/ and /w/.

vowel glide: vowels that involve a change of quality, including diphthongs, when a single movement of the tongue is made, and triphthongs, where a double movement is perceived.

phoneme: a unit of explicit sound contrast. If two sounds in a language make a contrast between two different words, they are said to be different phonemes.

allophone: variants of the same phoneme. If two or more phonetically different sounds do not make a contrast in meaning, they are said to be allophones of the same phoneme. To be allophones, they must be in complementary distribution and bear phonetic similarity.

complementary distribution: a relation in a language or speech variety when two or more phones never occur in the same context. When such phones bear phonetic similarity, they are considered to be allophones of the same phoneme.

assimilation: a process by which one sound takes on some or all the characteristics of a neighboring sound. If a following sound is influencing a preceding sound, it is called "regressive assimilation"; the converse process, in which a preceding sound is influencing a following sound, is known as "progressive assimilation".

Elsewhere Condition: The more specific rule applied first. It is applied when two or more rules are involved in deriving the surface form from the underlying form.

syllable: an important unit in the study of suprasegmentals. A syllable must have a nucleus or peak, which is often the task of a vowel or possibly that of a syllabic consonant, and often involves an optional set of consonants before and/or after the nucleus.

Maximal Onset Principle: a principle for dividing the syllables when there is a cluster of consonants between two vowels, which states that when there is a choice as to where to place a consonant, it is put into the onset rather than the coda.

sonority scale: a ranking of sound types according to their intrinsic sonority. Generally, vowels are considered to be the most sonorous (5), followed by approximants (4), nasals (3), fricatives (2), and the least sonorous, stops (1).

stress: the degree of force used in producing a syllable. When a syllable is produced with more force and is therefore more "prominent", it is a "stressed" syllable in contrast to a less prominent, "unstressed" syllable.

intonation: the occurrence of recurring fall-rise patterns, each of which is used with a set of relatively consistent meanings, either on single words or on groups of words of varying length.

tone: a set of fall-rise patterns affecting the meanings of individual words.

tone sandhi: a change of tone in a tone language like Chinese, in natural speech, when two consecutives syllables have identical tone patterns. For example, in Mandarin if two syllables (two characters) with the same 214 tone occur consecutively, the rule is for the first syllable to change to the 35 tone, as in 你好 and 洗澡.

OCP: Identical adjacent elements are not allowed. This is a general rule that covers a wide range of phonological phenomena, including insertion of a vowel between two consonants or a consonant between two vowels in the case of inflectional morphology and tone sandhi in the case of suprasegmental phonology.

2. Give the description of the following sound segments in English.
   1) [ð]   2) [ʃ]   3) [ŋ]   4) [d]   5) [p]
   6) [k]   7) [l]   8) [ɪ]   9) [u:]   10) [ɒ]

   1) voiced dental fricative   2) voiceless postalveolar fricative
   3) velar nasal   4) voiced alveolar stop/plosive
   5) voiceless bilabial stop/plosive 6) voiceless velar stop/plosive
   7) (alveolar) lateral (approximant) 8) high front unrounded lax vowel
   9) high back rounded tense vowel   10) low back rounded lax vowel

3. Give the IPA symbols for the sounds that correspond to the descriptions below.
   1) voiceless labiodental fricative   2) voiced postalveolar fricative
   3) palatal approximant   4) voiceless glottal fricative
   5) voiceless alveolar stop   6) high-mid front unrounded vowel
   7) high central rounded vowel   8) low front rounded vowel
   9) low-mid back rounded vowel   10) high back rounded tense vowel

   1) /f/   2) /ʒ/   3) /j/   4) /h/   5) /t/
   6) /e/   7) /ʉ/   8) /œ/   9) /ɔ/   10) /u/

4. Transcribe the following sentences into normal orthography.
   1) ɒn ə klɪə deɪ jʊ kn siː fə maɪlz
   2) səm piːpl θɪŋk ðət fɜːst ɪmpɹɛʃnz kaʊnt fə ə lɒt

   1) On a clear day you can see for miles.
   2) Some people think that first impressions count for a lot.

5. Here is the official IPA website. See what you can find there and then report to your class.
   https://www.internationalphoneticassociation.org/
   (Free answer)

6. Discuss the following questions.
   1) What organs are involved in speech production?
   2) Why did George Bernard Shaw say he could spell the word *fish* as *ghoti*?
   3) How is the description of consonants different from that of vowels?
   4) To what extent is phonology related to phonetics and how do they differ?
   5) The pronunciation of *tell* is [teɫ], but that of *teller* is [telə]. Discuss why the phoneme /l/ is realized as [ɫ] and [l] respectively in this situation.

   1) See Section 2.1.1 of the course book.

   2) This is because *gh* is pronounced as /f/ in *enough*, *o* as /ɪ/ in *women*, and *ti* as /ʃ/ in *nation*. Of course Shaw was only trying to be sarcastic about how irregular English can be and in practice nobody would pronounce *ghoti* in the same way as *fish*, because *gh* is never pronounced as /f/ before a vowel and *ti* is only pronounced as /ʃ/ in *-tion*. As for *o*, it is pronounced as /ɪ/ probably only in *women*.

   3) See Section 2.2 of the course book.

   4) Both phonetics and phonology study human speech sounds but they differ in the levels of analysis. Phonetics studies how speech sounds are produced, transmitted, and perceived. Imagine that the speech sound is articulated by a Speaker A. It is then transmitted to and perceived by a Hearer B. Consequently, a speech sound goes through a three-step process: speech production, speech transmission, and speech perception. Naturally, the study of sounds is divided into three main areas, each dealing with one part of the process: Articulatory Phonetics is the study of the production of speech sounds, Acoustic Phonetics is the study of the physical properties of speech sounds, and Perceptual or Auditory Phonetics is concerned with the perception of speech sounds. Phonology is the study of the sound patterns and sound systems of languages. It aims to discover the principles that govern the way sounds are organized in languages, and to explain the variations that occur. In phonology we normally begin by analyzing an individual language, say English, in order to determine its phonological structure, i.e. which sound units are used and how they are put together. Then we compare the properties of sound systems in different languages in order to make hypotheses about the rules that underlie the use of sounds in them, and ultimately we aim to discover the rules that underlie the sound patterns of all languages.

   5) The word *teller* is formed by adding a suffix *-er* to the base word *tell* to form a new word. We are all familiar with the rule that governs the allophones of the phoneme /l/: when preceding a vowel, it is [l] and when following a vowel it is [ɫ]. However, in *teller* it has a vowel both before and after it, so how do we decide that it should be pronounced as [l], not [ɫ]? We notice that *tell* is a monosyllabic word while *teller* is disyllabic. In a polysyllabic word, we follow the Maximal Onset Principle (MOP) for the division of syllable. By MOP, the /l/ must be placed in the onset position of the second syllable instead of the coda position of the

first syllable. Thus, the phoneme /l/ is realized as it should be before the vowel in the second syllable. The same is true with *telling*, *falling*, and many others. We can see from this that the phonological structure of a complex word is often different from its morphological structure, i. e., how the word is formed. In word-formation it is *tell*+*-er* while in syllable structure it is [te+lə].

7. The relationship between the spelling and pronunciation of English words is not always simple. Examine the following words and discuss in what ways the relationship is complex (irregular) and if there are any regularities. Use other examples to illustrate your discussion if necessary.

| although, beauty, bomb, ceiling, charisma, choice, cough, exercise, hour, light, phase, quiche, quake, sixteen, thigh, tongue, whose, writhe |

The relationship between sound and spelling in English is complex in that the correspondence between writing and pronunciation lacks regularity. In these examples,

gh is not pronounced in *although*, *light* and *thigh* but is pronounced as /f/ in *cough*, which is also found in words like *laugh*, *rough*, *tough*, etc. *c* is pronounced as /s/ in *ceiling* and *exercise*, but /k/ in *cough*. *ch* is pronounced as /k/ in *charisma*, /ʃ/ in *quiche*, and /tʃ/ in *choice*. *b* in *bomb* and *h* in *hour* are not pronounced, but *h* is pronounced in most other cases like *hot*, *hat*, *horror*, etc. *o* has a wide variety of pronunciation: /ɒ/ in *bomb* and *choice*, /ʌ/ in *tongue*, and /uː/ in *whose*, together with *i* that also corresponds to different sounds: /ɪ/ in *ceiling*, *charisma*, *choice*, and *sixteen*, but /iː/ in *quiche*, and /aɪ/ in *exercise*, *light*, *thigh* and *writhe*. *qu* also realizes as /k/ in *quiche* and /kw/ in *quake*. And /iː/ may be spelt as *ei* in *ceiling*, *i* in *quiche*, and *ee* in *sixteen*.

Out of this chaos, there are obviously some regularities too. For example, *e* is almost always silent in word-final positions, except for borrowed words with an accent mark, as in *cliché*, and in such cases, the preceding vowel is normally realized as its alphabetical pronunciation, like *exercise*, *phase*, *quake*, and *writhe*, but there are always exceptions, such as *choice*, *quiche*, *tongue*, and *whose* in this list and some others not listed here.

8. In some dialects of English the following words have different vowels, as shown by the phonetic transcription. Based on these data, answer the questions that follow.

A		B		C	
bite	[bʌɪt]	bide	[baɪd]	tie	[taɪ]
rice	[rʌɪs]	rise	[ɹaɪz]	by	[baɪ]
type	[tʌɪp]	bribe	[bɹaɪb]	sigh	[saɪ]
wife	[wʌɪf]	wives	[waɪvz]	die	[daɪ]
tyke	[tʌɪk]	time	[taɪm]	why	[waɪ]

1) How may the classes of sounds that end the words in columns A and B be characterized?

2) How do the words in column C differ from those in columns A and B?
3) Are [ʌɪ] and [aɪ] in complementary distribution? Give your reasons.
4) What are the phonetic transcriptions of (a) *life* and (b) *lives*?
5) What would the phonetic transcriptions of the following words be?
   (a) trial (b) bike (c) lice (d) fly (e) mine
6) State the rule that will relate the phonemic representations to the phonetic transcriptions of the words given above.

(Based on Fromkin, et al. 2014: 268—269)

1) All the sounds that end the words in column A are voiceless ([-voice]) consonants and all the sounds that end the words in column B are voiced ([+voice]) consonants.
2) All the words in column C are open syllables, i.e. they end in vowels.
3) The two sounds are in complementary distribution because [ʌɪ] appears only before voiceless consonants and [aɪ] occurs before voiced consonants and in open syllables.
4) (a) [lʌɪf] (b) [laɪvz]
5) (a) [traɪl] (b) [bʌɪk] (c) [lʌɪs] (d) [flaɪ] (e) [maɪn]
6) /aɪ/ → [ʌɪ] / ____ [-voice]
    [aɪ] in other places

9. The following words contain different forms of the negative prefix in-. Group the data according to the variants and try to determine which kinds of base word take which kinds of prefix variant and what kind of mechanism is responsible for the variation. Formulate a rule and then test it against words that are formed in this way but are not mentioned here.

irregular	incomprehensible	illiterate
ingenious	inoffensive	inharmonic
impenetrable	illegal	incompetent
irresistible	impossible	irresponsible
immobile	illogical	indifferent
inconsistent	innumerable	inevitable

(Based on Plag, 2003: 42)

As far as orthography is concerned, there are four variants: *in-*, *im-*, *ir-*, and *il-*, but closer scrutiny shows that *in-* may be pronounced as [ɪŋ] before velar consonants, so there are five groups of words according to their variation on pronunciation:
(1) [ɪn]: inharmonic, ingenious, inoffensive, indifferent, inevitable, innumerable
    [ɪn] or [ɪŋ]: incomprehensible, incompetent, inconsistent
    [ɪm]: impenetrable, impossible, immobile
    [ɪl]: illiterate, illegal, illogical
    [ɪr]: irresponsible, irresistible, irregular
It is clear that the first sound of the base word governs the distribution of the variants, because the final consonant of the prefix *in-* must assimilate to the first segment of the base word. As a result of this, we find [ɪm] before labial consonants like [m] or [p], [ɪl] before the lateral [l],

[ɪr] before [r]. When the first consonant of the base word is the velar consonant [k], it is [ɪŋ] in rapid speech and [ɪn] in careful speech. In all other cases [ɪn] is always the case. Assuming an underlying form /ɪn/, the rule for the prefix *in-* looks roughly like this (in the simplest notation):

(2) /ɪn/→{[ɪn], [ɪŋ]} / _____ [velar]
　　　　[ɪm] / _____ [labial]
　　　　[ɪl] / _____ [l]
　　　　[ɪr] / _____ [r]
　　　　[ɪn] in other places

This rule system could be further simplified if we eliminate the first rule, as the realization [ɪŋ] is actually optional. Unlike the other rules, this variation is due to a more general mechanism of assimilation in fast speech, which happens naturally. For example, *in conference* is also often pronounced as [ɪŋkɒnfərəns] in fast speech, and the nasal in *thank* and *think* is also realized as a velar. We can test these rules by looking at other base words which can take the prefix *in-*, such as *correct, moveable, legible, rational,* and *adequate.* When prefixed, they are respectively pronounced [ɪn]*correct* (or [ɪŋ]*correct*), [ɪm]*moveable,* [ɪl]*legible,* [ɪr]*rational,* and [ɪn]*adequate,* which further support the rules above.

(Based on Plag, 2003: 200—1)

10. In Old English, the fricatives /f/, /þ, ð/, and /s/ each represented two separate sounds:

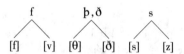

Voicing is predictable by context. Study the words below and state the rule.

sæt	[sæt]	'sat'
hūs	[huːs]	'house'
ēast	[æːəst]	'east'
cyssan	[kyssɑn]	'to kiss'
hlāf	[hlɑːf]	'loaf'
ceosan	[tʃeːozɑn]	'choose'
heofon	[heovɔn]	'heaven'
Wuldorfæder	[wuldɔrvæder]	'Father of Glory, God'
onstal	[ɔnstɑl]	'supply'
hrōfe	[hroːve]	'roof'
eorean	[ɛorðɑn]	'earth'
æfter	[æfter]	'after'
ēeel	[eːðɛl]	'native lord'
nīt	[niːθ]	'hatred'
niter	[nɪðɛr]	'downward'
nīeheard	[niːθhæərd]	'daring'

(Based on Fennell, 2001: 60 – 64 and Mitchell & Robinson, 2012: § 9)

In Old English, there are no voiced fricative phonemes. All voiced variants, which appear only between voiced sounds, are allophones of their voiceless counterparts. The rule can be stated as follows:

fricatives → [+voice] / [+voice]_____[+voice]
           [−voice]   in other places

11. Project Topics (Answers are not provided)

    1) Estuary English (EE) is a name given to the form(s) of English widely spoken in and around London and, more generally, in the southeast of England—along the river Thames and its estuary. The websites below contain much information about this variety of English. Find out what EE is like.

        http://www.phon.ucl.ac.uk/home/estuary
        http://www.ic.arizona.edu/~lsp/EstuaryEnglish.html

    See also Cruttenden (2014: Chapter 7) for some discussion on the changes of British English pronunciation.

    2) Based on your observation of Chinese students learning to speak English, discuss some of the typical phonetic and phonological difficulties they may encounter and make suggestions as to how you may help them tackle the problems. Make use of, as far as possible, what you have learned in this chapter.

    3) The discussion of phonological processes and phonological rules in this chapter are all illustrated with examples from English. Consider relevant facts in Chinese (Mandarin or a local dialect/accent) and see if they work in the same way.

Further Reading

Clark, John, Colin Yallop & Janet Fletcher. 2007. *An Introduction to Phonetics and Phonology*. 3rd ed. Oxford: Blackwell.

Collins, Beverley & Inger M. Mees. 2013. *Practical Phonetics and Phonology*. 3rd ed. London: Routledge.

Cruttenden, Alan. 1997. *Intonation*. 2nd ed. Cambridge: Cambridge University Press.

Cruttenden, Alan. 2014. *Gimson's Pronunciation of English*. 8th ed. London: Arnold.

Crystal, David. 2010. *The Cambridge Encyclopedia of Language*. 3rd ed. Cambridge: Cambridge University Press.

Fennell, Barbara A. 2001. *A History of English: A Sociolinguistic Approach*. Oxford: Blackwell.

Fromkin, Victoria, Robert Rodman & Nina Hyams. 2014. *An Introduction to Language*. 10th ed. Boston, MA: Wadsworth.

Gussenhoven, Carlos & Haike Jacobs. 2011. *Understanding Phonology*. 3rd ed. London: Hodder.

Ladefoged, Peter & Keith Johnson. 2015. *A Course in Phonetics*. 7th ed. Stamford, CT: Cengage Learning.

Mitchell, Bruce & Fred C. Robinson. 2012. *A Guide to Old English*. 8th ed. Malden, MA: Wiley-Blackwell.

Odden, David. 2013. *Introducing Phonology*. 2nd ed. Cambridge: Cambridge

University Press.

Plag, Ingo. 2003. *Word-formation in English*. Cambridge: Cambridge University Press.

Roach, Peter. 2001. *Phonetics*. Oxford: Oxford University Press.

Roach, Peter. 2009. *English Phonetics and Phonology: A Practical Course*. 4th ed. Cambridge: Cambridge University Press.

Wells, John. 2006. *English Intonation: An Introduction*. Cambridge: Cambridge University Press.

Chapter 3　Words and Morphology

1. Define the following terms.

    morpheme: the smallest unit of language in terms of the relationship between expression and content, a unit that cannot be divided into further smaller units without destroying or drastically altering the meaning, whether it is lexical or grammatical. For example, the word *tourists* contains three morphemes. There is one minimal unit of meaning, *tour*, another minimal unit of meaning *-ist* (meaning "person who does something"), and a minimal unit of grammatical function *-s* (indicating plural). Meanwhile, from the above example, we can further classify morphemes into different types on different dimensions: (a) free morphemes, which can stand by themselves as single words, e. g. *tour* in *tourist*, and bound morphemes, which cannot normally stand alone, but which are typically attached to another form, e. g. *-ist*, *-s*. (b) lexical morphemes and functional morphemes. Both of these two types of morphemes fall into the "free" category. The first category is that set of ordinary nouns, adjectives and verbs that carry the "content" of message we convey, e. g. *house*, *long* and *follow*. The second category consists largely of the functional words in the language such as conjunctions, prepositions, articles and pronouns, e. g. *but*, *above*, *the* and *it*. (c) derivational morphemes and inflectional morphemes. These two types of morphemes fall into the "bound" category. The derivational morphemes are used to make new words in the language and are often employed to produce words of a different grammatical category from the stem. For example, the addition of the derivational morpheme *-ness* changes the adjective *good* to the noun *goodness*. In contrast, inflectional morphemes never change the grammatical category of a word, but indicate aspects of the grammatical function of a word. For example, both *old* and *older* are adjectives. The *-er* inflection simply creates a different version of the adjective, indicating a comparative degree. As a useful way to remember the different categories of morphemes, the following chart can be used:

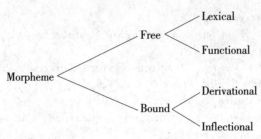

It should be pointed out, morphemes may also be divided into **roots** and **affixes**, the root being that part of a word structure which is left when all the affixes have been removed. Root morphemes may be bound or free, and are potentially unlimited in number in a language; Affixes are bound morphemes and limited in number. For instance, in *try*, *tries*, *trying*, *tried*, the root is *try*, and *-s*, *-ing*, *-ed* are affixes.

compound: refers to the words that consist of more than one lexical morpheme or the way to join two separate words to produce a single form, such as *classroom*, *mailbox*, *fingerprint*, *sunburn*. In terms of the word class of compounds, there are Noun compounds (e. g. *daybreak*), Verb compounds (e. g. *brainwash*), Adjective compounds (e. g. *dutyfree*) and Preposition compounds (e. g. *throughout*). Meanwhile compounds can be further divided into endocentric compound and exocentric compound in terms of its structural organization. The head of a nominal or adjectival endocentric compound is derived from a Verb, and it is usually the case that the first member is a participant of the process verb. Consider the following two examples: *self-control* and *virus-sensitive*. The exocentric nominal compounds are formed by V+N, V+A, and V+P, whereas the exocentric adjectives come from V+N and V+A. Here are some examples:

Nouns	Adjectives
scarecrow	*takehome*
playboy	*lackluster*
cutthroat	*breakneck*

inflection: is the manifestation of grammatical relationship through the addition of inflectional affixes such as number, person, finiteness, aspect and cases to which they are attached.

affix: the collective term for the type of formative that can be used when added to another morpheme. Affixes in a language are limited in number, and are generally classified into three subtypes, namely, prefix, suffix, and infix, depending on their position around the root or stem of a word. Prefixes are these affixes that have been added to the beginning of a word (e. g. *un-* in *unhappy*); suffixes are those added to the end of a word (e. g. *-ish* in *foolish*); infixes, as a third type of affix, is not normally found in English but fairly common in some other languages. As the term suggests, it is an affix that is incorporated inside another word. It is possible to see the general principle at work in certain expressions, occasionally used in fortuitous or aggravating circumstances by emotionally aroused English speakers: *Absogoddamlutely*! And *Unfuckingbelievable*! In fact, all affixes are bound morphemes.

derivation: is the most common word-formation process to be found in the production of new English words. It is accomplished by means of a large number of affixes of English language, and shows the relationship between roots and affixes. For example: *mis + represent → misrepresent*, *joy + ful → joyful*, *sad + ness → sadness*. In contrast to inflection, derivation can make the word class of the original word either changed or unchanged, e. g. *dis + card → discard* (changed) and *dis + obey → disobey* (unchanged). It is worth mentioning that word forms that come from derivation are relatively large and potentially open. Take the prefix *pre-* for example. One can easily list hundreds of words from any dictionary, such as *preamble*, *pre-arrange*, *precaution*, *precede*, *precedent*, *precept*, *precinct*, *precognition*, *precondition*, *precursor*, among many others.

root: refers to the base form of a word that cannot be further analyzed without loss of identity. That is to say, it is that part of the word that is left when all the affixes are removed. In the word *internationalism*, after the removal of *inter-*, *-al* and *-ism*, the part left is the root *nation*. Apparently, all words contain a root morpheme. And roots can be further classified into free root morpheme and bound root morpheme. First, free root morphemes are those that can stand by themselves and are the base forms of words, such as *black* in *black*, *blackbird*, *blackboard*, *blacksmith*. A language may contain many morphemes of this type. Second, there are relatively a few bound root morphemes in English, such as *-ceive* in *receive*, *perceive*, and *conceive*; *-mit* in *remit*, *permit*, *commit*, and *submit*; *-tain* in *retain*, *contain*, and *maintain*; *-cur* in *incur*, *recur*, and *occur*, etc. Third, a few English roots may have both free and bound variants. For instance, *sleep* and *child* are free root morphemes, whereas *slep-* in the past tense form of *sleep*, i. e. *slept* and *child-* in the plural form of *child*, namely *children*, cannot exist by themselves, and are hence bound.

allomorph: A morpheme, like a phoneme, is a linguistic abstraction, which must be realized as certain phonetic forms or variants in different phonetic environments. Each of the phonetic forms or variants is a morph. A single morpheme may be phonetically realized as two or more morphs. The different morphs that represent or which are derived from one morpheme is called the **allomorphs** of that morpheme. In practice, some morphemes have a single form in all contexts, such as "dog", "bark" etc. In other instances there may be considerable variation, that is to say, a morpheme may have alternate shapes or phonetic forms. For example, the plural in English can be represented by the voiceless /s/, the voiced /z/, the vowel-consonant structure

/ɪz/, the diphthong /aɪ/ found in the irregular form of /maɪs/, the nasal sound /n/ in /ɒksn̩/, the long vowel /iː/ in /tiːθ/ and the zero form /iː/ of /ʃiːp/ and others. Each would be said to be an ALLOMORPH of the plural morpheme.

stem: is any morpheme or combinations of morphemes to which an inflectional affix can be added. For example, *friend-* in *friends*, and *friendship-* in *friendships* are both stems. The former shows that a stem may be the same as a root, whereas the latter shows that a stem may contain a root and one, or more than one, derivational affix.

bound morpheme: refers to those which cannot occur alone and must appear with at least one other morpheme. For example, the word *distempered* has three morphemes, namely, *dis-*, *temper*, and *-ed*, of which *temper* is a free morpheme, *dis-* and *-ed* are two bound morphemes. There are two types of morphemes which fall into the "bound" category: derivational morphemes and inflectional morphemes. The derivational morphemes are used to make new words in the language and are often employed to produce words of a different grammatical category from the stem. For example, the addition of the derivational morpheme *-ness* changes the adjective *good* to the noun *goodness*. In contrast, inflectional morphemes never change the grammatical category of a word, but indicate aspects of the grammatical function of a word. For example, both *old* and *older* are adjectives. The *-er* inflection simply creates a different version of the adjective, indicating a comparative degree.

free morpheme: refers to those which may occur alone or which may constitute words by themselves. In English *cats*, *cat* is free since *cat* is a word in its own right. Free morphemes therefore necessarily constitute mono-morphemic words. So all mono-morphemic words are free morphemes. Poly-morphemic words/compound words may consist wholly of free morphemes, e. g. English *aircraft*, *godfather* and *housewife*. As for its subtypes, free morphemes can be further divided into lexical morphemes and functional morphemes. The former is that set of ordinary nouns, adjectives and verbs that carry the "content" of message we convey, e. g. *house*, *long* and *follow*. The latter consists largely of the functional words in the language such as conjunctions, prepositions, articles and pronouns, e. g. *but*, *above*, *the* and *it*.

grammatical word: refers to those which mainly work for constructing group, phrase, clause, clause complex, or even text, such as, conjunctions, prepositions, articles, and pronouns. Grammatical words serve to link together different content parts. So they are also known as Function Words.

lexical word: refers to those which mainly work for referring to substance, action and quality, such as nouns, verbs, adjectives, and adverbs. Lexical words carry the main content of a language. So lexical words are also known as Content Words.

closed-class: A word that belongs to the CLOSED-CLASS is one whose membership is fixed or limited, such as pronouns, prepositions, conjunctions, articles, and others. One cannot easily add or deduce a new member.

open-class: is one whose membership is in principle infinite or unlimited. When new ideas, inventions, or discoveries emerge, new members are continually and constantly being added to the lexicon. Nouns, verbs, adjectives and many adverbs are all open-class items.

blending: is a relatively complex form of compounding, in which two words are blended by joining together the initial part of the first word and the final part of the second word, or by only joining the initial parts of the two words. For example, *telephone + exchange →telex*; *transfer + resister →transistor*.

acronym: is made up from the first letters of the name of an organization, which has a heavily modified headword. For example, *WTO* stands for World Trade Organization. This process is also widely used in shortening extremely long words of word groups in science, technology and other special fields, e. g. *Aids—acquired immune deficiency syndrome*, *COBOL—common business oriented language*.

back-formation: refers to an abnormal type of word-formation where a shorter word is derived by deleting an imagined affix from a longer form already in the language. For example, the word *television* appeared before *televise*. The first part of the word *television* was pulled out and analyzed as a root, even though no such root occurs elsewhere in the English language.

2. Complete the words with suitable negative prefixes.

   a. removable   b. formal   c. practicable   d. sensible
   e. tangible   f. logical   g. regular   h. proportionate
   i. effective   j. elastic   k. ductive   l. rational
   m. syllabic   n. normal   o. workable   p. written
   q. usual   r. thinkable   s. human   t. relevant
   u. editable   v. mobile   w. legal   x. discreet

   a. irremovable b. informal   c. impracticable d. insensible
   e. intangible   f. illogical   g. irregular   h. disproportionate
   i. ineffective j. inelastic   k. inductive   l. irrational
   m. dissyllabic n. abnormal   o. unworkable   p. unwritten
   q. unusual   r. unthinkable s. inhuman   t. irrelevant
   u. uneditable   v. immobile   w. illegal   x. indiscreet

3. Read the following paragraph and list all the function words you can find. (Include all forms of *be* as function words.) Give the percentage of function words in this paragraph.

   She was a small woman, old and wrinkled. When she started washing for us, she was already past seventy. Most Jewish women of her age were sickly, weak, broken in body. But this washwoman, small and thin as she was, possessed a strength that came from generations of peasant ancestors. Mother would count out to her a bag of laundry that had accumulated over several weeks. She would lift the heavy bag, load it on her narrow shoulders, and carry it the long way home.

The function words in this passage include: *she*, *was*, *a*, *and*, *when*, *she*, *for*, *she*, *was*, *past*, *of*, *her*, *were*, *in*, *but*, *this*, *and*, *as*, *she*, *a*, *that*, *from*, *of*, *would*, *to*, *her*, *a*, *of*, *that*, *had*, *over*, *she*, *would*, *the*, *it*, *on*, *her*, *and*, *it*, and *the*. Altogether there are 85 words in this passage, and 40 of them are function words. Then the percentage of function words in this passage is $40/85 \approx 47\%$.

4. "A free form which consists entirely of two or more lesser free forms... is a phrase. A free form which is not a phrase is a word. A word, then,... is a minimum free form" (Bloomfield, 1935:178). Answer the following questions:
    (a) The term "word" is ambiguous. What kind of words is Bloomfield's definition intended to cover?
    (b) Are there any traditionally recognized words of English (in the appropriate sense of "word") that fail to satisfy Bloomfield's definition?
    (c) What other criteria have been involved in the definition of the word?

    (a) The "words" in Bloomfield's sense, namely, the minimum free forms as conceptual units in general thinking are those smallest units that can stand by themselves and constitute, by themselves, complete utterances. Those that can function as complete utterances by themselves like *hi*, *possibly*, *darling*, etc. are "words".
    (b) Yes, for example, those words that cannot stand only by themselves and constitute utterances by themselves in the usual sense like the articles *a* and *the* in English fail to satisfy Bloomfield's criterion, though he himself does not acknowledge this.
    (c) In addition to the criterion of *a minimum free form*, *stability* and *relative uninterruptibility* are also involved in defining the word. Besides, the three senses of "word", namely, a physically definable unit, the common factor underlying a set of forms and a grammatical unit can be conducive to identifying the word.

5. Find the sources of the following blends. In cases where the dictionary does not provide the answer, your own ingenuity will be your guide.
    (a) bash   (b) smash   (c) glimmer   (d) flimmer
    (e) clash   (f) flare   (g) brunch   (h) motel
    (i) transistor (j) medicare   (k) workaholic (l) spam
    (m) telethon   (n) aerobicise (o) chunnel   (p) chortle
    (q) bit   (r) modem   (s) guestimate (t) threepeat

    (a) bat and mash   (b) smack and mash
    (c) gleam and shimmer   (d) flame and glimmer
    (e) clap and crash   (f) flame and glare
    (g) breakfast and lunch   (h) motor and hotel
    (i) transfer and resistor   (j) medical and care
    (k) work and alcoholic   (l) spiced and ham
    (m) telephone and marathon   (n) aerobics and exercise
    (o) channel and tunnel   (p) chuckle and snort
    (q) binary and digit   (r) modulator and demodulator

Chapter 3 Words and Morphology • 21 •

    (s) guess and estimate   (t) three and repeat
6. Determine the historically accurate etymology of the words in the first column, and underline the correct one in the second or in the third column.

	Column 1	Column 2	Column 3
(a)	hangnail	aching nail	hanging nail
(b)	female	a male's companion	little woman
(c)	crayfish	crawling fish	crab
(d)	shamefaced	face reflecting shame	bound by shame
(e)	Jordan almond	imported almond	garden almond
(f)	sparrowgrass	a genus of herbs	bird nesting in grass
(g)	belfre	bell tower	bell
(h)	bridegroom	a woman is just or about to be married	a man is just, or about to be married
(i)	muskrat (Algonquian: musquash)	a large rat-like animal	a large musk deer
(j)	woodchuck (Algonquian: otchek)	a north American goat	a north American marmot

(a) hangnail (alter. of *agnail*, *angnail*)   aching nail
(b) female (ME: *femel*, *femelle*)   a male's companion
(c) crayfish (ME: *crevis*)   crawling fish
(d) shamefaced (alter. of *shamefast*)   bound by shame
(e) Jordan almond (ME: *jordan almande*)   garden almond
(f) sparrowgrass (alter. of *asparagus*)   a genus of herbs
(g) belfre (ME: *berfrey*)   bell tower
(h) bridegroom (ME: *bridegome*)   a man is just, or about to be married
(i) muskrat (Algonquian: *musquash*)   a large rat-like animal
(j) woodchunk (Algonquian: *otchek*)   a north American marmot

7. Determine the original term from which the following words were backformed.

(a) asset	(b) burgle	(c) enthuse	(d) greed
(e) hush	(f) automate	(g) donate	(h) escalate
(i) homesick	(j) peddle	(k) diagnose	(l) tuit
(m) amusing	(n) loat	(o) self-destruct	(p) attrit
(q) hairdress	(r) emote	(s) drowse	(t) frivol

(a) assets	(b) burglar	(c) enthusiasm	(d) greedy
(e) husht	(f) automation	(g) donation	(h) escalator
(i) homesickness	(j) peddler	(k) diagnosis	(l) intuition
(m) amuse	(n) loafer	(o) self-destruction	(p) attrition
(q) hairdresser	(r) emotion	(s) drowsy	(t) frivolous

8. Identify the immediate etymological source of the following words. (For example, the immediate source of "meaning" is French, although the more remote source is Latin.)

(a) air	(b) barbecue	(c) bungalow	(d) cola
(e) gusto	(f) babel	(g) buffalo	(h) cocoa
(i) costume	(j) ill	(k) mule	(l) decreed

(m) revolution (n) benevolent (o) lie (p) topic
(q) subject (r) theme (s) wind (t) datum

(a) Middle English (b) American Spanish
(c) Hindi and Urdu (d) African origin
(e) Spanish (f) Hebrew (The Bible)
(g) Italian (h) Spanish
(i) French (j) Middle English
(k) Middle English (l) Middle English
(m) Middle English (n) Middle English
(o) Middle English (p) Latin
(q) Middle English (r) Middle English
(s) Middle English (t) Ltin

9. If there are two affixes -ly, one producing adjectives and the other attaching to adjectives to produce adverbs, can we find words with both of these affixes?

   No. Words with both of these affixes -ly are not allocated in English. See below:
   * *friendlily (friend-friendly-friendlily*) * oilily (oil-oily-oilily*)
   * *chillily (chill-chilly-chillily*)

10. Make a list of nouns from the following words that -s can attach to.

    Epiphany   foot   hat   house
    kitchen   ox   phenomenon   region
    sheep   tomato

    hat   house   kitchen   region

11. Are there any affixes that attach (relatively) productively to verbs, contribute no or very specific meaning, and do not change category?

    -ing, He is walking home, of progressive aspect
    -ed, He walked home, of simple past tense
    -s, He walks home, of simple present tense

12. Some people claim that Chinese is a language with no morphology. Do you agree with this claim and why?

    (Here is a suggested answer—you might want to enrich or refute it as long as your argument is grounded on empirical data and rigorous logical reasoning.)

    It is true that compared with languages like English, morphological marking often does not seem to exist in Chinese. For example, Chinese has no overt case marking, and there is no morphological marking for gender (except the newly coined 他/她). Moreover, we don't see any overt categorial marker that often occurs in English derivation, and arguably Chinese does not have tense marking.

    But it is simply against the fact to say that Chinese has no morphology. First, Chinese does have a special plural marker, *men* (们), which is only attached to nouns that refer to humans, as in *xuesheng-men* (student-men, 学生们), meaning "students". This men is also used to mark plurality of personal pronouns as in *ni-men* (you, 你们), *wo-men* (we/us, 我们), and *ta-men* (they/them, 他/她们). Second, Chinese has some special particles that are attached to verbs to indicate aspectual information (like the perfective aspect). The verbal particle *le*（了）is an outstanding example: it is attached to the verb, often indicating that an action denoted by the verb is completed. This particle in a sense is like a bound morpheme (but people might have different ways to analyse its nature), as it cannot stand on its own, but has to be attached to a verb, and it lacks one aspect that a normal Chinese word often has, that is, a tone of its own. Third, we do sometimes see the morphological processing of derivation. For example, the morpheme *hua*（化）is often attached in some cases of derivation from nouns/adjectives to verbs: *shi* (stone, 石) — *shi-hua* (fossilise,石化); *mei* (beautiful, 美) — *mei-hua* (beautify, 美化); *chou* (ugly, 丑) — *chou-hua* (uglify, 丑化). There are of course more data to show morphology does exist in Chinese, and a potential project for you is not just to find out more data, but also the underlying reason(s) for the morphological differences between Chinese and English, or other languages.

13. A compound like blackbird can consist of an adjective and a noun, while a nominal phrase can have the same components, for example, *black tie*. Now ignore the lack of space between the two words in English compounds, what distinguishes a compound like *blackbird* from nominal phrases like *black tie*?

    The most salient difference is semantic: for a nominal phrase consisting of an adjective and a noun, the meaning of the phrase is always compositional and thus predictable. A *black tie* is "a tie that is black", *an expensive laptop* is "a laptop that is expensive", etc. The meaning of a compound, on the other hand, is non-compositional and thus non-predictable: a *blackbird* does not equate to a bird that is black, but only refers to a bird of a special species. The second difference is phonological: a compound like *blackbird* always has the stress on the first word, while a modified nominal phrase has its stress on the nominal head. Therefore, when hearing someone mentioning BLACK-BIRD in a conversation, you can tell whether he/she is talking about a special species of birds (*BLÁCKbird*) or birds that are black (*blackBÍRD*) by clarifying where the stress is located.

Further Reading

Adams, V. 1973. *An Introduction to Modern English Word-Formation*. London: Longman.

Bauer, L. 1983. *English Word-Formation*. Cambridge: Cambridge University Press.

Beard, R. 1995. *Lexeme-morpheme Base Morphology: A General Theory of Inflection and Word Formation*. Albany: State University of New York.

Bisetto, A. & S. Scalise 2005. The classification of compounds. *Lingue e Linguaggio*, 4: 319—332.

Fromkin, V. et al 2014. *An Introduction to Language*. New York: Michael Rosenberg.

Haiman, J. 1980. *Hua: A Papuan Language of the Eastern Highlands of New Guinea*. Amsterdam: John Benjamins.

Harley, H. 2006. *English Words. A Linguistic Introduction*. Oxford: Blackwell Publishing.

Katamba, F. 1993. *Morphology*. Hampshire: Macmillan.

Lieber, R. 2009. *Introducing Morphology*. Cambridge: CUP.

Matthews, P. H. 1991. *Morphology: An Introduction to the Theory of Word Structure* (2nd edition). Cambridge: Cambridge University Press, 1991; Beijing: Foreign Language Teaching and Research Press, 2000.

Nattinger, J. R. 1992. *Lexical Phrases and Language Teaching*. Oxford: Oxford University Press.

Tucker, G. H. 1998. *The Lexico-grammar of Adjectives: A Systemic Functional Approach to Lexis*. Washington, D.C.: Cassell.

Chapter 4 From Word to Text

1. Define the following terms.

   syntax: The study of the rules governing the ways different constituents are combined to form sentences in a language, or the study of the interrelationships between elements in sentence structures.

   co-occurrence: It means that words of different sets of clauses may permit, or require, the occurrence of a word of another set or class to form a sentence or a particular part of a sentence. For instance, what can precede a noun (*dog*) is usually the determiners and adjectives, and what can follow it when it takes the position of subject will be predicators such as *bark*, *bite*, *run*, etc. In short, co-occurrence is the syntactic environment in which a construction, with its relevant elements, can appear grammatically and conventionally. Thus relations of co-occurrence partly belong to syntagmatic relations, partly to paradigmatic relations.

   construction: It refers to any syntactic construct which is assigned one or more conventional functions in a language, together with whatever is linguistically conventionalized about its contribution to the meaning or use construct contains. It can be further divided into the external and internal properties. Take the sentence *The boy kicked the ball.* as an example, we will determine the external syntax as an independent clause, while NP ("the boy"), VP ("kicked") and NP ("the ball") will be assigned respectively to the different elements in this clause.

   constituent: Constituent is a term used in structural sentence analysis for every linguistic unit, which is a part of a larger linguistic unit. Several constituents together form a construction: for example, in the sentence *The boy ate the apple*, S (A), *the boy* (B), *ate the apple* (C), each part is a constituent. Constituents can be joined together with other constituents to form larger units. If two constituents, in the case of the example above, B (*the boy*) and C (*ate the apple*), are joined to form a hierarchically higher constituent A ("S", here a sentence), then B and C are said to be immediate constituents of A.

endocentric: Endocentric construction is one whose distribution is functionally equivalent to that of one or more of its constituents, i.e. a word or a group of words, which serves as a definable Centre or Head. In the phrase *two pretty girls*, *girls* is the Centre or Head of this phrase or word group.

exocentric: Exocentric construction refers to a group of syntactically related words where none of the words is functionally equivalent to the group as a whole, that is, there is no definable "Centre" or "Head" inside the group. Exocentric construction usually includes basic sentence, prepositional phrase, predicate (verb + object) construction, and connective (be + complement) construction. In the sentence *The boy smiled*, neither constituent can substitute for the sentence structure as a whole.

subordination: Subordination refers to the process or result of linking linguistic units so that they have different syntactic status, one being dependent upon the other, and usually a constituent of the other. Thus the subordinate constituents are words which modify the Head. Consequently, they can be called modifiers. In the phrase *swimming in the lake*, *swimming* is the head and *in the lake* are the words modifying the head.

category: The term category in some approaches refers to classes and functions in its narrow sense, e.g. noun, verb, subject, predicate, noun phrase, verb phrase, etc. More specifically, it refers to the defining properties of these general units: the categories of the noun, for example, include number, gender, case and countability; and of the verb, for example, tense, aspect, voice, and so on.

coordination: A common syntactic pattern in English and other languages is formed by grouping together two or more categories of the same type with the help of a conjunction such as *and*, *but* or *or*. This phenomenon is known as coordination. In the construction *the lady or the tiger*, both NPs *the lady* and *the tiger* have equivalent syntactic status, each of the separate constituents can stand for the original construction functionally.

agreement: Agreement (or concord) may be defined as the requirement that the forms of two or more words of specific word classes that stand in specific syntactic relationship with one another shall also, be characterized by the same paradigmatically marked category (or categories). For instance, the syntactic relationship between *this pen* and *it* in the following dialogue:

　　—Whose is <u>this pen</u>?
　　—Oh, <u>it</u>'s the one I lost.

embedding: Embedding refers to the means by which one clause is included in another clause in syntactic subordination. E.g. I saw the man <u>who had visited you last year</u>.

recursiveness: It mainly means that a constituent can be embedded within

(i. e. be dominated by) another constituent having the same category, but it can be used to any means to extend any constituent. Together with openness, recursiveness is the core of creativity of language. For example, "*I met a man who had a son whose wife sold cookies that she had baked in her kitchen that was fully equipped with electrical appliances that were new*".

grammatical subject & logical subject: Grammatical and logical subjects are two terms accounting for the case of subject in passive voice. Take the sentences *A dog bit John*. and *John was bitten by a dog*. as examples. Since the object noun (*John* in this case) sits in the slot before the verb in the passive, it is called grammatical subject, for the original object noun phrase occupies the grammatical space before a verb, the space that a subject normally occupies; the subject (*a dog*), now the object of a preposition (by *a dog*), is called a logical subject, since semantically the subject still does what a subject normally does: it performs an action.

cohesion: It refers to text connectedness in terms of reference, substitution, ellipsis, conjunction, and lexical collocation. For instance, "there" is used to refer back to "the park" in order to achieve cohesion in the following text: *Smith lives near the park. He often goes there.*

coherence: It is the conceptual relationships that comprehenders use to construct a coherent mental representation accommodated by what is said in the discourse. For example: *There was a loud knock. I opened the door. Two policemen. This text is short on overt indicators of cohesion*, but is coherent.

2. Indicate the category of each word in the following sentences. (Hint: It may help to refer back to section 4.2.2.)
   (1) The instructor told the students to study.
   (2) The customer requested for a cold beer.
   (3) The pilot landed the jet.
   (4) These dead trees must be removed.
   (5) That glass suddenly broke.

   (1) [NP(det. +n.)+V+NP(det. +n.)+inf.]
   (2) [NP(det. +n.)+V+PP(prep. +det. +adj. +n.)]
   (3) [NP(det. +n.)+V+NP(det. +n.)]
   (4) [NP(det. +adj. +n.)+mv(modal verb)+be(auxiliary verb)+Past Participle]
   (5) [NP(det. +n.)+adv. +V]

3. Put brackets around the immediate constituents in each sentence.
   Ex. ((I) ((rode) (back))) ((when) ((it) ((was) (dark)))).
   (a) The boy was crying.
   (b) Shut the door.
   (c) Open the door quickly.
   (d) The happy teacher in that class was beaming away.
   (e) He bought an old car with his first pay cheque.

(a) ((The) (boy)) ((was) (crying)).
(b) (Shut) ((the) (door)).
(c) ((Open) ((the) (door))) (quickly).
(d) ((The) (((happy) (teacher)) ((in) ((that) (class))))) ((was) ((beaming) (away))).
(e) (He) (((bought) ((an) ((old) (car)))) ((with) ((his) ((first) ((pay) (cheque))))))).

4. For each of the underlined constructions or word groups, do the following.
   —State whether it is headed or non-headed.
   —If headed, state its headword.
   —Name the type of constructions.
   Ex. His son <u>will be keenly competing</u>.
   Answer: headed, headword—competing; verbal group
   (a) <u>Ducks quack</u>.
   (b) The ladder <u>in the shed</u> is long enough.
   (c) I saw a bridge <u>damaged beyond repair</u>.
   (d) <u>Singing hymns</u> is forbidden in some countries.
   (e) <u>His handsome face</u> appeared in the magazine.
   (f) A lady <u>of great beauty</u> came out.
   (g) He enjoys <u>climbing high mountains</u>.
   (h) <u>The man nodded patiently</u>.
   (i) A man <u>roused by the insult</u> drew his sword.

   (a) (non-headed, independent clause)
   (b) (non-head, prepositional phrase)
   (c) (headed; headword—damaged; adjectival group)
   (d) (headed; headword—singing; gerundial phrase)
   (e) (headed; headword—face; nominal group)
   (f) (non-headed; prepositional phrase)
   (g) (headed; headword—climbing; gerundial phrase)
   (h) (non-headed; independent clause)
   (i) (headed; headword—roused; adjectival phrase)

5. In the pairs of sentences that follow, indicate with "N" those that need not follow a particular order when they are joined by "and". Indicate with "Y" those that need to be ordered. Aside from the examples below, in your opinion, which type is more relevant.
   (a) The sun is shining.
       The wind is blowing.
   (b) Susie went to sleep.
       She had a dream.
   (c) John came in.
       He closed the door.
   (d) He came in.
       John closed the door.
   (e) She felt embarrassed.
       She blushed.
   (f) The sky is blue.
       The grass is green.
   (g) He walked away.
       He got up.
   (h) He enjoyed the meal.
       He loved the pickles.

   (a) N   (b) Y   (c) Y   (d) Y
   (e) Y   (f) N   (g) Y   (h) N

6. Combine the following pairs of sentences. Make the second sentence of each pair into a relative clause, and then embed it into the first.
   (a) The comet appears every twenty years. Dr. Okada discovered the comet.
   (b) Everyone respected the quarterback. The quarterback refused to give up.
   (c) The most valuable experiences were small ones. I had the experiences on my trip to Europe.
   (d) Children will probably become abusers of drugs or alcohol. Children's parents abuse alcohol.
   (e) Many nations are restricting emissions of noxious gases. The noxious gases threaten the atmosphere.

   (a) The comet that Dr. Okada discovered appears every twenty years.
   (b) Everyone respected the quarterback who refused to give up.
   (c) The most valuable experiences that I had on my trip to Europe were small ones.
   (d) Children whose parents abuse alcohol will probably become abusers of drugs or alcohol.
   (e) Many nations are restricting emissions of noxious gases which threaten the atmosphere.

7. Use examples to illustrate different ways to extend syntactic constituents.

   In this chapter, several ways to extend syntactic constituents are brought under the category of recursiveness, including coordination and subordination, conjoining and embedding, hypotactic and paratactic and so on. Coordination and conjoining are the different names for the same linguistic phenomenon, that is, to use *and*, *but* or *or* to join together syntactic constituents with the same function. For instance, the sentence *A man got into the car* could be extended into a sentence like this "[$_{NP}$ A man, a woman, a boy, a cat and a dog] got into the car". While subordination and embedding can be understood as the extension of any syntactic constituent by inserting one or more syntactic elements with different functions, into another. *I saw the man who had visited you last year* is an extended sentence by changing the independent clause *The man had visited you last year* into a dependent element (here a relative clause).

   However, hypotaxis and parataxis are the two traditional terms for the description of syntactic relations between sentences. In the examples below, the former is hypotactic, while the latter is paratactic:
   We live near the sea. So we enjoy a healthy climate.
   He dictated the letter. She wrote it.

8. Mark the underlined parts of the sentences in Ex. 4—37 with the terms such as participial phrase, gerundial phrase, and so on.
   (a) The best thing would be to leave early.
   (b) It's great for a man to be free.
   (c) Having finished their task, they came to help us.
   (d) Xiao Li being away, Xiao Wang had to do the work.

(e) Filled with shame, he left the house.
(f) All our savings gone, we started looking for jobs.
(g) It's no use crying over spilt milk.
(h) Do you mind my opening the window?

(a) (infinitive phrase)   (b) (infinitive phrase)
(c) (past participial phrase)   (d) (absolute phrase)
(e) (past participial phrase)   (f) (absolute phrase)
(g) (gerundial phrase)   (h) (gerundial phrase)

9. Explain the main characteristics of subjects in English.

   The grammatical category "subject" in different language possesses different characteristics. In English, "subject" may have the following characteristics:
   A. Word order: Subject ordinarily precedes the verb in a statement such as "*Sally collects stamps.*"
   B. Pronoun forms: The first and third person pronouns in English appear in a special form when the pronoun is a subject. This form is not used when the pronoun occurs in other positions:
      He loves me.
      I love him.
      We threw stones at them.
      They threw stones at us.
   C. Agreement with verb: In the simple present tense, an -s is added to the verb when a third person subject is singular. However, the number and person of the object or any other element in the sentence have no effect at all on the form of the verb:
      She angers him.
      They anger him.
      She angers them.
   D. Content questions: if the subject is replaced by a question word (*who* or *what*), the rest of the sentence remains unchanged, as in (b) But when any other element of the sentence is replaced by a question word, an auxiliary verb must appear before the subject. If the basic sentence does not contain an auxiliary verb, we must insert *did* or *do(es)* immediately after the question word, as in (d, e)
      (a) *John stole/would steal Mrs. Thatcher's picture from the British Council.*
      (b) *Who stole/would steal Mrs. Thatcher's picture from the British Council?*
      (c) *What would John steal, if he had the chance?*
      (d) *What did John steal from the British Council?*
      (e) *Where did John steal Mrs. Thatcher's picture from?*
   E. Tag question: A TAG QUESTION is used to seek confirmation of a statement. It always contains a pronoun which refers back to the subject, and never to any other element in the sentence:
      John loves Mary, doesn't he?

Further Reading

Burton-Roberts, Noel. 1997. *Analysing Sentences: An Introduction to English Syntax*. New York: Longman.

Bresnan, Joan. 2001. *Lexical-Functional Syntax*. Malden, Mass.: Blackwell.

Halliday, M. A. K. & Matthiessen, Christian, M. I. M. 2014. *Halliday's Introduction to Functional Grammar*. 4th Edition. New York/London: Routledge.

Kehler, A. 2004. Discourse topics, sentence topics, and coherence. *Theoretical Linguistics*, 30 (2): 227—240.

Kroeger, Paul R. 2005. *Analyzing Grammar*. Cambridge: Cambridge University Press.

Louwerse, MAX M. & A. C. Graesser. 2005. Coherence in discourse. In P. Strazny (ed.) *Encyclopedia of Linguistics*. 2 Volume Set. New York/Oxon: The Taylor & Francis Group. pp. 216—218.

Morenberg, Marx. 2002. *Doing Grammar*. New York/Oxford: Oxford University Press.

Napoli, D. J. 1993. *Syntax: Theory and Problems*. New York: Oxford University Press.

O'Grady, William & Michael Dobrovolsky (eds.) 1992. *Contemporary Linguistic Analysis: An Introduction*. 2nd Edition. Toronto: Copp Clark Pitman Ltd.

Quirk, Randolph & Sidney Greenbaum. 1978. *A Concise Grammar of Contemporary English*. New York, Chicago, San Francisco, Atlanta: Harcourt Brace Jovanovich, Inc.

Sanders, T. & W. Spooren. 1999. Communicative Intentions and Coherence Relations. In W. Bublitz, U. Lenk & E. Ventola (eds.) *Coherence in Spoken and Written Discourse: How to Create It and How to Describe It*. Amsterdam/Philadelphia: John Benjamins Publishing Company. pp. 235—250.

Swan, M. 2005. *Practical English Usage*. 3rd Edition. Oxford/New York: OUP.

Tallerman, Maggie. 1998. *Understanding Syntax*. London, New York: Arnold.

Tanskanen, S.-K. 2006. *Collaborating Towards Coherence: Lexical Cohesion in English Discourse*. Amsterdam/Philadelphia: John Benjamins Publishing Company.

Thomas, Linda 1993. *Beginning Syntax*. Oxford: Blackwell.

Wardhaugh, Ronald. 1995. *Understanding English Grammar*. Oxford: Blackwell.

Yule, George. 1996. "Phrases and Sentences: Grammar"; and "Syntax" in *The Study of Language*, 2nd edition. Cambridge: Cambridge University Press: 86—113.

Chapter 5　Meaning

1. Define the following terms.

   conceptual meaning: This is the first type of meaning recognized by Leech, which he defined as the logical, cognitive, or denotative content. In other words, it overlaps to a large extent with the notion of reference. But Leech also uses "sense" as a briefer term for his conceptual meaning. As a result, Leech's conceptual meaning has two sides: sense and reference.

denotation: In the philosophers' usage, denotation involves the relationship between a linguistic unit and the non-linguistic entities to which it refers. Thus it is equivalent to referential meaning. For example, the denotation of *human* is any person such as John and Mary.

connotation: In the philosophers' usage, connotation, opposite to denotation, means the properties of the entity a word denotes. For example, the connotation of *human* is "biped", "featherless", "rational" etc.

reference: Reference is concerned with the relation between a word and the thing it refers to, or more generally the relation between a linguistic unit and a non-linguistic entity it refers to.

sense: In contrast to reference, sense may be defined as the semantic relations between one word and another, or more generally the relation between one linguistic unit and another. It is concerned with the intralinguistic relations.

synonoymy: Synonymy is the technical name for one of the sense relations between linguistic units, namely, the sameness relation.

gradable antonymy: Gradable antonymy is the sense relation between two antonyms which differ in terms of degree. There is an intermediate ground between the two. The denial of one is not necessarily the assertion of the other. Something which is not "good" is not necessarily "bad". It may simply be "so-so" or "average".

complementary antonomy: Complementary antonymy is the sense relation between two antonyms which are complementary to each other. That is, they divide up the whole of a semantic field completely. Not only the assertion of one means the denial of the other, the denial of one also means the assertion of the other. Not only *He is alive* means "He is not dead", *He is not alive* also means "He is dead".

converse antonymy: Converse antonymy is a special type of antonymy in that the members of a pair do not constitute a positive-negative opposition. They show the reversal of a relationship between two entities. *X buys something from Y* means the same as *Y sells something to X*. *X is the parent of Y* means the same as *Y is the child of X*. It is the same relationship seen from two different angles.

relational opposites: This is another name for converse antonyms. As converse antonymy is typically seen in reciprocal social roles, kinship relations, temporal and spatial relations, these antonyms are also known as relational opposites.

hyponymy: Hyponymy, the technical name for inclusiveness sense relation, is a matter of class membership. For example, the meaning of *desk* is included in that of *furniture*, and the meaning of *rose* is included in that of *flower*.

superordinate: The upper term in hyponymy, i. e., the class name, is called superordinate, and the lower terms, the members, hyponyms.

A superordinate usually has several hyponyms. Under *flower*, for example, there are *peony*, *jasmine*, *chrysanthemum*, *tulip*, *violet*, *carnation* and many others apart from *rose*.

semantic components: Semantic components, or semantic features, are semantic units smaller than the meaning of a word. For example, the meaning of the word *boy* may be analysed into three components: HUMAN, YOUNG and MALE.

compositionality: Compositionality refers to the principle that the meaning of a sentence depends on the meanings of the constituent words and the way they are combined.

propositional logic: Propositional logic, also known as propositional calculus or sentential calculus, is the study of the truth conditions for propositions: how the truth of a "composite" proposition is determined by the truth value of its constituent propositions and the connections between them.

proposition: A proposition is what is expressed by a declarative sentence when that sentence is uttered to make a statement.

predicate logic: Predicate logic, also called predicate calculus, studies the internal structure of simple propositions. In this logical system, propositions like *Socrates is a man* will be analyzed into two parts: argument and predicate. An argument is a term which refers to some entity about which a statement is being made. And a predicate is a term which ascribes some property, or relation, to the entity, or entities, referred to. In the proposition *Socrates is a man*, therefore, *Socrates* is the argument and *man* is the predicate.

logical connective: A logical connective is a logical element which helps to construct a composite proposition on the basis of simple proposition(s). There are 5 usual logical connectives: the negative connective ∼, the conjunctive &, the disjunctive connective ∨, the implicational (or conditional) connective → and the equivalent (or biconditional) connective ≡.

2. Read the following passage from *Through the Looking Glass* by Lewis Carroll, and discuss the meaning of *mean* in it.

> "Don't stand chattering to yourself like that," Humpty Dumpty said, looking at her for the first time, "but tell me your name and your business."
>
> "My name is Alice, but—"
>
> "It's a stupid name enough!" Humpty Dumpty interrupted impatiently. "What does it *mean*?"
>
> "Must a name *mean* something?" Alice asked doubtfully.
>
> "Of course it must," Humpty Dumpty said with a short laugh: "my name *means* the shape I am and a handsome shape it is, too. With a name like yours, you might be any shape, almost."

This *mean* means "refer to". This is the way in which *mean* is used in the referential theory of meaning.

3. Analyse the poem below from the semantic point of view, taking a special account of sense relations.

Coloured

Dear White Fella	You White Fella
Couple things you should know—	When you born, you pink
When I born, I black	When you grow up, you white
When I grow up, I black	When you go in sun, you red
When I go in sun, I black	When you cold, you blue
When I cold, I black	When you scared, you yellow
When I scared, I black	When you sick, you green
When I sick, I black	And when you die, you grey
And when I die, I still black	And you have the cheek
	To call me coloured?

    This poem is about the use of the word *coloured*. The author cleverly makes use of *coloured* in the sense of "different colours" to oppose the practice to refer to black people as "coloured". This shows from another point of view that *coloured* is not a superordinate to *red*, *green*, *yellow*, etc.

4. Do the following according to the requirements.
   (a) Write out the synonyms of the following words:
       youth, automobile, remember, purchase, vacation, big
   (b) Give the antonyms of the following words, and point out in which aspect the two of each pair are opposite:
       dark, boy, hot, go
   (c) Provide two or more related meanings for the following:
       bright, to glare, a deposit, plane

   (a) youth (adolescent); automobile (car); remember (recall); purchase (buy); vacation (holidays); big (large)
   (b) dark (light, with respect to brightness)
       boy (girl, with respect to sex)
       hot (cold, with respect to temperature)
       go (come, with respect to direction)
   (c) bright (a. shining; b. intelligent)
       to glare (a. to shine intensely; b. to stare angrily)
       a deposit (a. minerals in the earth; b. money in the bank)
       plane (a. a flying vehicle; b. a flat surface)

5. Some people maintain that there are no true synonyms. If two words mean really the same, one of them will definitely die out. An example often quoted is the disuse of the word *wireless*, which has been replaced by *radio*. Do you agree? In general what type of meaning we are talking about when we say two words are synonymous with each other?

    It is true that there are no absolute synonyms. The so-called synonyms always differ from each other one way or another, whether stylistically, connotatively, or dialectally. When we say two words are synonymous with each other, we usually mean they have the same conceptual meaning. Concerning the word *wireless* itself, its British English sense of "radio" indeed died out for many years. But *wireless* has come back into circulation again with the spread of network, used in the sense of "without a connection via wires". For example, "And the market for wireless earpieces depends on people's willingness to look as though they are talking to themselves", "The point of this standard is to make switching between wireless access points fast", and "The developer claims that this game has been a top-seller on wireless and on retail platforms" (https://www.bing.com/dict/search?q=wireless&FORM=BDVSP2, accessed 2/27/2017).

6. In the text, we did not mention antonyms like "friendly: unfriendly", "honest: dishonest", "normal: abnormal", "frequent: infrequent", "logical: illogical" and "responsible: irresponsible". Which type of antonymy do they belong to?

In terms of etymology, they may all belong to the complementary type in that the members of a pair divide the semantic field completely, and there is no middle ground. The assertion of one means the denial of the other, and vice versa. But in practice, some are used as gradable antonyms now, especially "friendly: unfriendly". They can be modified by degree adverbs like *very*, have comparative and superlative degrees, and the positive one *friendly* can serve as a cover term.

7. The British linguist F. R. Palmer argues in his Semantics(p. 97) that "there is no absolute distinction between [gradable antonyms and complementary antonyms]. We can treat *male/female*, *married/single*, *alive/dead* as gradable antonyms on occasions. Someone can be *very male* or *more married* and certainly *more dead than alive*." Comment on it.

It is not advisable to tell beginners of linguistics that the distinction between gradable antonyms and complementary antonyms is relative, even though there are situations in which a particular pair of antonyms may show characteristics of both types, such as *true: false*. In general, "It is true" means "It is not false", so this pair can be regarded as complementary. But it also shows the characteristics of the gradable, e.g., *true* can be modified by *very*, can serve as the cover term, and it has the true comparative *turer* and the superlative *truest*. However, there are not many antonyms like *true: false*. What is more, the expression "more dead than alive" is not a true comparative.

8. 姜望琪(1991:79) claims that "To some extent, we can say that any two words of the same part of speech may become antonyms, as long as the meaning difference between them is what needs to be emphasized in the particular context." He uses the two sentences below as examples. What do you think of the claim?

You have to *peel* a raw potato but you can *skin* a boiled one.
He's no *statesman*, but a mere *politician*.

This is a reasonable claim. As the author said in the paper, *man* can be the antonym of *woman*, but it can also be the antonym of *boy* in a situation when the age difference is important. When the difference between a man and an animal is important, *man* can also be the antonym of *dog*. And when the difference between something animate and something inanimate is important, then *man* can even be the antonym of *stone*. The two sentences "You have to *peel* a raw potato but you can *skin* a boiled one" and "He's no *statesman*, but a mere *politician*" are extreme cases, in which so-called synonyms become antonyms.

9. What is the superordinate term in the following list?

   man, stallion, male, boy, bull, boar

   The superordinate term is *male*. In this list of words, all the words belong to the male category. That is, they form a class in which *male* is the class name, or the superordinate.

10. Basing yourself on the model of componential analysis, analyze the following words:

    teacher, typewriter, chopsticks

    teacher: human, knowledgeable, instructive, respectable
    typewriter: machine, typewriting
    chopsticks: pair, eat, tool

11. Circle the two-place predicates in the list below:

    attack (verb), die (verb), between, put, love (verb), in, cat, elephant, forget

    attack, between, love, in, forget

12. Translate the following logical forms into English, where a = Ann, b = Bill, c = Carol, L = like, M = mother, and x and y are variables which may be translated as "someone", "anyone" or "everyone" depending on the quantifier:

    (a) M (a, b)
    (b) L (b, c) & L (c, b)
    (c) L (a, b) & ~L (a, c)
    (d) ∃x (L (x, b))
    (e) ~∀x (L (x, c))
    (f) ~∃x (∀y (L (y, x)))

    (a) Ann is Bill's mother.
    (b) Bill loves Carol, and Carol loves Bill.
    (c) Ann loves Bill, but Ann doesn't love Carol.
    (d) Someone loves Bill.
    (e) Not everyone loves Carol.
    (f) There is no one who is loved by everyone.

Further Reading

Akmajian, A., Demers, R. A., Farner, A. K. & Harnish, R. M. 2001. Semantics: the Study of Linguistic Meaning. In *Linguistics: An Introduction to Language and Communication*, 227−274. 5th edn. Cambridge, Mass.: MIT Press.

Geeraterts, D. (ed.) 2006. *Cognitive Linguistics: Basic Readings*. Berlin: Mouton de Gruyter.

Goldberg, A. 1995. *Constructions: A Construction Grammar Approach to Argument Structure*. Chicago: The University of Chicago Press.

Haspelmath, M. 2005. Ditransitive Constructions: The Verb "Give". In Haspelmath, M., Dryer, M. S., Gil, D. & Comrie, B. (eds.) *The World Atlas of Language Structures*. Oxford: Oxford University Press.

Haspelmath, M. 2015. Ditransitive Constructions. *Annual Review of Linguistics*, 1:19—41.

Haspelmath, M. 2016. The Serial Verb Construction: Comparative Concept and Cross-linguistic Generalizations. *Language and Linguistics*, 17(3): 291—319.

Lakoff, G. & Johnson, M. 1980. *Metaphors We Live By*. Chicago: The University of Chicago Press.

Lakoff, G. & Johnson, M. 1999. *Philosophy in the Flesh: The Embodied Mind and Its Challenge to Western Thought*. New York: Basic Books.

Lyons, J. 1977. *Semantics*. 2 vols. Cambridge: Cambridge University Press.

Lyons, J. 1995. *Linguistic Semantics: An Introduction*. Cambridge: Cambridge University Press.

Leech, G. 1981. *Semantics: The Study of Meaning*. 2nd edn. Harmondsworth: Penguin.

Ogden, C. K. & Richards, I. A. 1923. *The Meaning of Meaning*. London: Routledge & Kegan Paul.

Palmer, F. R. 1981 (1976) *Semantics: A New Outline*. 2nd edn. Cambridge: Cambridge University Press.

Saeed, J. I. 1997. *Semantics*. Oxford: Blackwell.

高远、李福印(主编),2007,《乔治·莱考夫认知语言学十讲》,北京:北京外语教学与研究出版社。

姜望琪,1991,True or false?《北京大学学报(英语语言文学专刊)》第2期。

徐烈炯,1995,《语义学》(第二版),北京:语文出版社。

Chapter 6 Language and Cognition

1. Define the following terms.

   cognition: Cognition is a term used in several different related ways. In psychology, it refers to the mental processes of an individual with particular relation to the internal mental states (such as beliefs, desires and intentions); in cognitive psychology, cognition can be understood in terms of information processing involving knowledge, expertise or learning for example are at work. In cognitive linguistics, cognition refers to the conceptualization of linguistic structures and patterns.

   psycholinguistics: Psycholinguistics is the interdisciplinary study of psychological aspects of language that investigates the psychological states and mental activity associated with language performance. Psycholinguistics has its roots in linguistics and cognitive psychology, and, it is also closely related to anthropology and neurosciences. There are six subjects of research in psycholinguistics: language acquisition, language comprehension, language production, disorders of language performance, language and thought, and, neurocognitive foundation of language. Generally, the former three subjects, say, acquisition, comprehension and production are in the central position of the field.

cognitive linguistics: Cognitive linguistics is a newly established approach to the study of language that emerged in the 1970s. Cognitive linguistics is based on human experiences of the world and the way they perceive and conceptualize the world. The basic principle of cognitive linguistics is that language is symbolic rather than automatic and is shaped by the way in which it is used and the general cognitive abilities of human being. The main research areas of cognitive linguistics are metaphor and metonymy, cognitive semantics, cognitive grammar and construction grammar, cognitive pragmatics.

language acquisition: Language acquisition is one of the central topics in psycholinguistics which investigates the process of children's acquisition of language. Learning a language is something every child does successfully, in a matter of a few years and without the need for formal lessons. With language so close to the core of what it means to be human, children's acquisition of language has received so much attention. In the field of language acquisition, scholars kept diaries of children's speech for their research data. The portable tape-recorders are available for analyzing children's spontaneous speech systematically. Today, the naturalistic studies of children's spontaneous speech can be put into computer files and be disseminated and analyzed automatically.

holophrastic stage: This is a term that refers to the first phase of language acquisition at which babies use one word for the meaning of the whole sentence. During their first year of life, the main accomplishments of the babies in acquiring language are to control the speech musculature and sensitivity to the phonetic distinctions used in the parents' language. Before their first birthday, babies begin to understand words, and around that birthday, they start to produce words in isolation. About half the words are for objects: food (*juice, cookie*), body parts (*eye, nose*), clothing (*diaper, sock*), vehicles (*car, boat*), toys (*doll, block*), household items (*bottle, light*), animals (*dog, kitty*), and people (*dada, baby*). Children's first words are similar all over the planet, and, this one-word stage can last from two months to a year.

two-word stage: This is a term that refers to the second phase of language acquisition at which infants use two words to stand for the whole sentence. Around 18 months, the children begin to learn words at a rate of one every two waking hours and keep learning at that rate or faster through adolescence. Vocabulary growth increases and the primitive syntax begins with two-word strings like the following, *all dry*, *I sit*, *I shut*, *no bed*, *dry pants*, etc. Children's two-word combinations are highly similar across cultures. Everywhere, children announce when objects appear, disappear, and move about, point out their properties and owners, comment on people doing things and seeing things, reject and request objects and activities, and ask about who, what, and where. These sequences already reflect the language being acquired: in 95% of them, the words are properly ordered.

three-word utterances: This is a term that refers to the third phase of language acquisition at which children can use three words to utter their linguistic performances. Children's three-word utterances look like samples drawn from longer potential sentences expressing a complete and more complicated idea. At this stage of language development among children, they can produce strings containing all of its components in the correct order as the following: *Mother gave John lunch in the kitchen*, *Give doggie paper*, *Adam put it box*. etc.

connectionism: It is a postulate in psycholinguistics which claims that readers use the same system of links between spelling units and sound units to generate the pronunciations of written words like *tove* and to access the pronunciations of familiar words like *stove*, or words that are exceptions to these patterns, like *love*. In this view, both similarity and frequency play important roles in processing and comprehending language, with the novel items being processed based on their similarity to the known ones.

cohort model: It is a model proposed by Marslen-Wilson and Welsh in 1990 for explaining the mental mechanism of word recognition during language comprehension. It is hypothesized that the first few phonemes of a spoken word activate a cohort of word candidates that are consistent with the input. These candidates compete with one another for activation. As more acoustic input is analyzed, candidates that are no longer consistent with the input drop out of the cohort. This process continues until only one word candidate matches the input; the best fitting word may be chosen if no single candidate is a clear winner. For example, to an instruction "*pick up the candle*" listeners sometimes glance first at a picture of a candy. This suggests that a set of words beginning with /kæn/ is briefly activated. Listeners may glance at a picture of a handle, too, suggesting that the cohort of word candidates also includes words that rhyme with the target.

interactive model: This a model for word recognition in psycholinguistics which postulates that higher processing levels have a direct "top-down" influence on lower levels when language user recognizes a spoken word. Lexical knowledge can affect the perception of phonemes. There is a interactivity in the form of lexical effects on the perception of sublexical units. In certain cases, listeners' knowledge of words can lead to the inhibition of certain phonemes; in other cases, listeners continue to "hear" phonemes that have been removed from the speech signal and replaced by noise.

race model: It is a model for word recognition in psycholinguistics which postulates that it has two routes that race each other in the process of word recognition—a pre-lexical route which computes phonological information from the acoustic signal, and a lexical route in which the phonological information associated with a word becomes available when the word itself is accessed. It is assumed that when word-level information appears to affect a lower-level process, the lexical route won the race.

serial model: It is a psycholinguistic model about sentence comprehension. Serial model proposes that the sentence comprehension system continually and sequentially follows the constraints of grammar of a language with remarkable speed. It holds that language processor can quickly construct one or more representations of a sentence based on a restricted range of grammatical information that is relevant to its interpretation. Any such representation is then quickly interpreted and evaluated by using the full range of information being relevant.

parallel model: This is a psycholinguistic model about sentence comprehension which emphasizes that the sentence comprehension system is sensitive to a vast range of information, including grammatical, lexical, and contextual, as well as knowledge of the speaker/writer and of the world in general. Parallel models describe how the processor uses all relevant information to quickly evaluate the full range of possible interpretations of a sentence. It is generally acknowledged that listeners and readers integrate grammatical and situational knowledge in understanding a sentence.

resonance model: It is a model addressing comprehension of text in psycholinguistic. Text or discourse makes contact with knowledge in readers' long-term memory and materials introduced earlier in a discourse. Retrieval of information from long-term memory can be a passive process that occurs automatically throughout comprehension. In *resonance model*, information in long-term memory is automatically activated by the presence of material that apparently bears a rough semantic relation to it. Semantic details, including factors such as negation that drastically change the truth of propositions, do not seem to affect the resonance process. It emphasized a more active and intelligent search for meaning as the basis on which a reader discovers the conceptual structure of a discourse. In reading a narrative text, reader attempts to build a representation of the causal structure of the text, analyzing events in terms of goals, actions, and reactions. A resonance process serves as a first stage in processing a text, and, reading objectives and details of text structure determine whether a reader goes further and searches for a coherent structure for the text.

construal: As a basic concept in cognitive linguistics, construal means the ability to conceive and portray the same situation in alternate ways through specificity, mental scanning, directionality, vantage point, figure-ground segregation etc.

construal operations: It is an important term relevant to the concept construal in cognitive linguistics. To cognitive linguists, construal operations are conceptualizing processes used in language process by human beings. That is, construal operations are the underlying psychological processes and resources employed in the interpretation of linguistic expressions. The fundamental construal operations include the following: attention and salience, judgment and comparison, perspective and situatedness, etc.

figure-ground alignment: This is a type of the construal operations of judgment/comparison. As a very fundamental cognitive capacity and the cognitive operations of judgment, the figure-ground alignment seems to apply to space with the ground as the prepositional object and the preposition expressing the spatial relational configuration. It also applies to human perception of moving objects since the moving object is typically the most prominent one. Because of its moving, an object is typically the figure, while the remaining stimuli constitute the ground. For example, in sentence *"There's a cat on the mat."*, *a cat* is figure, and, *the mat* is ground.

trajector: This is a cognitive linguistic term explaining the construal operation of judgment/comparison. It refers to moving figure in an event, for instance, in sentence *"We went across the field."*, *we* is a trajector because *we* can move in the event.

landmark: It is a term related to "trajector", cognitive linguist Langacker uses the term "trajector" for a moving figure and "landmark" for the ground of a moving figure to distinguish between stationary and dynamic figure/ground relations, for example, in sentence *"He is going to London"*, *London* is landmark.

basic level category: In cognitive linguistics, categorization is the process of classifying human experiences into different categories based on commonalities and differences. There are three levels in categories: the basic level, the superordinate level, and the subordinate level. The basic level categories are those that are most culturally salient and are required in order to fulfill our cognitive needs the best. For example, all categories of dogs are different, but they still share enough to be distinguished from cats, birds, snakes, primates, etc. Basic level category can help us find the idealized configuration of feature of a category and it is the most economical one in that it is at this level that we can find the most relevant information.

subordinate level category: In cognitive linguistics, subordinate categories are less good categories than basic categories, their members have low distinctiveness from members of neighboring categories. Subordinate level categories are much less informative relative to their immediate superior category and are frequently polymorphemic.

image schema: This is a term in cognitive linguistics that is defined as a recurring and dynamic pattern of our perceptual interactions and motor programs that gives coherence and structure to our experience. Image schemas exist at a level of abstraction and operate at a level of mental organization between propositional structures and concrete images, and, serve repeatedly as identifying patterns in an indefinitely large number of experiences, perceptions, and image formation for objects or events that are similarly structured in the relevant ways.

metaphor: In cognitive linguistics, metaphor is the comparison of two concepts in that one is construed in terms of the other. It consist in a target domain and a source domain. The target domain is the experience being described by the metaphor and the source domain is the means that we use in order to describe the experience. For example, the sentence "We are wasting our time here." is based on a metaphor "TIME IS MONEY" in which the target domain, TIME, is conceptualized in terms of the source domain of MONEY. In cognitive linguistics, metaphors are represented by a simple formula: "X IS Y", in which X is the target domain and Y is the source domain.

metonymy: Metonymy is modelled as Idealized Cognitive Models (ICMs) in cognitive linguistics. Metonymy is a basic way of thinking of human beings in which we substitute one entity for another entity, and it is a cognitive process in which one more salient conceptual entity mentally accesses another entity. The interrelations between entities of the same or from different ontological realms lead to various ICMs and possibilities for metonymy.

ontological metaphors: Ontological metaphors mean that human experiences with physical objects provide the basis for ways of viewing events, activities, emotions, ideas, etc., as entities and substances. By ontological metaphors we give bounded surfaces to less clearly discrete entities (mountains, hedges, street corners) and categorize events, actions and states as substances. In ontological metaphors it is our experiences of interacting with physical bounded bodies which provide the basis for categorizing events, activities, ideas, etc., as entities and substances. Take the experience of rising prices as an example, which can be metaphorically viewed as an entity via the noun *inflation*. Regarding *inflation* as an entity allows human beings to refer to it, quantify it, identify it, treat it as a case, act with respect to it, and even believe that we understand it.

structural metaphors: In cognitive linguistics, structural metaphors imply how one concept is metaphorically structured in terms of another and give us the possibility to structure one concept according to another, for example, ARGUMENT IS WAR leads to an English expression like "He attacked every weak point in my argument." It is obvious that we don't just talk about argument in terms of war. We can actually win or lose arguments. We see the person we are arguing with as an opponent. We attack his positions and we defend our own. We gain and lose ground. We plan and use strategies. If we find a position indefensible, we can abandon it and take a new line of attack. Many of the things we do in arguing are partially structured by the concept of war.

generic space: In the Blending Theory proposed and elaborated by Fauconnier & Turner as cognitive linguists, generic space is a kind of space established on the basis of the two input spaces and can supply and provide the input for generating and producing a new space, the blend space. Generic space is an alternative space established by an analogy process and can map onto each other of the input I_1 and input I_2. Therefore, it can reflect the common and abstract structure and organization shared by input I_1 and input I_2. Generally, generic space defines the core cross-space mapping between input I_1 and input I_2.

blend space: In the Blending Theory proposed and elaborated by Fauconnier & Turner in cognitive linguistics, blend space receives all the background knowledge, structural patterns and cognitive models that have been transmitted from the relevant domains of the input I_1 and input I_2 and generic space as well. Finally, the inputs I_1 and I_2 partially project onto a fourth space, the blend, and a new cognition can be generated and achieved.

ICMs: In cognitive linguistics, ICMs is an acronym from the string Idealized Cognitive Models which contains stands-for relations is what we referred as metonymic models. On the basis of the ontological realms, we may distinguish three categories: the world of "concept", the world of "form" and the world of "things" and "events". These realms correspond to the three entities, say, thought, symbol and referent that comprise the well-known semiotic triangle. The interrelations between entities of the same or from different ontological realms lead to various ICMs and possibilities for metonymy. Thus, we have three ICMs in ontological realms: Sign ICMs, Reference ICMs and Concept ICMs.

2. What does psycholinguistics study and what are the subjects of it?

Psycholinguistics is the study of psychological aspects of language which usually studies the psychological states and mental activities associated with the use of language. Most problems in psycholinguistics are more concrete, involving the study of language acquisition especially in children and linguistic performance such as producing and comprehending utterances or sentences among adults. An important focus of psycholinguistics is the largely unconscious application of grammatical rules that enable people to produce and comprehend intelligible sentences. Psycholinguists investigate the relationship between language and thought, a perennial subject of debate being whether language is a function of thinking or thought a function of the use of language. Psycholinguistics is also concerned with how languages are learned, and the role they play in our thinking. Experts in psycholinguistics use experiments to investigate such topics as short-term and long-term memory, perceptual strategies, speech perception based on linguistic models, the brain activity involved in language use, and language impaired due to brain damage, cognition and language.

It is customary to distinguish six subjects of research within psycholinguistics: 1) Acquisition: how does a child acquire the language skills (first language acquisition) and how are they extended to other languages (second/foreign language acquisition)? 2) Comprehension: how is the acoustic or visual signal linguistically interpreted by the hearer or reader? 3) Production: how is the information that somebody wants to convey transformed into acoustic waves, or written characters? 4) Disorders: what causes the occurrence of transient or more permanent disturbances of the speech and language processing systems? 5) Language and thought: what role does human language play in thinking? And what differences do different languages make to how we think? 6) Neurocognition: how is the cognitive architecture of language and language processing implemented in the human brain, i. e. what is the cerebral-functional architecture of our language faculty? Here, we will focus on the former three subjects, say, acquisition comprehension and production.

3. Describe the stages of first language acquisition.

Language acquisition is one of the central topics in psycholinguistics. Possessing a language is the quintessentially human trait. Learning a first language is something every child does successfully, in a matter of a few years and without the need for formal lessons. Children's acquisition of language has received so much attention. Generally, there are 4 stages of first language acquisition.

1) Holophrastic stage. Language acquisition begins very early in the human lifespan, and begins with the acquisition of a language's sound patterns. The main linguistic accomplishments during the first year of life are control of the speech musculature and sensitivity to the phonetic distinctions used in the parents' language. Shortly before their first birthday, babies begin to understand words, and around that birthday, they start to produce them. Words are usually produced in isolation; this one-word stage can last from two months to a year. About half the words are for objects: food (*juice, cookie*), body parts (*eye, nose*), clothing (*diaper, sock*), vehicles (*car, boat*), toys (*doll, block*), household items (*bottle, light*), animals (*dog, kitty*), and people (*dada, baby*). There are words for actions, motions, and routines, like *up, off, open, eat,* and *go*, and modifiers, like *hot, all gone, more, dirty,* and *cold*. Finally, there are routines used in social interaction, like *yes, no, want, bye-bye,* and *hi*—a few of which, like *look at that and what is that*, are words in the sense of memorized chunks, though they are not single words for the adult.

2) Two-word stage. Around 18 months, language changes in two ways. Vocabulary growth increases; the child begins to learn words at a rate of one every two waking hours, and will keep learning that rate or faster through adolescence. And primitive syntax begins, with two-word strings like the following:

All dry	*All messy*	*All wet*
I sit	*I shut*	*No bed*
Our car	*Papa away*	*Dry pants*

Children's two-word combinations are highly similar across cultures. Everywhere, children announce when objects appear, disappear, and move about, point out their properties and owners, comment on people doing things and seeing things, reject and request objects and activities, and ask about who, what, and where. These sequences already reflect the language being acquired: in 95% of them, the words are properly ordered. Even before they put words together, babies can comprehend a sentence using its syntax. For example, in one experiment, babies who spoke only in single words were seated in front of two television screens, each of which featured a pair of adults dressed up as Cookie Monster and Big Bird from *Sesame Street*. One screen showed Cookie Monster tickling Big Bird; the other showed Big Bird tickling Cookie Monster. A voice-over said, "OH LOOK!!! BIG BIRD IS TICKLING COOKIE MONSTER!! FIND BIG BIRD TICKLING COOKIE MONSTER!!" The children must have understood the meaning of the ordering of subject, verb, and object, because they looked more at the screen that depicted the sentence in the voice-over.

3) Stage of three-word utterances. Children's two-and three-word utterances look like samples drawn from longer potential sentences expressing a complete and more complicated idea. An expert in the field of language development Roger Brown noted that although the three children he studied never produced a sentence as complicated as *Mother gave John lunch in the kitchen*, they did produce strings containing all of its components in the correct order (Brown, 1973: 205):

Agent	Action	Recipient	Object	Location
Mother	gave	John	lunch	in the kitchen.
Tractor	go			floor.
Adam			put	it box.

4) Fluent grammatical conversation stage. Between the late two-word and mid-three-word stage, children's language blooms into fluent grammatical conversation rapidly, sentence length increases steadily. Because grammar is a combinatorial system, the number of syntactic types increases exponentially, doubling every month, reaching the thousands before the third birthday. Normal children can differ by a year or more in their rate of language development, though the stages they pass through are generally the same regardless of how stretched out or compressed and many children speak in complex sentences before they turn two.

During the grammar explosion, children's sentences are getting not only longer but also more complex, and, they can embed one constituent inside another. Whereas before they might have said *Give doggie paper* (a three-branch Verb Phrase) and *Big doggie* (a two-branch Noun Phrase), they now say *Give big doggie paper*, with the two-branch NP embedded inside the three-branch VP. The earlier sentences resembled telegrams, missing unstressed function words like *of*, *the*, *on*, and *does*, as well as inflections like *-ed*, *-ing*, and *-s*. By the 3, children can use these function words more often than they omit them in more than 90% of the sentences that require them. A full range of sentence types flower—questions with words like *who*, *what* and *where*, relative clauses, comparatives, negations, complements, conjunctions, and passives. These constructions appear to display the most, perhaps even all, of the grammatical machinery needed to account for adult grammar.

4. Illustrate the models explaining the process of word recognition.

Word lays in the central position in language comprehension because of its extremely important role in transmitting the meaning. Word recognition can be viewed in terms of recognition of spoken words and printed ones.

According to *cohort model* proposed by Marslen-Wilson and Welsh in 1990, the first few phonemes of a spoken word activate a set or cohort of word candidates that are consistent with the input. These candidates compete with one another for activation. As more acoustic input is analyzed, candidates that are no longer consistent with the input drop out of the set. This process continues until only one word candidate matches the input; the best fitting word may be chosen if no single candidate is a clear winner. For example, to an instruction "*pick up the candle*" listeners sometimes glance first at a picture of a candy. This suggests that a set of words beginning with /kæn/ is briefly activated. Listeners may glance at a picture of a handle, too, suggesting that the cohort of word candidates also includes words that rhyme with the target.

The *interactive model* holds that higher processing levels have a direct "top-down" influence on lower levels. Lexical knowledge can affect the perception of phonemes. There is interactivity in the form of lexical effects on the perception of sublexical units. In certain cases, listeners' knowledge of words can lead to the inhibition of certain phonemes; in other cases, listeners continue to "hear" phonemes that have been removed from the speech signal and replaced by noise.

The *race model* does not agree "top-down" effects, it has two routes that race each other—a pre-lexical route which computes phonological information from the acoustic signal, and a lexical route in which the phonological information associated with a word becomes available when the word itself is accessed. When word-level information appears to affect a lower-level process, it is assumed that the lexical route won the race.

Listeners' knowledge of language and its patterns facilitates perception in some ways. For example, listeners use phonotactic information such as the fact that initial /tl/ is illegal in English to help identify phonemes and word boundaries. Listeners also use their knowledge that English words are often stressed on the first syllable to help parse the speech signal into words. These types of knowledge help us solve the segmentation problem in a language that we know.

Print serves as a map of linguistic structure, readers use the clues to morphological structure that are embedded in orthography in reading the printed words. For example, they know that the prefix *re-* can stand before free morphemes such as *print* and *do*, yielding the two-morpheme words *reprint* and *redo*. Encountering *vive*, readers may wrongly judge it to be a word because of its familiarity with *revive*. Phonology and other aspects of linguistic structure are retrieved in reading. In printed word recognition, there is a question about how linguistic structure is derived from print. One idea is that two different processes are available for converting orthographic representations to phonological representations. A lexical route is used to look up the phonological forms of known words in the mental lexicon; this procedure yields correct pronunciations for exception words such as *love*. A nonlexical route accounts for the productivity of reading: It generates pronunciations for novel letter strings (e. g. *tove*) as well as for regular words (e. g. *stove*) on the basis of smaller units. This latter route gives incorrect pronunciations for exception words, so that these words may be pronounced slowly or erroneously (e. g. *love* said as /lʌv/) in speeded word naming tasks. Connectionist theories claim that a single set of connections from orthography to phonology can account for performance on both regular words and exception words.

Another question about orthography-to-phonology translation concerns its grain size. English, which has been the subject of much of the research on word recognition, has a rather irregular writing system. For example, *ea* corresponds to /ɪ/ in *bead* but /ɛ/ in *dead*; *c* is /k/ in *cat* but /s/ in *city*. Such irregularities are particularly common for vowels. Quantitative analyses have shown, however, that consideration of the consonant that follows a vowel can often help to specify the vowel's pronunciation. The /ɛ/ pronunciation of *ea*, for example, is more likely before *d* than before *m*. Such considerations have led to the proposal that readers of English often use letter groups that correspond to the syllable *rime* (the vowel nucleus plus an optional consonantal coda) in spelling-to-sound translation.

5. **What are the factors influencing sentence comprehension?**

Psycholinguists have addressed the phenomena of sentence comprehension in different ways. It is generally acknowledged that listeners and readers integrate grammatical and situational knowledge in understanding a sentence.

Structural factors in sentence comprehension. Psycholinguists have proposed principles interpreting sentence comprehension with respect to the grammatical constraints. The most popular principle is *Minimal attachment* which defines "structurally simpler" which claims that structural simplicity guides all initial analyses in sentence comprehension. In this view, the sentence processor constructs a single analysis of a sentence and attempts to interpret it. The first requires the fewest applications of grammatical rules to attach each incoming word into the structure being built. Consider the sentence *The second wife will claim the inheritance belongs to her.* When *the inheritance* first appears, it could be interpreted as either the direct object of *claim* or the subject of *belongs*. It was found that readers' eyes fixated for longer than usual on the verb *belongs*, which disambiguates the sentence. They interpreted this result to mean that readers first interpreted *the inheritance* as a direct object. Readers were disrupted when they had to revise this initial interpretation to the one in which *the inheritance* is subject of *belongs*. They described the readers as being led down a garden path because the direct object analysis is structurally simpler than the other possible analysis.

Lexical factors in sentence comprehension. Psycholinguists have proposed that the human sentence processor is primarily guided by information about specific words that is stored in the lexicon. In the sentences like *The salesman glanced at a/the customer with suspicion/ripped jeans*, the prepositional phrases *with suspicion* or *with ripped jeans* could modify either the verb *glance* or the noun *customer*. This is true only for action verbs, not for perception verbs like *glance at*. It has been noted that an actual preference for noun phrase modification only appeared when the noun had the indefinite article *a*.

6. **Explain the various aspects of process of language production.**

Various aspects of process of language production such as conceptualization and linearization, grammatical and phonological encoding, self-monitoring, self-repair and gesturing during speech are topics of process of language production.

1) Access to words: Words are planned in several processing steps. Each step generates a specific type of representation and information is transmitted between representations via the spreading of activation. The first processing step called conceptualization, is deciding what notion to express. In making such a choice, the speaker considers a variety of things, including whether the person has been mentioned before and whether the listener is likely know his proper name. The next step is to select a word that corresponds to the chosen concept. The speaker first selects a syntactic word unit which specifies the syntactic class of the word and additional syntactic information. A unit is selected as soon as its activation level exceeds the summed activation of all competitors. A checking mechanism ascertains that the selected unit indeed maps onto the intended concept. The following processing step is morpho-phonological encoding which begins with the retrieval of the morphemes corresponding to the selected word. Sometimes morphologically related items have different effects on the production of target words than do semantically or phonologically related items. Generally, morphemes are accessed in sequence, according to their order in the utterance.

2) Generation of sentences: In generating sentences, the first step is again conceptual preparation—deciding what to say. Theories of sentence generation assume that speakers prepare utterances incrementally. That is, they initiate linguistic planning as soon as they have selected the first few lexical concepts and prepare the rest later, either while they are

speaking or between parts of the utterance. Speakers can probably choose conceptual planning units of various sizes, but the typical unit for many situations appears to correspond roughly to a clause. When speakers plan sentences, they retrieve words. Speakers must apply syntactic knowledge to generate sentences. Two distinct sets of processes are involved in generating syntactic structure. The first set, often called functional planning processes, assigns grammatical functions, such as subject, verb, or direct object. The second set of processes, often called positional encoding, uses the retrieved lexicon-grammar units and the functions they have been assigned to generate syntactic structures that capture the dependencies among constituents and their order. The mapping from the functional to the positional level is usually quite straightforward: The subject usually precedes the verb, and the direct object and indirect object follow it.

3) Written language production: The steps in the production of written language are similar to those in the production of spoken language. A major difference is the orthographic rather than the phonological form that must be retrieved and produced. Phonology plays an important role in this process, just as it does in the process of deriving meaning from print in reading. Writing differs from speaking in that writers often have more time available for conceptual preparation and planning. They may have more need to do so as well, as the intended reader of a written text is often distant in time and space from the writer. Monitoring and revising, too, typically play a greater role in writing than in speaking. For these reasons, much of the research on writing has concentrated on the preparation and revision processes rather than on the sentence generation and lexical access processes that have been the focus of spoken language production.

7. What is the definition of cognitive linguistics?

Cognitive linguistics is a newly established approach to the study of language that emerged in the 1970s as a reaction against the dominant generative paradigm which pursues an autonomous view of language. Cognitive linguistics is based on human experiences of the world and the way they perceive and conceptualize the world. The basic principle of cognitive linguistics addresses that language is symbolic rather than automatic, it is shaped by the way it is used and the general cognitive abilities of human being, and, it is not developed on the back of "Universal Grammar" but has to be learned. The international academic organization of cognitive linguistics is the International Cognitive Linguistic Association (ICLA) founded in 1989 which holds biennial conferences of cognitive linguistics worldwide. The academic journals for scholars in cognitive linguistics community are *Cognitive Linguistics* and *Annual Review of Cognitive Linguistics*.

8. Describe the three categories of conceptual metaphors.

Metaphor involves the comparison of two concepts in that one is construed in terms of the other. It's often described in terms of a target domain and a source domain. In cognitive linguistics, metaphors are represented by a simple formula: "X IS Y", in which X is the target domain and Y is the source domain. Conceptual metaphor is classified by Lakoff & Johonson into 3 categories, ontological metaphors, structural metaphors and orientational metaphors.

Ontological metaphors: Ontological metaphors mean that human experiences with physical objects provide the basis for ways of viewing events, activities, emotions, ideas, etc. as entities and substances. By ontological metaphors we give bounded surfaces to less clearly discrete entities (mountains, hedges, street corners) and categorize events, actions and states as substances. In ontological metaphors it is our experiences of interacting with physical bounded bodies that provides the basis for categorizing events, activities, ideas etc. , as entities and substances. For example, the experience of rising prices can be metaphorically viewed as an entity via the noun inflation, INFLATION IS AN ENTITY. This gives us a way to refer to experiences of "*Inflation is lowering our standard of living*". In this case, regarding inflation as an entity allows us to refer to it, quantify it, identify it, treat it as a case, act with respect to it, and even believe that we understand it. Ontological metaphors are necessary for dealing with human experiences.

Structural metaphors: Structural metaphors give us the possibility to structure one concept according to another. Structural metaphors imply how one concept is metaphorically structured in terms of another. For example, ARGUMENT IS WAR leads to an English expression like "*He attacked every weak point in my argument.*" It is obvious that we don't just talk about argument in terms of war. We can actually win or lose arguments. We see the person we are arguing with as an opponent. We attack his positions and we defend our own. We gain and lose ground. We plan and use strategies. If we find a position indefensible, we can abandon it and take a new line of attack. Many of the things we do in arguing are partially structured by the concept of war.

Orientational metaphors: Orientational metaphors give a concept a spatial orientation. They are characterized by a co-occurrence in our experience. The orientational metaphors are grounded in an experiential basis which links together the two parts of the metaphor. The link verb "is", part of the metaphor should be seen as the link of two different co-occurring experiences. For example, MORE IS UP. This metaphor is grounded in the co-occurrence of two different kinds of experiences: adding more of a substance and perceiving the level of the substance rise. HAPPY IS UP; SAD IS DOWN, "*I'm feeling up*" and "*I'm feeling down*", From these sentences above, it is obvious that drooping posture typically goes along with sadness and depression, erect posture with a positive state.

9. Illustrate the model of blending theory.

The Blending Theory was proposed and elaborated by Fauconnier & Turner (1994, 1996). According to Blending Theory, blending operates on the two input mental spaces for producing a third space, the blend, and the blend can inherit the partial structures from the input spaces and can have a newly emergent structure of its own. To blend two input spaces I_1 and I_2, four conditions and/or spaces are needed.

1) Cross-Space Mapping: This is the first step of blending in which input space I_1 and I_2 are projected or mapped optionally to the third space, the blended space of emergent structure. The projection or mapping is run via the cross-space mapping.

2) Generic Space: Generic Space is a kind of space established on the basis of the two input spaces and it is an alternative space established by an analogy process and can map onto each other of the input I_1 and input I_2. So, Generic Space can reflect the common and abstract structure and organization shared by input I_1 and input I_2. Generic Space defines the core cross-space mapping between input I_1 and input II_2.

3) Blend Space: Blend Space receives and accepts all the background knowledge, structural patterns and cognitive models that have been transmitted from the relevant domains of the input I_1 and input I_2 and Generic Space as well. Finally, the inputs I_1 and I_2 partially project onto a fourth space, the blend, and a new cognition can be generated and achieved.

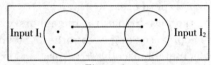

Figure 1.

4) Emergent Structure: Emergent Structure is in the blended space and has a simpler structure. It is a dynamic structure of the whole blending network rather than the blending space itself. It helps set up a simple but best blending space which can take use of the existing and accessible structures. Emergent Structure can link and connect all mental spaces in the blending network.

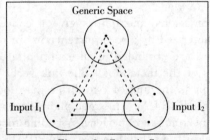

Figure 2. Generic Space

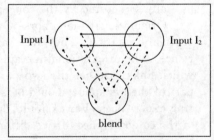

Figure 3 Blend Space

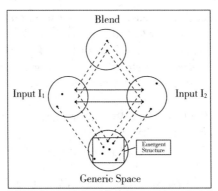

Figure 4 Emergent Structure

10. Analyze the following paragraph by image schemas.

You wake out of a deep sleep and peer out from beneath the covers into your room. You gradually emerge out of your stupor, pull yourself out from under the covers, climb into your robe, stretch out your limbs, and walk in a daze out of the bedroom and into the bathroom. You look in the mirror and see your face staring out at you. You reach into the medicine cabinet, take out the toothpaste, squeeze out some toothpaste, put the toothbrush into your mouth, brush your teeth in a hurry, and rinse out your mouth. At breakfast you perform a host of further in-out moves—pouring out the coffee, setting out the dishes, putting the toast in the toaster, spreading out the jam on the toast, and on and on. Once you are more awake you might even get lost in the newspaper, might enter into a conversation, which leads to your speaking out on some topic.

Some of these senses of *in* and *out* involve clear-cut physical orientation in space, while others involve more abstract nonspatial relations such as walk *in* daze, brush your teeth *in* a hurry, get lose *in* the newspaper, enter *into* a conversation, speak *out* on some topics. However, they all require certain activity of establishing relations, either among physical or among abstract entities or events.

Further Reading

Barcelona, A. (eds.) 2000. *Metaphor and Metonymy at the Crossroads: A Cognitive Perspective*. Berlin: Mouton de Gruyter.

Bloom, P. 1994. *Language Acquisition: Core Readings*. Cambridge, Massachusetts: MIT Press.

Croft, W. 2002. *Radical Construction Grammar: Syntactic Theory in Typological Perspective*. Oxford: Oxford University Press.

Croft, W. & Cruse, D. A. 2004. *Cognitive Linguistics*. Cambridge: Cambridge University Press.

Fauconnier, G. 1997. *Mappings in Language and Thought*. Cambridge: Cambridge University Press.

Fauconnier, G. & Turner, M. 1994. *Conceptual Projection and Middle Spaces*. Technical Report No. 9401, University of California, San Diego.

Fauconnier, G. & Turner, M. 1996. Blending as a Central Process of Grammar, in. Goldberg, A. (eds.), *Conceptual Structure, Discourse, and Language*, 113—130. Stanford, California: CSLI Publications.

Fauconnier, G. & Turner, M. 2002. *The Way We Think: Conceptual Blending and the Mind's Hidden Complexities*. New York: Basic Books.

Forrester, M. 1996. *Psychology of Language: A Critical Introduction*. London: Sage Publications.

Garman, M. 1991. *Psycholinguistics*. Cambridge: Cambridge University Press; Reprinted Peking University Press, 2001.

Gleason, J. & Ratner, N. 1993. *Psycholinguistics*. New York: Harcourt Brace Jovanovich.

Johnson, M. 1987. *The Body in the Mind: The Bodily Basis of Meaning, Imagination and Reason*. Chicago, Illinois: University of Chicago Press.

Kovecses, Z. 2002. *Metaphor: A Practical Introduction*. Oxford: Oxford University Press.

Langacker, R. W. 1987. *Foundations of Cognitive Grammar*, vol. 1: *Theoretical Prerequisites*. Stanford, California: Stanford University Press.

Langacker, R. W. 2000. *Grammar and Conceptualization*. Berlin: Mouton de Gruyter.

Lakoff, G. & Johnson, M. 1980/2003. *Metaphors We Live by*. Chicago, Illinois: University of Chicago Press.

Lakoff, G. 1987. *Woman, Fire and Dangerous Things: What Categories Reveal About the Mind*. Chicago, Illinois: University of Chicago Press.

Ogden, C. & Richards, I. A. 1923[1989]: *The Meaning of Meaning*. San Diego, California: Harcourt Brace Jovanovich [Originally Published London: Kegan Paul].

Panther, K. & Radden, G. (eds.) 1999. *Metonymy in Language and Thought*. Amsterdam: John Benjamins.

Radden, G. & Kovecses, Z. 1999. Towards a Theory of Metonymy. in Panther, K & Radden, G. (eds.) *Metonymy in Language and Thought*, 15—59. Amsterdam: John Benjamins.

Rumelhart, D. E., Hinton, G. E., & Williams, R. J. 1986. Learning Internal Representations by Error Propagation. in Rumelhart, D. E. & J. L. McClelland (eds.), *Parallel Distributed Processing: Explorations in the Microstructure of Cognition*, Vol. 1, 318—362. Cambridge, Massachusetts: MIT Press.

Ruiz de Mendoza, F. J. 2000. The Role of Mappings and Domains in Understanding Metonymy. in Barcelona, A. (eds.). *Metaphor and Metonymy at the Crossroads*, 109—132. Berlin: Mouton de Gruyter.

Scovel, T. 2000. *Psycholinguistics*. Shanghai: Shanghai Foreign Language Education Press.

Talmy, L. 2000. *Toward a Cognitive Semantics*, vol. 1: *Concept Structuring Systems*. Cambridge, Massachusetts: MIT Press.

桂诗春,2011,《什么是心理语言学》,上海:上海外语教育出版社。
胡壮麟,2004,《认知隐喻学》,北京:北京大学出版社。
蓝　纯,2005,《认知语言学与隐喻研究》,北京:外语教学与研究出版社。
卢　植,2006,《认知与语言—认知语言学引论》,上海:上海外语教育出版社。

束定芳,2013,《认知语言学研究方法》,上海:上海外语教育出版社。
王　寅,2011,《什么是认知语言学》,上海:上海外语教育出版社。

Chapter 7　Language, Culture, and Society

1. Define the following terms.

    Anthropological Study of Linguistics: A linguistic branch aims to look at the relationships between language and culture in a speech community. For this reason, it can alternatively be called anthropological linguistics. More specifically, practitioners of the field want to know more about a given community by examining the correlation between the tradition of the community, beliefs, and social behavior of community members and their language use in different contexts of communication.

    Communication: An information process taking place between at least two parties or persons.

    Communicative Competence: A sociolinguistic rule put forward by Dell Hymes in contrast with the "competence" vs. "performance" dichotomy in theoretic linguistics.

    Context of Situation: A framework put forward by Firth. This theory has the following elements (Firth, 1950: 43—44 [Palmer, 1981: 53—54]).

    　　A. The relevant features of the participants: persons, personalities:

    　　　　(i) The verbal action of the participants.

    　　　　(ii) The non-verbal action of the participants.

    　　B. The relevant objects.

    　　C. The effects of the verbal action.

    Nida's Classification of Culture: According to Nida(1964), there are five types of sub-culture we should be fully aware of when engaged in translation: 1) ecological culture; 2) linguistic culture; 3) religious culture; 4) material culture; and 5) social culture.

    Ethnography of Communication: An authoritative research framework of our time in a linguistic study of social and cultural factors (Hymes, 1972). The essential elements suggested by this framework include 1) speech community, 2) situation, event and act, and 3) mnemonic SPEAKING components.

    FLB: An important concept, which was put forward by theoretic linguistics in the early 2000s, stands for the faculty of language in the broad sense. It forms a contrast with FLN—the faculty of language in the narrow sense.

    FLN: An important concept, which was put forward by theoretic linguistics in the early 2000s, stands for the faculty of language in the narrow sense. It forms a contrast with FLB—the faculty of language in the broad sense.

    Gender Difference: A term used to refer to the variety of differences observed between men and women's linguistic behavior. This study covers almost all the levels of linguistic studies, ranging from pronunciation variants to communicative patterns.

Linguistic Determinism: A theory which believes that our language will influence or decide our way of looking at the world. In a loose sense, linguistic determinism, linguistic relativity, and the Sapir-Whorf hypothesis can be regarded as synonyms.

Linguistic Relativity: A view which "was first expounded by the German ethnologist, Wilhelm von Humboldt" (Crystal, 1985: 262). In a loose sense, this term has the same meaning with linguistic determinism and the Sapir-Whorf hypothesis.

Linguistic Sexism: A term used to refer to sex-biased phenomena in language use. More specifically, it aims to reveal and deal with linguistic issues related to male chauvinism.

Six-Person System: A typological pattern developed to study personal pronouns from the perspective of linguistic universality (Ingram, 1978). The following table summarizes this system explicitly. This typological system provides us with a comparative model to study the pronominal usage across languages.

Six-Person System

singular	plural
I	we
thou	you
he	they

Speech Community: A term refers to a group of people who "share not only the same rules of speaking, but at least one linguistic variety as well." (Hymes, 1972: 52)

SPEAKING: A mnemonic way of summarizing certain components of speech which make possible the description and analysis of communicative behavior: S=Situation(场景), P=Participants(参与者), E=Ends(目的), A=Act sequence(相关形式与内容), K=Key(语气), I=Instrumentalities(语式), N=Norms(准则), and G=Genres(体裁).

Sapir-Whorf Hypothesis: A theoretic assumption which suggests that our language helps mould our way of thinking and, consequently, different languages may probably express speakers' unique ways of understanding the world. In a loose sense, this term can be interchangeably used with linguistic relativity and linguistic determinism.

Sociolinguistics of Language: A branch of linguistics examines issues related to the subject from a more linguistic perspective and, hence, is complementary with the Sociolinguistics of Society in terms of its coverage and concerns. Alternatively, we may also define the Sociolinguistics of Language as a study of sociolinguistic issues at a micro level of discussion.

Sociolinguistics of Society: A branch of linguistics examines issues related to the subject from a more societal perspective, which is complementary with the Sociolinguistics of Language in terms of its coverage and concerns. Alternatively, we may also define the Sociolinguistics of Society as a study of sociolinguistic issues at a macro level of discussion.

Tripartite Model for Successful Communication: A working framework which is based on Roger's concept of real communication (1961) and is composed of the following principles: 1) try to look at things from other persons' point of view, 2) try to sense their feeling to a given issue, and 3) try to understand their way of knowing the world.

Variationist Linguistics: A theoretic framework advanced by William Labov to study how language variation and change take place in different social contexts or geographic districts under the influence of social factors such as economics, education, class, gender, style, and so on. The method it uses is basically quantitative, but qualitative instruments have recently been introduced in this branch of linguistic research for a better description and explanation of the data collected.

Women Register: A hypothesis which assumes that the following features are prevailing in women's linguistic behavior:
1) Women use more "fancy" color terms such as "mauve" and "beige".
2) Women use less powerful curse words.
3) Women use more intensifiers such as "terrible" and "awful".
4) Women use more tag questions.
5) Women use more statement questions like "Dinner will be ready at seven o'clock?" (with a rising intonation at the end)
6) Women's linguistic behavior is more indirect and, hence, more polite than men's.

2. What are some important contributions that sociolinguistics has made to linguistic studies?

    A couple of contrastive points can be given to show important contributions of sociolinguistics to linguistics. First, traditional linguistics emphasizes a formal analysis of language, whereas sociolinguistics calls for a multi-faceted study of language so that a more balanced research framework can be achieved. Second, traditional linguistics focuses much on the study of structure, whereas sociolinguistics emphasizes the study of function so that a holistic study of linguistic issues will be possible. Third, traditional linguistics attempts to look at internalized elements of language, but sociolinguistics pays more attention to externalized factors in language use so that a better understanding of the relationships between language, society, and the speaker can be achieved.

3. Why do we need to teach culture in our language classroom?

    A consensus has been reached that language not only reflects culture but also is part of culture. The close relationships between language and culture have widely been acknowledged. When it comes to language teaching and learning, the influence of cultural knowledge on the linguistic performance of language learners has been identified and highlighted. It has repeatedly been found that learners who lack sufficient knowledge about the target culture can hardly become active and appropriate language users in their target language. For these reasons, the information concerning cultural differences has rightly been introduced in language classrooms of different kinds for enhancing learners' cultural consciousness and improving their performance in cross-cultural contexts of communication.

4. As students of linguistics, how should we understand the relationships between functionalism and formalism?

A healthier understanding of the relationships between functionalism and formalism is to regard them as two sides of a coin, rather than two contrasting theories or concepts. Meanwhile, we must also admit that each of them has something rather unique in terms of the selection of theoretical frameworks, perspectives, research concerns, and methods. For instance, when we want to study grammatical issues from a typological perspective, a formal description of the differences in language structure proves to be a more economic and feasible approach. On the other hand, if we attempt to examine issues related to language use, a functional perspective will be a better choice. In either case, there is no absolute contrast between the two, if you want to have a holistic study of linguistic problems.

5. Over the past two decades, hundreds of new words have rushed into the daily life of Chinese people. Try to collect a bunch of these words, examine the context of their usage, and provide a feasible explanation to their booming.

If we compare newspaper articles published recently with those published five years ago, we will catch a big difference in their lexical choice—there are so many new words and expressions in these new articles. Based on the results of this comparison, we can equally predict that today's readers will find it a little bit difficult to understand what future newspapers or e-newspapers will carry. Over the past decades, Chinese people have enjoyed a much more colorful life, materially and spiritually. The rapid development in science, technology, economics, culture, and education has brought in our daily communication thousands and thousands of new words. Words such as 微信、动漫、网游、按揭、海选(in an election)、海面(in a job interview)、网购、裸捐、裸退, have now become part of our active vocabulary and are used frequently in our speech. Facing a situation like this, you may ask this question: Where do these new words and expressions come from? It is not an easy job to tell a complete story of these words. If you look at the question from a sociolinguistic point of view, you may claim that language changes with society. Words are the most active, sensible, and changeable component of language. Following this line of reasoning, we may conclude that, as society changes, the vocabulary of our language will become richer, more colorful and expressive in the days to come.

6. It has been widely recognized that the so-called "magic words" like "thank you" and "please" are more frequently used in English speaking society than they will in Chinese speaking society. One of explanations for this phenomenon may go like this: Look, these foreigners are really more polite than our countrymen. Try to use your knowledge in sociolinguistics and make some comments on this understanding of cultural differences.

   Basically speaking, the above explanation is not a correct one. As we all know, people from different cultural backgrounds speak differently. A maxim we should keep in mind is that one culture's meat can be another culture's poison. Take the quoted example again. English people and Chinese people have their distinctive ways to express politeness. In most cases, expressions like "thank you" and "please" are used as a lip service (口惠) in English, not really meaning that the speaker owes you something. On the other hand, a friendly smile or a slight nodding will be a more common practice in Chinese culture to express politeness. If we are not aware of this subtle difference, new cultural misunderstanding will come into being. For instance, you may either feel that English speakers are so polite for trivial things that they appear false and less sincere(虚情假意)or consider that Chinese speakers are so rude that they never know how to speak politely.

7. What will you say to a statement like "one culture's meat is another culture's poison"?

   In cross-cultural communication, when people have some trouble and do not know how to behave correctly, they inevitably turn to their source culture for help. This is a strategy often used by communicators in a new cultural setting. Convenient as it is, this strategy may not always work. Far too many bad stories can be told to illustrate this point. This is because people from different communities think, behave, and speak differently. As our case studies in Chapter 7 show, if we are not aware of this difference, we may run into trouble. Therefore, a principle that cross-cultural communicators should follow is to understand the target culture by transcending the source culture. Put alternatively, try to do as the Romans do when in Rome.

8. Why should language instructors look to sociolinguistics?

   According to Berns (1990: 339), sociolinguistics can make the following contributions to language teaching. If you like, you may add more.

   It has contributed to a change of emphasis in the content of language teaching.

   It has also contributed to innovations in materials and activities for the classroom.

   It has contributed to a fresh look at the nature of language development and use.

It has contributed to a more fruitful research in this field.
9. For linguistic studies of the new century, what is the significance of the division made between the faculty of language in the broad sense (FLB) and in the narrow sense (FLN)?

According to the new development in linguistic studies (Hauser, Chomsky & Fitch, 2002), a revolutionary point of view should be adopted in the linguistic research of the new century. In addition, a distinction has been made between the faculty of language in the broad sense (FLB) and in the narrow sense (FLN). The former covers a much wide range of linguistic studies by calling for an interdisciplinary study of linguistic issues, while the latter "only includes recursion and is the only uniquely human component of the faculty of language" (ibid, 1569). Clearly enough, this re-classification of linguistic studies will broaden the horizon of linguistic research, enrich linguistic science, and encourage healthier communication between relevant fields so that new breakthroughs in linguistic theorizing will be possible.

10. As we all know, compared with the rapid change in vocabulary, address forms in a language usually keep constant and stable. However, a dramatic change did take place in the address system of Chinese recently. A typical case in this respect is the use of *qin*（亲）and its plural form *qinmen*（亲们）as address forms. As a student of sociolinguistics, how are you going to explain this phenomenon?

Believe it or not, the rapid spread of a new Chinese address form has been promoted by virtual e—commerce communication rather than by real interpersonal interaction. And this new usage is *qin*（亲）, which was initiated by China's largest online shopping business—Taobao Marketplace. If we look at the use of *qin* from a sociolinguistic perspective, we may realize that it is indeed something unexpected. Here are some explanations for this change.

Morphologically speaking, *qin* comes from the expression *qinaide*（亲爱的）which, when used as an address form meaning "dear" in English, is a linguistic entity that allows no further segmentation. Semantically speaking, even the use of *qinaide* is heavily constrained by a sociolinguistic factor—intimacy. For instance, *qinaide* is only used among couples, lovers, family members, and close friends, but never between unfamiliar persons. Based on the above analysis, three features can be summarized concerning the formation and use of this new address form. An unbelievable thing is that *qin* is taken from an inseparable linguistic entity, forming a new expression that is grammatically wrong but pragmatically acceptable. An innovative thing is that you can use *qin* to address anyone, intimate or not. An unexpected thing is that its plural forms *qinmen*（亲们）, *zhongqin*（众亲）, and even *zhongqinmen*（众亲们）have come into use as well. When it comes to this point, we may draw a conclusion like this: Society changes. So does language.

Further Reading

Berlin, Brent & Paul, Kay. 1991[1969]. *Basic Color Terms: Their Universality and Evolution*. Berkeley: University of California Press.

Downes, William. 1998. *Language and Society*. 2nd Edition. Cambridge: Cambridge University Press.

Fasold, Ralph. 1999[1990]. *The Sociolinguistics of Language*. Oxford: Blackwell.

Ferrara, K. & B. Bell. 1995. Sociolinguistic Variation and Discourse Function of Constructed Dialogue Introducers: The Case of *be* + *like*. *American Speech*, 70 (3): 265—289.

Hauser, Marc D., Noam Chomsky & W. Tecumseh Fitch. 2002. "The Faculty of Language: What Is It, Who Has It, and How Did It Evolve?" *Science*, 298: 1569—1579.

Hymes, Dell. (ed.)1964. *Language in Culture and Society: A Reader in Linguistics and Anthropology*. New York: Harper & Row.

Hymes, Dell. 1972. "Toward Ethnographies of Communication: The Analysis of Communicative Event." In Pier Pulo Giglioli (ed.) *Language and Social Context*, 21—24. Harmondsworth: Peguin.

Labov, William. 1966. *The Social Stratification of English in New York City*. Washington, DC: Center for Applied Linguistics.

Rogers, Carl R. 1961. *On Becoming a Person: A Therapist's View of Psychotherapy*. Boston, MA.: Houghton Mifflin Company.

Romaine, S. & D. Lange. 1991. The Use of *Like* as a Marker of Reported Speech and Thought: A Case of Grammaticalization in Progress. *American Speech*, 66 (3): 227—279.

Rosch, Eleanor. 1977. "Human Categorization". In N. Warren(ed.), *Studies in Cross-cultural Psychology*, Vol. I, 1—49. London: Academic Press.

Sampson, Geoffrey. 1980. *Schools of Linguistics: Competition and Evolution*. London: Hutchinson.

Stewart, Edward C. 1983. "Talking Culture: Language in the Function of Communication". In R. J. Di Pietro, W. Frawley & A. Wedel (eds.), *The First Delaware Symposium on Language Studies: Selected Papers*, 23—34. Newark: University of Delaware Press.

XinRan. 2005. "Food for Talk". *The Guardian*, Friday, July 29.

Yang, Yonglin. 2002. *A Socio-cognitive Study of Chinese Students' Color Codability in English*(《中国学生英语色彩语码认知模式研究》). 北京:清华大学出版社.

Yang, Yonglin. 2004a. *A Study of Sociolinguistic Issues*(《社会语言学研究:功能·称谓·性别篇》), Vol. I, 上海:上海外语教育出版社.

Yang, Yonglin. 2004b. *A Study of Sociolinguistic Issues*(《社会语言学研究:文化·色彩·思维篇》), Vol. II, 北京:高等教育出版社.

杨永林,2008,"千门万门,同出一门——从美国'水门事件'看文化'模因'现象",《外语教学与研究》, 30 (5): 385—389.

杨永林,2013,"社会语言学视角下的语法化研究",《现代外语》, 36 (2):111—119.

Chapter 8 Language in Use

1. Define the following terms.

    performative: A performative is a sentence like "I *name* this ship the Queen Elizabeth", which does not describe things and cannot be said to be true or false. The uttering of a performative sentence is, or is a part of, the doing of an action. Verbs like *name* are known as performative verbs.

    constative: In contrast to performative, sentences like "I pour some liquid into the tube" is a description of what the speaker is doing at the time of speaking. The speaker cannot pour any liquid into a tube by simply uttering these words. He must accompany his words with the actual pouring. Otherwise one can accuse him of making a false statement.

    locutionary act: The locutionary act is the ordinary act we perform when we speak, i.e. we move our vocal organs and produce a number of sounds, organized in a certain way and with a certain meaning. For example, when somebody says "Morning!", we could say he produced a sound, word or sentence, "Morning!"

    illocutionary act: The illocutionary act is the act performed in the performing of a locutionary act. When we speak we not only produce some units of language with certain meanings, but also make clear our purpose in producing them, the way we intend them to be understood, or they also have certain forces as Austin prefers to say. In the example of "Morning!", we can say it has the force of a greeting, or it ought to have been taken as a greeting.

    perlocutionary act: The perlocutionary act concerns the consequential effects of a locution upon the hearer. By telling somebody something the speaker may change the opinion of the hearer on something, or mislead him, or surprise him, or induce him to do something, etc. Whether or not these effects are intended by the speaker, they can be regarded as part of the act that the speaker has performed.

    cooperative principle: This is the principle suggested by Grice about the regularity in conversation, which reads "Make your conversational contribution such as is required, at the stage at which it occurs, by the accepted purpose or direction of the talk exchange in which you are engaged". There are four categories of maxims under it, namely, quantity maxims, quality maxims, relation maxim, and manner maxims.

    conversational implicature: This is a type of implied meaning, which is deduced on the basis of the conventional meaning of words together with the context, under the guidance of the CP and its maxims. In this sense, implicature is comparable to illocutionary force in speech act theory in that they are both concerned with the contextual side of meaning, or 言外之意 in Chinese.

    entailment: This is a logical relationship between two sentences in which the truth of the second necessarily follows from the truth of the first, while the falsity of the first follows from the falsity of the second. For example, when "I saw a boy" is true, "I saw a child" is necessarily true; and if "I saw a child" is not true, "I saw a boy" will not be true either.

ostensive communication: "Ostensive communication" or "inferential communication" is a shorthand for "ostensive-inferential communication". That is, communication is not simply a matter of encoding and decoding, it also involves inference on the part of the hearer and ostension (making clear of one's intention to express something) on the part of the speaker.

communicative principle of relevance: This is the principle first proposed by Sperber and Wilson in 1986, which reads "Every act of ostensive communication communicates the presumption of its own optimal relevance."

relevance (as a comparative notion): Sperber and Wilson have defined the notion relevance in different ways. In their view, relevance is a comparative concept, so they also have an extent-conditions format as follows:

Extent condition 1: an assumption is relevant in a context to the extent that its contextual effects in this context are large.

Extent condition 2: an assumption is relevant in a context to the extent that the effort required to process it in this context is small.

(Horn's) Q-principle: The Q-principle (Hearer-based)
  MAKE YOUR CONTRIBUTION SUFFICIENT (cf. Quantity$_1$)
  SAY AS MUCH AS YOU CAN (given R)

R-principle: The R-principle (Speaker-based)
  MAKE YOUR CONTRIBUTION NECESSARY (cf. Relation, Quantity$_2$, Manner)
  SAY NO MORE THAN YOU MUST (given Q)

division of pragmatic labor: Horn observes that the Q-based and R-based principles often directly collide and suggests the resolution comes from a division of pragmatic labor, which reads "The use of a marked (relatively complex and/or prolix) expression when a corresponding unmarked (simpler, less 'effortful') alternate expression is available tends to be interpreted as conveying a marked message (one which the unmarked alternative would not or could not have conveyed)."

Levinson's three heuristics: In 2000, Levinson renamed his three principles as heuristics and simplified the contents as follows:

Heuristic 1
What isn't said, isn't.

Heuristic 2
What is simply described is stereotypically exemplified.

Heuristic 3
What's said in an abnormal way, isn't normal; or Marked message indicates marked situation.

2. Consider the following dialogue between a man and his daughter. Try to explain the illocutionary force in each of the utterances.

> [The daughter walks into the kitchen and takes some popcorn.]
> Father: I thought you were practicing your violin.
> Daughter: I need to get the [violin] stand.
> Father: Is it under the popcorn?

The illocutionary force of "I thought you were practicing your violin" is a criticism of the daughter for her not practicing the violin. That of the daughter's answer is a defence for herself—I need to get the stand first. And that of the father's retort is a denial of the daughter's excuse, since she is not getting the stand, but eating popcorn.

3. If you ask somebody "Can you open the door?", he answers "Yes" but does not actually do it, what would be your reaction? Why? Try to see it in the light of speech act theory.

I would be angry with him. "Can you open the door" is normally a request of the hearer to do it rather than a question about his ability. The fact that he answers "Yes" but does not actually do it shows that he declines my request.

4. On 14 January, 1993, US President-elect Bill Clinton spoke to journalists in the wake of rumours that he might go back on some of his promises made during the electoral campaign. When cornered by some insistent journalists, he came up with the following statement.

> *I think it would be foolish for the President of the United States, for any President of the United States, not to respond to changing circumstances. Every President of the United States, as far as I know, and particularly those who have done a good job, have known how to respond to changing circumstances. It would clearly be foolish for a President of the United States to do otherwise.*

Some linguists argue that campaign speeches, like all political speeches, are one of the occasions on which the CP and its maxims are suspended, do you agree? Can you think of any other similar occasion?

Yes, this is an occasion on which the CP and its maxims are suspended. When he formulated his CP, Grice qualified it with expressions like "normally", "characteristically" and "ceteris paribus". In other words, the CP and its maxims are not meant to be observed in all situations. Alternatively, we may say that assumptions like "The speaker believes in what he says" are implicatures, which will be cancelled in situations where there are indications to the contrary. Similar occasions include funeral orations, poetry writing, and joking.

5. "The Club" is a device for blocking an automobile's steering wheel, thus protecting the car from being stolen. And one of its ads reads:

THE CLUB!
Anti-theft device for cars
POLICE SAY:
'USE IT'
OR LOSE IT

In terms of the Gricean theory, what maxim is exploited here? Find two Chinese ads of the same type.

The main maxim exploited here is the Manner maxim of "Avoid ambiguity". The two tokens of *it* refer to two different things. Two Chinese ads of similar kind are 买一送一 and 要想皮肤好,早晚用大宝.

6. A is reading the newspaper. When B asks "What's on television tonight?" he answers "Nothing." What does A mean in normal situations? Think of two situations in which this interpretation of "Nothing" will be cancelled.

Normally "Nothing" here means "Nothing interesting". If A adds after "Nothing", "The workers are on strike" or "There's going to be a blackout tonight", then the interpretation of "Nothing interesting" will be cancelled.

7. Of the following pairs of sentences, say whether A entails B in each case.
   (1) A. John is a bachelor.
       B. John is a man.
   (2) A. Janet plays the fiddle.
       B. Someone plays a musical instrument.
   (3) A. I've done my homework.
       B. I haven't brushed my teeth.
   (4) A. Some of the students came to my party.
       B. Not all of the students came to my party.
   (5) A. Mary owns three canaries.
       B. Mary owns a canary.
   (6) A. John picked a tulip.
       B. John didn't pick a rose.

   (1) Yes. (2) Yes. (3) No. (4) No. (5) Yes. (6) No.

8. Each of the following conversational fragments is to some degree odd. To what extent can the oddness be explained by reference to Grice's CP and maxims?
   (1) A: Have you seen Peter today?
       B: Well, if I didn't deny seeing him I wouldn't be telling a lie.
   (2) A: Are you there?
       B: No, I'm here.
   (3) A: Thank you for your help, you've been most kind.
       B: Yes, I have.
   (4) A: Can you tell me where Mr. Smith's office is?
       B: Yes, not here.

(5) A: Would you like some coffee?
    B: Mary's a beautiful dancer.
(6) A: Has the postman been?
    B: He leant his bicycle against the fence, opened the gate, strode briskly down the path, stopped to stroke the cat, reached into his bag, pulled out a bundle of letters and pushed them through our letter box.

Without a proper context, these conversations can all be regarded as jokes resulting from the exploitation of Grice's CP and maxims.

In (1) Speaker B uses a long and prolix way to express the meaning of "Yes, I have", thus violating the Manner maxim of "Be brief (avoid prolixity)".

(2B) results from the exploitation of Quality maxims in that the speaker seems to be telling the truth while deliberately misinterpreting Speaker A's "there".

(3B) is another instance of exploiting the Quality maxims. Though logically speaking it may be true that Speaker B has been helpful to A, we don't usually respond to others' thanks in this way.

On one hand, (4B) is still another instance of exploiting the Quality maxims in that Mr. Smith's office is really "not here". On the other hand, Speaker B has violated the Quantity maxim of being as informative as is required since A needs more specific information than "not here".

(5B) is an indirect way of declining the offer. In terms of Grice's maxims, this is a case of not being relevant.

In the last conversation, Speaker B uses a long and prolix way for the simple answer "Yes, he has", and has thus violated the Manner maxim of "Be brief (avoid prolixity)".

Further Reading

Austin, J. L. 1975 [1962]. *How to Do Things with Words*. 2nd ed. Oxford: Clarendon Press. Reprinted in China by 外语教学与研究出版社, 2002.

Barr, D. J. & Keysar, B. 2005. Making Sense of How We Make Sense: The Paradox of Egocentrism in Language Use. In Colston, H. L. & Katz, A. N. (eds.) *Figurative Language Comprehension: Social and Cultural Influences*, 21–43. Mahwah, NJ: Erlbaum.

Bonnefon, J. F., Feeney, A. & Villejoubert, G. 2009. When Some is Actually All: Scalar Inferences in Face-threatening Contexts. *Cognition*, 112: 249–58.

Grice, H. P. 1975. Logic and Conversation. In Cole, P. & Morgan, J. L. (eds.) (1975) *Syntax and Semantics 3: Speech acts*, 41–58. New York: Academic Press.

Grice, H. P. 1989. *Studies in the Way of Words*. Cambridge, Mass.: Harvard University Press. Reprinted in China by 外语教学与研究出版社, 2002.

Horn, L. R. 1984. Towards a New Taxonomy for Pragmatic Inference: Q-based and R-based Implicature. In Schiffrin, D. (ed.) 1984. *Meaning, Form, and Use in Context: Linguistic Applications*, 11–42. Washington,

D. C.: Georgetown University Press.
Horn, L. R. 1988. Pragmatic Theory. In Newmeyer, F. (ed.) 1988. *Linguistics: The Cambridge Survey*. Vol. 1, 113—145. Cambridge: Cambridge University Press.
Kecskes, I. 2014. *Intercultural Pragmatics*. Oxford: Oxford University Press.
Keysar, B. 2007. Communication and Miscommunication: The Role of Egocentric Processes. *Intercultural Pragmatics*, 4.1: 71—84.
Keysar, B., Barr, D. J. & Horton, W. S. 1998. The Egocentric Basis of Language Use: Lnsights From a Processing Approach. *Current Directions in Psychological Science*, 7.2: 46—50.
Keysar, B., Barr, D. J., Balin, J. A. & Brauner, J. S. 2000. Taking Perspective in Conversation: The Role of Mutual Knowledge in Comprehension. *Psychological Science*, 11.1: 32—8.
Keysar, B., Lin Shuhong & Barr, D. J. 2003. Limits on Theory of Mind use in Adults. *Cognition*, 89: 25—41.
Leech, G. N. 1983. *Principles of Pragmatics*. London: Longman.
Levinson, S. C. 1983. *Pragmatics*. Cambridge: Cambridge University Press.
Levinson, S. C. 1987. Pragmatics and the Grammar of Anaphora: A Partial Pragmatic Reduction of Binding and Control Phenomena. *Journal of Linguistics*, 23: 379—434.
Levinson, S. C. 1989. A Review of Relevance. *Journal of Linguistics*, 25, 455—472.
Levinson, S. C. 2000. *Presumptive Meanings*. Cambridge, Mass.: MIT Press.
McCawley, J. 1978. Conversational Implicature and the Lexicon. In Cole, P. (ed.) *Syntax and Semantics 9: Pragmatics*, 245—259. New York: Academic Press.
Sperber, D. & Wilson, D. 1995 [1986]. *Relevance: Communication and Cognition*. 2nd ed. Oxford: Blackwell. Reprinted in China by 外语教学与研究出版社, 2002.
Verschuren, J. 1987. *Pragmatics as a Theory of Linguistic Adaptation*. In *Working Document #1*, Antwerp: International Pragmatics Association.
Wilson, D. and Sperber, D. 1981. "On Grice's Theory of Conversation". In P. Werth (ed), *Conversation and Discourse*. London: Croom Helm, 155—78. Reprinted in A. Kasher (ed), *Pragmatics: Critical Concepts*. London: Routledge. 1998, vol. 4, 347—368.
程雨民,2011,《语言系统及其运作》(修订版),上海:上海外语教育出版社。
姜望琪,2000,《语用学——理论及应用》,北京:北京大学出版社。
姜望琪,2003,《当代语用学》,北京:北京大学出版社。

Chapter 9   Language and Literature

1. Define the following terms.

    third-person narrator: If the narrator is not a character in the fictional world, he or she is usually called a THIRD-PERSON NARRATOR, because reference to all the characters in the fictional world of the story will involve the use of the third-person pronouns, *he*, *she*, *it* or *they*. This type of narrator is arguably the dominant narrator type.

I-narrator: The person who tells the story may also be a character in the fictional world of the story, relating the story after the event. In this case the critics call the narrator a FIRST-PERSON NARRATOR or I-NARRATOR because when the narrator refers to himself or herself in the story the first person pronoun *I* is used. First-person narrators are often said to be "limited" because they don't know all the facts or "unreliable" because they trick the reader by withholding information or telling untruths. This often happens in murder and mystery stories.

free indirect speech: It usually occurs in a form which appears at first sight to be indirect speech but also has direct speech features. One example of free indirect speech is *The child asked how he was and hoped he was better*. The first half of the sentence *The child asked how he was* ... is clearly indirect speech, giving the propositional content of the utterance but not the words used.

direct thought: It tends to be used for presenting conscious, deliberative thought. E. g. *"He will be late", she thought*.

stream of consciousness writing: The term was originally coined by the philosopher William James in his *Principle of Psychology* (1890) to describe the free association of ideas and impressions in the mind. It was later applied to the writing of William Faulkner, James Joyce, Virginia Woolf and others experimenting early in the 20th century with the novelistic portrayal of the free flow of thought. Note, however, that the majority of thought presentation in novels is not stream of consciousness writing. The examples we have discussed above are not stream of consciousness writing because they are too orderly to constitute the free association of ideas. Perhaps the most famous piece of stream of consciousness writing is that associated with Leopold Bloom in Joyce's *Ulysses*. Here he is in a restaurant thinking about oysters:

"Filthy shells. Devil to open them too. Who found them out? Garbage, sewage they feed on. Fizz and Red bank oysters. Effect on the sexual. Aphrodis. (sic) He was in the Red bank this morning. Was he oyster old fish at table. Perhaps he young flesh in bed. No. June has no ar (sic) no oysters. But there are people like tainted game. Jugged hare. First catch your hare. Chinese eating eggs fifty years old, blue and green again. Dinner of thirty courses. Each dish harmless might mix inside. Idea for a poison mystery."

This cognitive meandering is all in the most free version of direct thought. It is also characterised by a highly elliptical sentence structure, with as many grammatical words as possible being removed consistently allowing the reader to be able to infer what is going on. The language is not very cohesive, and breaks the Gricean maxims of Quantity and Manner. But we must assume that apparently unreasonable writing behaviour is related to a relevant authorial purpose. It is the assumption that Joyce is really cooperating with us at a deeper level, even though he is apparently making our reading difficult, that leads us to conclude that he is trying to evoke a mind working associatively.

text style: It looks closely at how linguistic choices help to construct textual meaning. Just as authors can be said to have style, so can text. Critics can talk of the style of *Middlemarch*, or even parts of it, as well as the style of George Eliot. When the style of texts or extract from texts is examined, we are even more centrally concerned with meaning than with the world view version of authorial style discussed above, and so when we examine text style we will need to examine linguistic choices which are intrinsically connected with meaning and effect on the reader. All of the areas discussed in the textbook could be relevant to the meaning of a particular text and its style; as can areas like lexical and grammatical patterning. Even the positioning of something as apparently insignificant as a comma, for example, can sometimes be very important in interpretative terms.

2. What different forms of sound patterning can you find in the first stanza of the poem, "Easter Wings", by George Herbert (1593—1663)?

> Lord, who createdst man in wealth and store,
> Though foolishly he lost the same,
> Decaying more and more,
> Till he became
> Most poore:
> With thee
> O let me rise
> As larks, harmoniously,
> And sing this day thy victories:
> Then shall the fall further the flight in me.

Alliteration: store/same; Lord/lost; this/thy/then/the; fall/further/flight; more/me
Assonance: Lord/store/fall; Though/most; same/decaying
Consonance: man/in
Rhyme: more/poore/store; became/same; thee/me/harmoniously
Half-rhyme: rise/victories
Repetition: more/more; me/me

(Thornborrow and Wareing 1998/2000: 218)

3. Identify the type of trope employed in the following examples.
   1) The boy was as cunning as a fox.
   2) ...the innocent sleep,... the death of each day's life,... (Shakespeare)
   3) Buckingham Palace has already been told the train may be axed when the rail network has been privatised. (*Daily Mirror*, 2 February 1993)
   4) Ted Dexter confessed last night that England are in a right old spin as to how they can beat India this winter. (*Daily Mirror*, 2 February 1993)

   1) simile   2) metaphor   3) metonymy   4) synecdoche

4. Choose a scene from a play, one you have seen or read, one you have heard on the radio(there are published collections of radio plays available), or one you are studying.

1) Write a *paraphrase* of it, as described in Stage One in this course;
2) Write a *commentary* on the same scene, as described in Stage Two in this course;
3) Choose one of the discourse features discussed above, and *analyse* the same scene to see how that feature is made use of in the scene, and the effect this has on your interpretation of it.

(Free answer)

5. Discuss questions related to Exercise 4. Does your analysis change your attitude to anything you wrote in your paraphrase or commentary of the play? If so, what, and how?

(Free answer)

6. Do you know anything about the British poet Philip Larkin?

Philip Larkin (1922—1985) was the most representative and highly regarded of the poets who gave expression to a clipped, antiromantic sensibility prevalent in English verse in the 1950s. He was educated at Oxford University. (*Merriam-Webster's Encyclopedia of Literature*, 1995)

7. What do you think of the cognitive approach to literature?

The linguistic and cognitive approaches to literature are complementary. The cognitive approach can augment the overall quality, depth and value of the linguistic approach. (Burke, 2005)

Further Reading

Bradford, R. 1997. *Stylistics*. London: Routledge.
Brumfit, C. J. & R. A. Carter. 1986/1997/2000. *Literature and Language Teaching*. Oxford University Press and Shanghai Foreign Languages Education Press.
Burke, M. 2005. How Cognition Can Augment Stylistic Analysis, *European Journal of English Studies*, Vol. 9, No. 2 August 2005, pp. 185—195.
Carter, R. & P. Simpson, Eds. 1989. *Language, Discourse and Literature: An Introductory Reader in Discourse Stylistics*. London: Unwin Hyman.
Cook, G. 1994/1995/1999. *Discourse and Literature*. Oxford University Press and Shanghai Foreign Languages Education Press.
Gavins, J. & Steen, G. (eds.) 2003. *Cognitive Poetics in Practice*. London and New York: Routledge.
Leech, G. 1969. *A Linguistic Guide to English Poetry*. London: Longman.
Leech, G. & M. Short. 1981. *Style in Fiction*. London: Longman.
Semino, E. & Culpeper, J. (eds.) 2002. *Cognitive Stylistics: Language and Cognition in Text Analysis*. Amsterdam/Philadelphia: Amsterdam: John Benjamins Publishing Company.
Short, M. 1996. *Exploring the Language of Poems, Plays and Prose*. London: Longman.
Stockwell, P. 2002. *Cognitive Poetics: An Introduction*. London and New York: Routledge.
Thornborrow, J. & S. Wareing. 1998/2000. *Patterns in Language—An Introduction to Language and Literary Style*. Routledge and Foreign Languages Teach-

ing and Research Press.
Toolan, M. 1998. *Language in Literature—An introduction to Stylistics*. London: Arnold.
Wales, K. 1989/2000. *A Dictionary of Stylistics*. London: Longman.
Widdowson, H. G. 1992/1999. *Practical Stylistics*. Oxford University Press and Shanghai Foreign Languages Education Press.
Wright, L. & J. Hope. 1996/2000. *Stylistics: A Practical Coursebook*. Routledge and Foreign Languages Teaching and Research Press.
高远、李福印(主编),2005,《乔治•莱考夫认知语言学十讲》,北京:外语教学与研究出版社。
胡壮麟,2004,《认知隐喻学》,北京:北京大学出版社。
李福印(主编),2004,《隐喻与认知——中国大陆出版物注释目录 1980—2004》,北京:中国文史出版社。
刘世生、曹金梅,2006,"思维风格与语言认知",《清华大学学报》哲社版第 2 期。

Chapter 10 Language and Computer

1. Define the following terms.

   computational linguistics: a branch of applied linguistics, dealing with computer processing of human language. It includes programmed instruction, speech synthesis and recognition, automatic translation, and computer mediated communication.

   computer literacy: (one with) sufficient knowledge and skill in the use of computers and computer software.

   speech synthesis: electronic production of artificial speech.

   CALL: computer-assisted language learning, the use of a computer in the teaching or learning of a second or foreign language.

   programmed instruction: teaching based on the analysis of language data so as to establish the order in which learners acquire various grammatical rules or the frequency of occurrence of some particular item.

   LAN: local area network, computers linked together by cables in a classroom, lab, or building.

   CD-ROM: COMPACT DISK-READ ONLY MEMORY, which allows huge amounts of information to be stored on one disk with quick access to the information.

   MT: machine translation, the use of machine (usually computers) to translate texts from one natural language to another.

   concordance: sorting the data in some way, for example, alphabetically on words occurring in the immediate context of the word.

   e-mail: sending mail to someone or a number of correspondents, or sending files and graphs by way of attachment in Messenger mail-box. With the help of listserv or majodomo the mail-box can also help the user with academic activities.

   blog: an online journal comprised of links and postings in reverse chronological order, meaning the most recent posting appears at the top of the page.

chatroom: a site on the internet where a number of users can communicate in real time (typically one dedicated to a particular topic)

IE: internet explorer, a series of graphical web browser developed by Microsoft.

FYI: for your information

corpus: a collection of linguistic data, either compiled as written texts or as a transcription of recorded speech. The main purpose of a corpus is to verify a hypothesis about language, for example, to determine how the usage of a particular sound, word, or syntactic construction varies.

CMC: computer-mediated communication, distinguished by its focus on language and language use in computer networked environments, and by its use of methods of discourse analysis to address that focus.

drill and practice: a teaching practice focused on vocabulary or discrete grammar points.

MOOC: massive open online course.

2. What is the basic difference between CAI and CAL in educational philosophy?

CAI aims at seeing educational problems on the part of the teacher, whereas CAL emphasizes the use of a computer in both teaching and learning in order to help the learners to achieve educational objectives through their own reasoning and practice, a reflection of newly advocated autonomous learning.

3. What are the 4 phases in the course of CALL development?

Phase I. During this period, computers were large mainframe machines kept in research institutions. Programs were stored on large mainframe computers and could only be accessed from terminals on certain university sites.

Phase II. Small portable computers appeared and cost cheaper than before. This made a generation of programs possible. They could be stored on tapes or floppy disks.

Phase III. The learning was based on cognitive problem-solving techniques and the interaction between students in a group. Activities such as role-play interaction are carried out.

Phase IV. Students are enabled to compose and try out their own writings in a non-permanent form. Multimedia technology is used. This leads to the phase of ICALL-intelligent CALL.

4. Is the linguistic approach in MT research successful? Why?

Not quite successful, because there are so many theories involved. It has also been found that those new theories which were successful in their initial trials on small samples have turned out to be problematic in the end.

5. What do you think about the knowledge-based approach?

Three types of knowledge are needed for the improvement of MT system, namely, linguistic knowledge independent of context (semantics), linguisitic knowledge that relates to context (pragmatics), and common sense/real world knowledge (non-liguistic). The first two problems are language-oriented but a system containing a bilingual dictionary and knowledge of grammar does not guarantee good quality translation. What is more, it is the lack of real world language on the part of computers that baffles the researchers. Computers do not understand the relationships things have with each other or how things fit together.

6. What's your view about the relation between MT and human translation?

When translation has to be of "publishable" quality, both human translation and MT have their roles. The human translator is and will remain unrivalled for non-repetitive linguistically sophisticated texts(e. g. in literature and law), and even for one-off texts in specific highly-specialized technical subjects. For the translation of texts where the quality of output is much less important, machine translation is often an ideal solution.

7. Choose the correct answer from each of the following set of options.
   a. Qualitative analysis is not useful in recognizing ambiguities in data.
      False.
   b. Corpus A has 350,000 words in it and 615 examples of "get". Corpus B has 20,000 words in it and 35 examples of "get". Which corpus has the greatest proportion of the word "get"?
      Corpus B
   c. A word frequency lexeme analysis is carried out on the data below. Which lexeme has the highest frequency?
      bat 16   bats 2   batting 1   batty 4
      can 22   clock 16   clocked 4   dark 7
      darkening 11   gave 11   give 6   given 3
      gives 1

      bat/can/clock/dark/give

8. What do you think about Chomsky's criticism and the revival of corpus linguistics?

Chomsky held the view that the corpus could never be a useful tool for the linguist, as the linguist must seek to model language competence rather than performance. Second, the only way to account for a grammar of a language is by description of its rules—not by enumeration of its sentences. Third, language is not a finite construct.

It was the wonder of computer that heralded the revival of corpus linguistics. The computer has the ability to search for a particular word, sequence of words, or perhaps even a part of speech in a text. The computer can also retrieve all examples of a particular word, usually in context, which is a further aid to the linguist. It can also calculate the number of occurrences of the word so that information on the frequency of the word may be gathered. We may then be interested in sorting the data in some way, for example, alphabetically on words occurring in the immediate context of the word.

9. What is the difference between blog and chatroom?

Some people think blogs with comment facilities could be seen as chatrooms, though it puts the blogger more in the role of moderator than writer, but some others think that a blog is not a chatroom, because the presence of a comment facility doesn't make it so.

10. Why should chatroom sometimes be monitored?

Although the users are free to enter a chatroom site and are free to talk whatever they like, many chatrooms are monitored for unacceptable, offensive, racial, violence, sexual content, etc.

11. What is the difference between cMOOCs and xMOOCs?

In cMOOC, the letter c stands for "connectivist". cMOOCs emphasize the connectivist philosophy, peer-review and group collaboration. The material should be *aggregated* (rather than pre-selected), *remixable*, *repurposable*, and *feeding forward*.

In contrast, "x" stands for "extended", xMOOCs resemble more traditional courses. xMOOCs have a clearly specified syllabus of recorded lectures and self-test problems. The instructor is the expert provider of knowledge, and student interactions are usually limited to asking for assistance and advising each other on difficult points.

12. In what sense WeChat is more advanced than Chatroom and Facebook?

WeChat provides text messaging, hold-to-talk voice messaging, broadcast (one-to-many) messaging, video conferencing, video games, sharing of photographs and videos, and location sharing. Photographs may also be embellished filters and captions, and a machine translation service is available.

13. What does each of the following acronyms and numbers stand for?

ADN	AISI	B4	CU
DIY	EOD	F/F	FYA
G2G	GA	HAGD	HLM
IDC	IHU	JAM	JK
KIT	LHM	LMA	NM
PM	Q4Y	SYS	TA
TTUL	U2	VBS	W8
WB	Y	YATB	WW4U

ADN	any day now	AISI	as I see it
B4	before	CU	see you
DIY	do it yourself	EOD	end of discussion
F/F	face to face	FYA	for your amusement
G2G	got to go	GA	go around
HAGD	have a good day	HLM	he loves me
IDC	I don't care	IHU	I hate you
JAM	just a minute	JK	just kiddy
KIT	keep in touch	LHM	lord help me
LMA	leave me alone	NM	never mind
PM	private message	Q4Y	question for you
SYS	see you soon	TA	thank again
TTUL	talk to you later	U2	you too

VBS	very big smile	W8	wait
WB	welcome back	Y	why
YATB	you are the best	WW4U	too wise for you

14. Can you guess the meaning of the following Emoticons or Smiley?

:-*   :{ }:   :<   (-:
:-()   :OI   XD   :)
:-D |-I

:-*	Kissing Smiley	:{ }:	Two people talking
:<	Very Sad Smiley	(-:	Left handed Smiley
:-()	Yelling	:OI	Mouth Full
XD	Laughing hilariously	:)	Standard Smiley for lazy people
:-D	Laughing	|-I	Asleep

Further Reading

Arnold, D., Balkan L., Meijer S., Humphreys R.L., L. Sadler. 1995. *Machine Translation: An Introductory Guide*. University of Essex.

Biber, Douglas, Susan Conrad & Randi Reppen. 1998. *Corpus Linguistics*. Cambridge: Cambridge University Press.

Butler, C. S. 1992. *Computers and Written Texts*. Oxford: Blackwell.

Garrett, N. 1991. Technology in the Service of Language Learning: Trends and Issues. *Modern Language Journal*, 75: 74—101.

Garside, R., Leech, G. & Sampson, G. 1987. *The Computational Analysis of English*. London: Longman.

Gazdar, G. & Mellish, C. 1987. Computational Linguistics. In J. Lyons, et al. (eds.) *New Horizon in Linguistics 2: An Introduction to Contemporary Linguistic Research*. London: Penguin Books, 25—248.

Grishman, R. 1986. *Computational Linguistics: An Introduction*. Cambridge: Cambridge University Press.

Hardisty, D. & Windeatt, S. 1989. *CALL*. Oxford: Oxford University Press.

Higgins, Chris. 1993. Computer-assisted Language Learning: Current Programs and Projects. *ERIC Digest*, April, 1993. Washington DC: ERIC Clearinghouse on Languages and Linguistics.

Jurafsky, D., & Martin, J. H. 2009. *Speech and Language Processing: An Introduction to Natural Language Processing, Computational Linguistics, and Speech Recognition*. Upper Saddle River, N.J: Pearson Prentice Hall.

Kay, Martin. 1982. *Computational Linguistics Archive*. Cambridge, MA: MIT Press.

Kennedy, Graeme. 1998. *An Introduction to Corpus Linguistics*. Addison-Wesley: Longman.

Leech, G. 1991. The State of the Art in Corpus Linguistics. In K. Aijmer & B. Altenberg (eds.) *English Corpus Linguistics: Studies in Honour of Jan Svartvik*, pp. 8—29. London: Longman.

Leech, G. 1993. Corpus Annotation Schemes. In *Literary and Linguistic Computing*, 8 (4): 275—281.

Leech, G. & Candlin, C.N. 1986. *Computers in English Language Teaching and*

Research. Harlow: Longman.

MoocGuide. 2013. "Benefits and Challenges of a MOOC". *MoocGuide*. 7 Jul 2011. Retrieved 4 February 2013.

Prpić, John; Melton, James; Taeihagh, Araz; Anderson, Terry (16 December 2015). "MOOCs and crowdsourcing: Massive courses and massive resources". *First Monday* 20 (12).

Siemens, George. "MOOCs are really a platform". *Elearnspace*. Retrieved 2012-12-09.

易绵竹, 南振兴, 2005,《计算语言学》, 上海: 上海外语教育出版社。

Chapter 11 Second and Foreign Language Teaching

1. Why should language teachers learn some knowledge of linguistics?

   Some knowledge of linguistics not only helps language teachers to better understand the nature of language, but also helps them better understand how to teach language. Theoretical views of language explicitly or implicitly inform the approaches and methods adopted in language teaching. Language teachers do need a theory (*maybe* theories) of language in order to teach language effectively, and they need to know at least how the language they teach works. To discover the real language and to obtain some understanding of it, language teachers may well turn to linguistics. Many language learning theories are proposed based on certain linguistic theories. In fact, knowledge in linguistics lies at the root of understanding what language learners can learn, how they actually learn and what they learn ultimately. Therefore, linguistics has always played an important role in the studies of language acquisition and learning.

2. What is FOCUS ON FORM?

   The key point in *focus on form* is that although language learning should generally be meaning-focused and communication-oriented, it is still necessary and beneficial to focus on form occasionally. Focus on form often consists of an occasional shift of attention to linguistic code features—by the teacher and/or one or more students—triggered by perceived problems with comprehension or production.

3. What is the INPUT HYPOTHESIS?

   According to Krashen's INPUT HYPOTHESIS (1985), learners acquire language as a result of comprehending input addressed to them. Krashen brought forward the concept of "$i+1$" principle, i.e. the language that learners are exposed to should be just far enough beyond their current competence that they can understand most of it but still be challenged to make progress. Input should neither be so far beyond their reach that they are overwhelmed, nor so close to their current stage that they are not challenged at all.

4. What is INTERLANGUAGE? Can you give some examples of interlanguage?

   The type of language constructed by second or foreign language learners who are still in the process of learning a language is often referred to as INTERLANGUAGE. Interlanguage is often understood as a language system between the target language and the learner's native language. It is imperfect compared with the target language, but it is not mere translation from the learner's native language. However, interlanguage should not really be seen as a bridging language between the target language and native language. Interlanguage is a dynamic language system, which is constantly moving from the departure level to the native-like level. Therefore, "inter" actually means between the beginning stage and the final stage. There are many examples of interlanguage, such as *I no have a book. I like read books.*

5. **What is the discourse-based view of language teaching?**

   The essential point of the discourse-based view of language takes into account the fact that linguistic patterns exist across stretches of text. These patterns of language extend beyond the words, clauses and sentences which have been the traditional concern of much language teaching (McCarthy & Carter, 1994:1). The discourse-based view of language focuses on complete spoken and written texts and on the social and cultural contexts in which such language operates. Accordingly, the discourse-based view of language teaching aims at developing discourse competence.

6. **What are real-world tasks and pedagogical tasks? Can you give some examples?**

   A real-world task is very close to something we do in daily life or work. For example, students may be asked to work in groups, discuss how the sports facilities in their school can be improved (e. g. buy some new facilities) and make some suggestions to the headmaster. This is a real world task because there are things like this in the real world. Pedagogical tasks are those activities that students do in the classroom but that may not take place in real life. For example, the students work in pairs. Each is given a picture. Most of the things in the pictures are the same, but there are some differences. The students are asked to describe their picture to each other and identify the differences. In this task, the students use language to do something, that is, to identify differences between two pictures. In doing this task, they focus on meaning rather than form, because they are not asked to practise particular linguistic items. We say this is a pedagogical task rather than a real-world task because in daily life we do not normally do things like this. It is pedagogical in the sense that it is designed to help the students to learn or review certain language knowledge or skills. This does not mean, however, that real-world tasks do not have any pedagogical purposes.

7. **What are the most important tasks for a syllabus designer?**

   The process of syllabus design in foreign language teaching mainly includes selecting and grading what is to be taught. A process of selection must be undertaken since learning the whole system of a foreign language is neither possible nor necessary. Selection involves two sub-processes: First, the restriction of the language to a particular dialect and register; and second, the selection from within the register of the items that are to be taught according to criteria such as frequency of occurrence, learnability and classroom needs. The whole process of selection must be applied at all levels of language, such as phonology, grammar, lexis, contexts (semantic and cultural). After a list of language items have been selected, the next process is to put them into the most appropriate order for practical teaching purposes. This process is often referred to as grading or sequencing.

8. What is a structural syllabus?

   Influenced by structuralist linguistics, the structural syllabus is a grammar oriented syllabus based on a selection of language items and structures. The vocabulary and grammatical rules included in the teaching materials are carefully ordered according to factors such as frequency, complexity and usefulness. The syllabus input is selected and graded according to grammatical notions of simplicity and complexity. These syllabuses introduce one item at a time and require mastery of that item before moving on to the next.

9. The structural syllabus is often criticised. Do you think it has some merits as well?

   The major drawback of such a syllabus is that it concentrates only on the grammatical forms and the meaning of individual words, whereas the meaning of the whole sentence is thought to be self-evident, whatever its context may be. Students are not taught how to use these sentences appropriately in real situations. As a result, students trained by a structural syllabus often prove to be communicatively incompetent. However, the structural syllabus also have some merits. For example, many students feel comfortable when learning a language through learning its grammar. In many contexts, both teachers and students expect to see grammar in the syllabus and teaching materials. Besides, the system of grammar provides a convenient guidance for syllabus design.

10. What are the important features of a task as defined in a task-based syllabus?

    (1) A task should have a clear purpose.
    (2) A task should have some degree of resemblance to real-world events.
    (3) A task should involve information seeking, processing and conveying.
    (4) A task should involve the students in some modes of doing things.
    (5) A task should involve the meaning-focused use of language.
    (6) A task should end with a tangible product.

11. What are non-language outcomes?

    (1) Affect cultivation, such as confidence, motivation, interest;
    (2) Learning strategies, thinking skills, interpersonal skills, etc.;
    (3) Cultural understanding.

12. What is Contrastive Analysis?

    Contrastive Analysis a way of comparing languages (e.g. L1 and L2) in order to determine potential errors for the ultimate purpose of isolating what needs to be learned and what does not need to be learned in a second language learning situation. The goal of contrastive analysis is to predict what areas will be easy to learn and what areas will be difficult to learn. Contrastive Analysis was associated in its early days with behaviourism

13. What are the differences between errors and mistakes? Can you identify the errors and mistakes in the sentences below?
    (1) I bought in Japan.
    (2) These dog are big.
    (3) He was arrived early.
    (4) Joe doesn't likes it.
    (5) Why didn't you came to school.
    (6) I doesn't know how.
    (7) She has been smoking less, isn't it?
    (8) I falled from the bike.
    (9) I no have it.
    (10) Why they look at each other?
    (11) I know what is that.
    (12) Although he was ill, but he still came.
    (13) I go to the university yesterday.
    (14) Teacher said he is right.

    Errors usually arise from the learner's lack of knowledge; it represents a lack of competence. In other words, the learner does not know the right form or is unable to use language correctly. Mistakes often occur when learners fail to perform their competence. In other words, the learner has already learned the knowledge or skill but simply fails to function correctly due to lack of attention or other factors.

14. What is a corpus? Can you give some examples of how the use of a corpus contributes to language teaching?

    Corpus is a collection of texts input into a computer. Language corpora make it possible for material developers to select authentic, natural and typical language. The two most important factors in a corpus are the size and types of texts selected. Usually the uses that will be made of the corpus decide the number and type of texts in a corpus. Corpora usually provide the following types of information:

    (1) Frequency information. Corpora can tell us how frequently certain language items or structures are used. This kind of information is useful when we try to select what to teach, select what to focus on, and decide what senses to focus on in the language classroom.

    (2) Context and co-text information. Contexts are the situational environments in which language is used. Co-texts are the linguistic environments. Sometimes it is very difficult to tell the differences of two words or phrases which have similar meaning. However, if we look at the context and co-text in which they are used, the difference becomes clear.

    (3) Grammatical information. We usually refer to grammar books for grammatical information. However, what the corpora show is far more complicated than what grammar books tell about grammar. For example, information from corpora has shown that conditionals in English are far more than 3 (first, second and third conditionals).

(4) Collocation and phraseology information. It is usually difficult for second and foreign language learners to learn which words are frequently used together, e. g. should we say *make effort* or *take effort*? A search in corpus will do the job.

(5) Pragmatics information. Information from corpora can tell us how language is actually used in communication. For example, students are often told that if someone says "How do you do?", they should say "How do you do?". Data from corpora show that in this situation there is more than one way to responsible. For example, we can also say "Nice to meet you."

Further Reading

Cook, V. 2000. *Linguistics and Second Language Acquisition*. Beijing: Foreign Language Teaching and Research Press.

Doughty, C. & Williams, J. (eds.). 1998. *Focus on Form in Classroom Second Language Acquisition*. Cambridge: Cambridge University Press.

Ellis, R. 1994. *The Study of Second Language Acquisition*. Oxford: Oxford University Press.

Ellis, R. 2003. *Task-based Language Learning and Teaching*. Oxford: Oxford University Press.

Gass, S. & Selinker, L. 2001. *Second Language Acquisition: An Introductory Course*. (2nd edition). N.J.: Lawrence Erlbaum.

James, C. 1998. *Errors in Language Learning and Use: Exploring Error Analysis*. London: Longman.

Nunan, D. 1988. *Syllabus Design*. Oxford: Oxford University Press.

Nunan, D. 1989. *Designing Tasks for the Communicative Classroom*. Cambridge: Cambridge University Press.

Nunan, D. 1999. *Second Language Teaching and Learning*. Boston: Heinle/Thomson Learning.

Richards, J. & Rodgers, T. 2001. *Approaches and Methods in Language Teaching*. Second Edition. Cambridge: Cambridge University Press.

Sinclair, J. 1991. *Corpus, Concordance, Collocation*. Oxford: Oxford University Press.

Willis, J. 1996. *A Framework for Task-based Learning*. London: Longman.

Chapter 12   Theories and Schools of Modern Linguistics

1. Why is Saussure hailed as the father of modern linguistics?

Saussure was the first to notice the complexities of language. He believed that language is a system of signs. To communicate ideas, signs must be part of a system of signs, called conventions. He held that the sign is the union of a form (signifier) and an idea (signified), and it is the central fact of language.

By providing answers to questions concerning many aspects of language, Saussure made clear the object of study for linguistics as a science. His ideas on the arbitrary nature of sign, on the relational nature of linguistic units, on the distinction of *langue* and *parole* and of synchronic and diachronic linguistics, etc. pushed linguistics into a brand new stage.

Chapter 12 Theories and Schools of Modern Linguistics

2. **What are the three important points of the Prague School?**

    The Prague School has three points of special importance. First, it stressed that the synchronic study of language is fully justified as it can draw on complete and controllable material for investigation. Second, it emphasized the systemic character of language, arguing that no element of any language can be satisfactorily analysed or evaluated if viewed in isolation. In other words, elements are held to be in functional contrast or opposition. Third, it looked on language as a tool performing a number of essential functions or tasks for the community using it.

3. **What is the Prague School best known for?**

    The Prague School is best known and remembered for its contribution to phonology and the distinction between phonetics and phonology. Following Saussure's distinction between *langue* and *parole*, Trubetzkoy argued that phonetics belonged to *parole* whereas phonology belonged to *langue*. On this basis he developed the notion of "phoneme" as an abstract unit of the sound system as distinct from the sounds actually produced.

    In classifying distinctive features, he proposed three criteria: (1) their relation to the whole contrastive system; (2) relations between the opposing elements; and (3) their power of discrimination. These oppositions can be summarised as: a) bilateral opposition; b) multilateral opposition; c) proportional opposition; d) isolated opposition; e) privative opposition; f) gradual opposition; g) equipotent opposition; h) neutralisable opposition; and i) constant opposition.

4. **What is the essence of Functional Sentence Perspective (FSP)?**

    FSP is a theory that refers to a linguistic analysis of utterances (or texts) in terms of the information they contain. The principle is that the role of each utterance part is evaluated for its semantic contribution to the whole. From a functional point of view, some Czechoslovak linguists believed that a sentence contains a point of departure and a goal of discourse. The point of departure is equally present to the speaker and to the hearer which it is their rallying point, the ground on which they meet. This is called the Theme. The goal of discourse presents the very information that is to be imparted to the hearer. This is called the Rheme. It is believed that the movement from the Theme to the Rheme reveals the movement of the mind itself. Language may use different syntactic structures, but the order of ideas remains basically the same. Based on these observations, they created the notion of Functional Sentence Perspective (FSP) to describe how information is distributed in sentences. FSP deals particularly with the effect of the distribution of known (or given) information and new information in discourse. The known information refers to information that is not new to the reader or hearer, and the new information is what is to be transmitted to the reader or hearer.

5. **What is the tradition of the London School?**

    The London School has a tradition of laying stress on the functions of language and attaching great importance to contexts of situation and the system aspect of language. It is these features that have made this school of thought known as systemic linguistics and functional linguistics. It is an important and admirable part of the London School tradition to believe that different types of linguistic description may be appropriate for different purposes.

6. What is the difference between Malinowski and Firth on context of situation?

Malinowski distinguished three types of context of situation: situations in which speech interrelates with bodily activity, narrative situations, and phatic situations. Firth defined the context of situation as including the entire cultural setting of speech and the personal history of the participants rather than as simply the context of human activity going on at the moment. Recognizing that sentences can vary infinitely, Firth used the notion of "typical context of situation", meaning that social situations determine the social roles participants are obliged to play; since the total number of typical contexts of situation they will encounter is finite, the total number of social roles is also finite. He put forward the idea that in analysing a typical context of situation, one has to take into consideration both the situational context and the linguistic context of a text.

7. What is important about Firth's prosodic analysis?

Prosodic analysis, or prosodic phonology, is Firth's second important contribution to linguistics. Since any human utterance is a continuous speech flow made up of at least one syllable, it cannot be cut into independent units. Phonological description only deals with paradigmatic relations, leaving syntagmatic relations out of consideration. Firth pointed out that in actual speech, it is not phonemes that make up the paradigmatic relations, but phonematic units. There are fewer features in phonematic units than in phonemes, because some features are common to phonemes of a syllable or a phrase (even a sentence). When these features are considered in syntagmatic relations, they are all called prosodic units, which include features such as stress, length, nasalisation, palatalisation, and aspiration. In any case, these features cannot be found in one phonematic unit alone.

8. What is the relation between Systemic Grammar and Functional Grammar?

Systemic Grammar and Functional Grammar are two inseparable components for an integral framework of Systemic-Functional linguistic theory. Systemic Grammar aims to explain the internal relations in language as a system network, or meaning potential. This network consists of subsystems from which language users make choices. Functional grammar aims to reveal that language is a means of social interaction, based on the position that language system and the forms that make it up are inescapably determined by the uses or functions which they serve. Systemic Grammar contains a functional component, and the theory behind Functional Grammar is systemic.

9. What is special about Systemic-Functional linguistics?

Systemic-Functional linguistics aims to provide a taxonomy for sentences, a means of descriptively classifying particular sentences. Although it may not seem as influential as Chomsky's transformational-generative

Chapter 12 Theories and Schools of Modern Linguistics • 81 •

theory in some parts of the world, it is much more relevant to the needs of various groups of people who deal with language.

Halliday believes that language is what it is because it has to serve certain functions. In other words, social demand on language has helped to shape its structure.

Systemic-Functional linguistics is based on two facts: (1) language users are actually making choices in a system of systems and trying to realise different semantic functions in social interaction; and (2) language is inseparable from social activities of man. Thus, it takes actual uses of language as the object of study, in opposition to Chomsky's approach that takes the ideal speaker's linguistic competence as the object of study.

10. Analyze the following sentences by identifying the Subject and Predicate on the first level and Theme and Rheme on the second level.
    (1) Mary gave her daughter a birthday present.
    (2) A birthday gift was given to Jenny.
    (3) The play was written by William Shakespeare.
    (4) Do have another drink.

    (1) Mary   gave her daughter a birthday gift.
        Subject   *Predicate*
        Theme   *Rheme*
    (2) A birthday gift   was given to Jenny.
        Subject   *Predicate*
        Theme   *Rheme*
    (3) The play   was written by William Shakespeare.
        Subject   *Predicate*
        Theme   *Rheme*
    (4) Do have   another drink.
        Predicate
        Theme   *Rheme*

11. Please put the following items in a diagram according to Halliday's notion of system and scale of delicacy.
    (1) she   (2) we   (3) always   (4) a perception process
    (5) an action process

    (1) Person: third person; Number: singular
    (2) Person: first person; Number: plural
    (3) Modality: frequency
    (4) Transitivity: mental process: internalized process
    (5) Transitivity: material process

12. Analyze the following Relational-process sentences according to their mode and type.
    (1) Linguistics is a difficult course.
    (2) This laptop is Professor Huang's.

    (1) Type: intensive; Mode: attributive
    (2) Type: possessive; Mode: identifying

13. Analyze the following sentences on two levels. First, identify the Subject, Finite, Predicator, and Adjunct. Second, identify Mood and Residue. Ex-

plain the difference, if any, between the two levels of analysis.
(1) Mr Hu made a speech at a conference yesterday.
(2) The university president has been awarded an international prize.
(3) Three days ago, an honorary title was given to a professor from Yale.

Mr Hu		made		a speech at the conference yesterday.
Subject	Finite		Predicator	Adjunct
Mood		Residue		

The university president		has	been awarded	an international prize.
Subject	Finite		Predicator	Adjunct
Mood		Residue		

Three days ago,	an honorary title	was	given	to a professor from Yale.
Adjunct	Subject	Finite	Predicator	Adjunct
Residue	Mood		Residue	

14. Analyze the following sentences on three levels of metafunctions.
    (1) John likes linguistics.
    (2) The paper was handed in three days later.

Ideational	John	likes	linguistics
Mental Process *Reaction*	Senser	Process: Mental: reaction	Phenomenon
Interpersonal	Mood	Residue	
Declarative	Subject	Predicator	Adjunct
Textual	Theme	Rheme	
Unmarked Theme	Given		New

Ideational	The paper	was handed in	three days later
Material Process *Action/passive*	Goal/Affected	Process: Material Action	
Interpersonal	Mood	Residue	
Declarative	Subject	Predicator	Adjunct
Textual	Theme	Rheme	
Unmarked Theme	Given		New

15. What is "appliable linguistics"?

"Appliable linguistics" is different from "applied" or "applicable" linguistics. It was marked by Halliday's lecture "Working with Meaning: Towards an Appliable Linguistics" at the City University of Hong Kong in March 2006 for launching the Halliday Center for Intelligent Application of Language Studies. Based on his belief that a theory of language is "essentially consumer oriented" (1985: 7), Halliday discusses in *Comple-*

mentarities in Language (2008) the complementarities between lexis and grammar, "language as system" and "as text", and speaking and writing, in his commitment to "working towards a coherent account of language which is 'appliable'" rather than constructing "some more powerful theoretical apparatus". His efforts were backed up by the publication of an anthology entitled *Appliable Linguistics* (Mahboob & Knight, 2010) and the founding of Martin Center of Appliable Linguistics at Shanghai Jiaotong University in 2014.

Appliable linguistics deals with the development and evaluation of linguistic theories, mainly consisting of the following principles: (1) the inseparability of theory and practice; (2) language as meaning and meaning as choice; (3) social accountability; and (4) multimodal research. The research objective and application of Systemic-Functional linguistic theories have undergone constant changes and revisions in order to meet various challenges and solve new problems. The notion "appliability" requires that theory and practice should develop according to new situations. "Appliable linguistics" is not a monopoly of Systemic-Functional linguists, but a theory for all schools of linguistics. Further, it is not only applicable to the field of linguistics, but also to semiotics and other related disciplines.

16. What are the special features of American structuralism?

American Structuralism is a branch of synchronic linguistics that developed in a very different style from that of Europe. While linguistics in Europe started more than two thousand years ago, linguistics in America started at the end of the nineteenth century. While traditional grammar plays a dominating role in Europe, it has little influence in America. While many European languages have their own historical traditions and cultures, English is the dominating language in America, where there is no such a tradition as in Europe. In addition, the pioneer scholars in America were faced with the urgent task of recording the rapidly perishing native American Indian languages because there was no written record of them. However, these languages were characterised by features of vast diversity and differences which are rarely found in other parts of the world. To record and describe these exotic languages, it is probably better not to have any presuppositions about the nature of language in general. This explains why there was not much development in linguistic theory during this period but a lot of discussion on descriptive procedures.

Structuralism is based on the assumption that grammatical categories should be defined not in terms of meaning but in terms of distribution, and that the structure of each language should be described without reference to the alleged universality of such categories as tense, mood and parts of speech. Firstly, structural grammar describes everything that is found in a language instead of laying down rules. However, its aim is confined to the description of languages, without explaining why language operates the way it does. Secondly, structural grammar is empirical, aiming at objectivity in the sense that all definitions and statements should be verifiable or refutable. However, it has produced almost no complete grammars comparable to any comprehensive traditional grammars. Thirdly, structural grammar examines all languages, recognising and doing justice to the uniqueness of each language. But it does not give an adequate treatment of meaning. Lastly, structural grammar describes even the smallest contrasts that underlie any construction or use of a language, not only those discoverable in some particular use.

17. How is behaviourist psychology related to linguistics?

For Bloomfield, linguistics is a branch of psychology, and specifically of the positivistic brand of psychology known as "behaviourism". Behaviourism is a principle of scientific method, based on the belief that human beings cannot know anything they have not experienced. Behaviourism in linguistics holds that children learn language through a chain of "stimulus-response reinforcement", and the adult's use of language is also a process of "stimulus-response". When the behaviourist methodology entered linguistics via Bloomfield's writings, the popular practice in linguistic studies was to accept what a native speaker *says* in his language and to discard what he *says about* it. This is because of the belief that a linguistic description was reliable when based on observation of unstudied utterances by speakers; it was unreliable if the analyst had resorted to asking speakers questions such as "Can you say in your language?"

18. What is Harris's most important contribution to linguistics?

Harris's *Methods in Structural Linguistics* (1951) makes the maturity of American descriptive linguistics, for he gave the fullest and most interesting expression of the "discovery procedure" approach characterised by accurate analytical procedures and high degree of formalisation. He formulated a set of strict descriptive procedures which took the logic of distributional relations as the basis of structural analysis. This method has greatly influenced American descriptive linguistics and Harris is therefore regarded as one of the most distinguished linguists in the post-Bloomfieldian era.

19. What is the theoretical importance of Tagmemics?

Tagmemics is a special name for the technique of linguistic analysis developed by Pike, the most significant figure in continuing the structuralist tradition. For Pike, a language has its own hierarchical systems independent of meaning. Not only are there hierarchies in language, but that everything in the world is hierarchical, consisting of different layers in the system from small to big, from bottom to top, from simple to complex, from part to whole. The ultimate aim of tagmemics is to provide a theory which integrates lexical, grammatical, and phonological information. This theory is based on the assumption that there are various relations in language, and these relations can be analysed into different units. However, to believe that language is part of human behaviour, one needs to recognise that language cannot be strictly formalised. Since no representational system can account for all the relevant facts of language, tagmemics accepts various different modes of representation for different purposes, and does not insist that

Chapter 12　Theories and Schools of Modern Linguistics　• 85 •

there is only one correct grammar or linguistic theory.
20. **What are the main features of Stratificational Grammar?**

　　Lamb's Stratificational Grammar consists of three levels: phoneme, morpheme, and morphophoneme. It sees the complex relationship in language as series of connected stratal systems on the assumption that while the system of relationships are not directly observable, it is generalizable. In this grammar, there is no direct relation between a concept and its sounds, and that there are various strata that make up a number of stratal systems. Among these, the four principal ones are the sememic, lexemic, morphemic, and the phonemic, from top to bottom.

21. **How many stages of development has Chomsky's TG Grammar undergone?**

　　Chomsky's TG Grammar has seen five stages of development. The Classical Theory aims to make linguistics a science. The Standard Theory deals with how semantics should be studied in a linguistics theory. The Extended Standard Theory focuses discussion on language universals and universal grammar. The Revised Extended Standard Theory (or GB) focuses discussion on government and binding. The latest is the Minimalist Program, a further revision of the previous theory.

　　The development of TG Grammar can be regarded as a process of constantly minimalising theories and controlling the generative powers. Although TG Grammar has involved putting forward, revising, and cancelling of many specific rules, hypotheses, mechanisms, and theoretical models, its aims and purposes have been consistent, i. e. , to explore the nature, origin and the uses of human knowledge on language.

22. **What does Chomsky mean by Language Acquisition Device?**

　　Chomsky believes that language is somewhat innate, and that children are born with what he calls a Language Acquisition Device (LAD), which is a unique kind of knowledge that fits them for language learning. He argues the child comes into the world with specific innate endowment, not only with general tendencies or potentialities, but also with knowledge of the nature of the world, and specifically with knowledge of the nature of language. According to this view, children are born with knowledge of the basic grammatical relations and categories, and this knowledge is universal. The categories and relations exist in all human languages and all human infants are born with knowledge of them. According to him, the study of language, or the structure of language, can throw some light on the nature of the human mind.

　　According to Chomsky, there are aspects of linguistic organization that are basic to the human brain and that make it possible for children to acquire linguistic competence in all its complexity with little instruction from family or friends. He argues that LAD probably consists of three elements: a hypothesis-maker, linguistic universal, and an evaluation procedure.

23. **Draw a tree diagram for each of the following sentences.**
　　(1) The police attacked the suspect.
　　(2) These children cannot understand her painting.

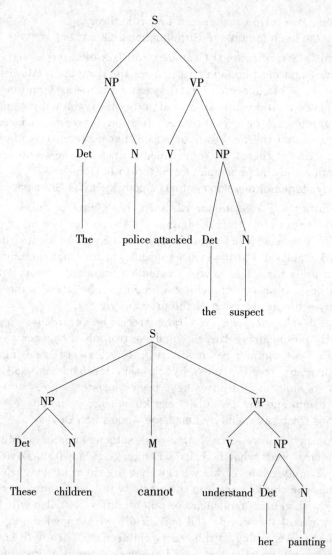

24. Explain why Generative Grammar can produce well-formed sentences (e.g. *Mary reads a book*) but not ill-formed ones (e.g. * *A book reads Mary*).

    The Standard Theory has a selectional restriction to rule out ill-formed sentences of this kind. It ensures that in an active voice the animate noun appears before the verb and the inanimate noun appears after the verb.

25. Why can a sentence like *John kills John* be transformed into *John kills himself*?

    The Reflexive Rule says that in simple sentences, if a noun appears twice, the second noun should be in the reflexive form. Thus, the second *John* becomes *himself*.

26. What is special about TG Grammar?

The starting point of Chomsky's TG Grammar is his innateness hypothesis, based on his observations that some important facts can never be otherwise explained adequately.

Chomsky's TG Grammar has the following features. First, Chomsky defines language as a set of rules or principles. Second, Chomsky believes that the aim of linguistics is to produce a generative grammar which captures the tacit knowledge of the native speaker of his language. This concerns the question of learning theory and the question of linguistic universals. Third, Chomsky and his followers are interested in any data that can reveal the native speaker's tacit knowledge. They seldom use what native speakers actually say; they rely on their own intuition. Fourth, Chomsky's methodology is hypothesis-deductive, which operates at two levels: (a) the linguist formulates a hypothesis about language structure—a general linguistic theory; this is tested by grammars for particular languages, and (b) each such grammar is a hypothesis on the general linguistic theory. Finally, Chomsky follows rationalism in philosophy and mentalism in psychology.

27. What are the latest developments of Chomsky's linguistic theory?

Chomsky's *The Minimalist Program* (1995) marks a new stage of his generative theory. It is motivated by two related questions: (1) What are the general conditions that the human language faculty should be expected to satisfy? (2) To what extent is the language faculty determined by these conditions, without a special structure that lies beyond them? This new theory is characterised by several remarkable changes. First, some of the discrete analytical models in the previous theory are discarded and the two levels of analysis, the deep structure and the surface structure, are left out. Second, the important concept of "government" is rejected and the facts interpreted by the theory of government are replaced by several revised concepts, thus the theory of government has turned from a subsystem of universal grammar into the interpretative constraint of the output condition.

In the late 1990s, Chomsky reconsidered the motivation for the Minimalist Program in order to give it a clearer explanation. He holds that the initial states of human languages are the same whereas the states of acquiring different languages are not. A universal grammar is a theory for studying the initial states, and particular grammars are theories for studying the states of acquisition. While the faculty of language consists of a cognitive system that stores information such as sound, meaning, and structure, the performance system retrieves and uses the information. He raises a profound question: How well is the language faculty designed? He imagines a case in which a certain primate is comparable to human beings except for its lack of the faculty of language. Suppose some event has reorganized its mind by giving it the faculty of language. In order for the new mechanism to be operable, it must meet the "legibility conditions", and the other systems of the mind/brain must be able to understand the expressions generated by the new mechanism. On the other hand, the directions given by the new mechanism must be recognised and accepted by the other systems of the mind/brain. Thus, Chomsky puts forward the strongest minimalist thesis: Linguistic mechanism is the ideal solution to the problem of legibility conditions.

Since the beginning of the 21st century, Chomsky's attention has been on interdisciplinary perspectives and the biological aspects of the faculty of language. In 2002, together with two psychologists, Chomsky argues that an understanding of the faculty of language requires substantial interdisciplinary cooperation, on the belief that linguistics can be profitably wedded to work in evolutionary biology, anthropology, psychology, and neuroscience. In 2007, he traces the development of biolinguistics from its early philosophical origins through its reformulation during the cognitive revolution of the 1950s and outlines his views on where the biolinguistic enterprise stands. He suggests that the growth of language in the individual depends on three factors: genetic factors, experience, and principles that are not specific to the faculty of language. He says that little is known about the evolution of human thought and about the brain to proceed from the very first thing in a useful way. By formulating the goals with reasonable clarity and moving step by step towards principled explanation, we gain a clearer grasp of the universals of language, although much work is needed before we can understand the problems concerning the "organical structure of the brain" and the "creative and coherent ordinary use of language".

The development of TG Grammar can be regarded as a process of constantly minimalising theories and controlling the generative powers, and the Minimalist Program and the Minimalist Inquiries are just some logical steps in this process. Although TG Grammar has involved putting forward, revising, and cancelling of many specific rules, hypotheses, mechanisms, and theoretical models, its aims and purposes have been consistent, i. e. , to explore the nature, origin and the uses of human knowledge on language.

28. What is Case Grammar?

Case Grammar is a type of generative approach that stresses the semantic relationship of elements in a sentence. This grammar takes the verb as the most important part of the sentence, marking the relationships between the verb with various noun phrases as "cases".

Fillmore's argument is based on the assumptions that syntax should be central in the determination of case and that covert categories are important. The various ways in which cases occur in simple sentences define sentence types and verb types of a language.

Case Grammar shows clear semantic relevance of notions such as agency, causation, location, advantage to someone, etc. These are easily identifiable across languages, and are held by many psychologists to play an important part in child language acquisition.

29. **What is Generative Semantics?**

Generative Semantics was developed as a reaction to Chomsky's syntactic-based TG Grammar. This theory considers that all sentences are generated from a semantic structure. Linguists working within this theory hold that there is no principled distinction between syntactic processes and semantic processes. This notion was accompanied by a number of subsidiary hypotheses. First, the purely syntactic level of deep structure posited by Chomsky (1965) cannot exist. Second, the initial representations of derivations are logical representations identical from language to language. Third, all aspects of meaning are representable in phrase-marker forms. In other words, the derivation of a sentence is a direct transformational mapping from semantics to surface structure.

While Generative Semantics is no longer regarded as a viable grammatical model, it is important in a number of ways. First, it was generative semanticists that started an intensive investigation of syntactic phenomena which defied formalisation by means of transformational rules. Second, many proposals originally disputed by generative semanticists have since appeared in the interpretivist literature. Finally, the important initial studies which Generative Semantics inspired on various topics are becoming more and more appreciated.

30. **Why should we study theories and schools of linguistics?**

The study of any theory or school of thought involves the study of its history. Modern linguistics actually began in the 18th century. Like other parts of human knowledge and learning, linguistics is the product of its past and the matrix of its future. The importance of the history of a science is that it helps to place the present in perspective. One will find that many of the ideas about language which the linguist will question, if not abandon entirely, will seem less self-evident if one knows something of their historical origin. And it does so, not only by challenging and refuting traditional doctrines, but also by developing and reformulating them. In the study of linguistic theories, we do not only see the great advances in the last few decades but also the continuity of linguistic history from the past to the present.

The study of theories and schools of linguistics broadens our horizons. Linguistics has also grown up in many widely separated parts of the world. Each individual linguist or a group of linguists has its own theories of and approaches to language, due to different intellectual environments in which their ideas have been nurtured. And each of these theories and approaches has its own philosophical, historical, and sociocultural traditions. For many reasons and in many cases, one school of thought has directed its attention to issues that have not been properly considered by another school. It is not a problem if a student does not know a certain theory but it is a big problem if he sticks to only one theory. As Sampson (1980: 10) points out, "by far the greatest danger in scholarship (perhaps especially in linguistics) is not that the individual may fail to master the thought of a school but that a school may succeed in mastering the thought of the individual."

Further Reading

Bloch, B. & Trager, J. L. 1942. *Outlines of Linguistic Analysis*. Baltimore: Waverly Press.

Bloomfield, L. 1933/1955. *Language*. London: George Allen & Unwin Ltd.

Boas, F. 1911. *A Handbook of American Indian Languages*. Washington, D.C.: Smithonian Institution.

Bolinger, D. 1968/1975. *Aspects of Language*. New York: Harcourt Brace Jovanovich.

Chomsky, N. 1957. *Syntactic Structures*. The Hague: Mouton & Co.

Chomsky, N. 1965. *Aspects of the Theory of Syntax*. Cambridge, MA: MIT Press.

Chomsky, N. 1972. *Studies on Semantics in Generative Grammar*. The Hague: Mouton.

Chomsky, N. 1986. *Knowledge of Language: Its Nature, Origin, and Use*. New York: Praeger.

Chomsky, N. 1994. *Language and Thought*. London: Moyer Bell.

Chomsky, N. 1995. *The Minimalist Program*. Cambridge, MA: MIT Press.

Chomsky, N. 1998. *Minimalist Inquiries: The Framework*. Cambridge, MA: MIT Press.

Chomsky, N. 2007. "Biolinguistic Explorations: Design, Development, Evolution", *International Journal of Philosophical Studies*, 15(1): 1−21.

Culler, J. 1976. *Saussure*. London: Fontana/Collins.

Feng, Z. 2014. "The Logical Nature of Systemic-Functional Grammar and 'Grammatical Logic'", *Journal of World Languages*, 1(3): 232−241.

Fillmore, C. 1966. "Toward a Modern Theory of Case", in D. Reibel and S. Schane (eds.) *Modern Studies in English*. Englewood Cliffs: Princeton Hall.

Fillmore, C. 1968. "The Case for Case", in E. Bach and R. T. Harms (eds.) *Universals in Linguistic Theory*. New York: Holt, Rinehart and Winston.

Fillmore, C. 1977. "The Case for Case Reopened", in P. Cole and J. M. Sadock (eds.) *Syntax and Semantics*, Vol. 8: *Grammatical Relations*. New York: Academic Press.

Firth, J. R. 1957. *Papers in Linguistics 1934−1951*. London: Oxford University Press.

Gibb, M. & Zheng Z. 2006. Promoting New Applications of Linguistics: The Search for Meaning. *City U Today*, (14).

Halliday, M. A. K. 1978. *Language as Social Semiotic*. London: Edward Arnold.

Halliday, M. A. K. 1985/1994. *An Introduction to Functional Grammar*. London: Edward Arnold.

Halliday, M. A. K. 2008a. Working with Meaning: Towards an Appliable Linguistics. In J. Webster (ed). *Meaning in Context: Implementing Intelligent Applications of Language Studies*. London: Continuum.

Halliday, M. A. K. 2008b. *Complementarities in Language*. Beijing: The Commercial Press.
Halliday, M. A. K. & Hasan, R. 1985. *Language, Context, and Text: Aspects of Language in a Socio-semiotic Perspective*. Victoria: Deakin University Press.
Halliday, M. A. K. & Matthiessen, C. 2004. *An Introduction to Functional Grammar* (3rd ed.). London: Arnold.
Halliday, M. A. K. & Matthiessen, C. 2014. *Halliday's Introduction to Functional Grammar* (4th ed.). London: Routledge.
Harris, Z. S. 1951. *Methods in Structural Linguistics*. Chicago: The University of Chicago Press.
Hauser, M. D., Chomsky, N. & Fitch, W. T. 2002. "The Faculty of Language: What Is It, Who Has It, and How Did It Evolve?", *Science*, 298 (5598): 1569—1579.
Lamb, S. 1966. *Outline of Stratificational Grammar*. Washington, DC: Georgetown University Press.
Lamb, S. 1999. *Pathways of the Brain: The Neurocognitive Basis of Language*. Amsterdam: John Benjamins.
Lepschy, G. C. 1970. *A Survey of Structural Linguistics*. London: Faber and Faber.
Lyons, J. 1968. *Introduction to Theoretical Linguistics*. London: Cambridge University Press.
Lyons, J. 1981. *Language and Linguistics*. Cambridge: Cambridge University Press.
Lyons, J. 1991. *Chomsky* (3rd ed.). London: Fontana.
Mahboob, A. & Knight, N. (eds). 2010. *Appliable Linguistics*. London: Continuum.
Malinowski, B. 1923. "The Problem of Meaning in Primitive Languages", supplement to C. K. Ogden and I. A. Richards. *The Meaning of Meaning*. London and New York: Routledge and Kegan Paul.
Martin, J. 1992. *English Text: System and Structure*. Amsterdam: Benjamins.
Martin, J. & White, P. R. R. 2005. *The Language of Evaluation: Appraisal in English*. London: Palgrave.
Pike, K. 1982. *Linguistic Concepts: An Introduction to Tagmemics*. Lincoln, NE and London: University of Nebraska Press.
Robins, H. R. 1990. *A Short History of Linguistics* (4th ed.). London: Longman.
Sampson, G. 1980. *Schools of Linguistics: Competition and Evolution*. London: Hutchinson.
Sapir, E. 1921. *Language: An Introduction to the Study of Speech*. New York: Harcourt Brace Jovanovich.
Saussure, F. de. 1960 [1916]. *Course in General Linguistics* (trans. W. Baskin). London: Peter Owen.
Saussure, F. de. 1983 [1916]. *Course in General Linguistics* (trans. R. Harris). London: Duckworth.
Vachek, J. 1964. *A Prague School Reader in Linguistics*. Bloomington: Indiana University Press.
封宗信, 2006,《现代语言学流派概论》,北京:北京大学出版社.

封宗信,2012,"语言的不确定性与系统功能语法的模糊性",《外语学刊》,(5):41—47。
封宗信,2013,"功能语言学中的'语法逻辑'",《当代外语研究》,(4):5—11。
胡壮麟,2000,《功能主义纵横谈》,北京:外语教学与研究出版社。
胡壮麟,2007,解读韩礼德的 Appliable Linguistics,《四川外语学院学报》,(6),1—6。
胡壮麟,2014,"系统功能语言学的认知观",《外语学刊》,(3):44—50。
胡壮麟等,2005,《系统功能语言学概论》,北京:北京大学出版社。
刘润清、封宗信,2003,《语言学理论与流派》(英文版),南京:南京师范大学出版社。
刘润清,1995,《西方语言学流派》,北京:外语教学与研究出版社。
赵世开,1989,《美国语言学简史》,上海:上海外语教育出版社。

Part II 中文练习及参考答案

第一章 语言学导论

1. 术语解释。

    定义特征(design features)：从本质上将人类语言与动物的语言区分开的人类语言的区别性特点。

    功能(function)：语言在交际(如表达观点、态度等)或特定的社会情境(如宗教、法律场合)中所起的作用。

    共时的(synchronic)：在某一理论上的时间点研究语言的方法。

    历时的(diachronic)：研究语言随时间发展变化的方法。

    规定式(prescriptive)：对语言正确用法的权威性规定。

    描写式(descriptive)：客观系统地记录一种语言的模式和用法或变化。

    任意性(arbitrariness)：语言符号和这些符号所指的实体间不存在任何物质的联系。

    二层性(duality)：语言的结构组织可分为两个抽象的层面：有意义的单元(如词语)和无意义的片段(如语音、字母)。

    移位性(displacement)：语言能够指称说话人即时情境以外的语境。

    寒暄(phatic communion)：用来创造气氛或维持社会联系的谈话。

    元语言(metalanguage)：用来谈论语言的语言。

    宏观语言学(macrolinguistics)：语言研究的宽泛概念，包括心理、文化等方面。

    语言能力(competence)：对于一门语言的语法规则系统的无意识获得的知识。

    语言运用(performance)：人们说话、写作时实际使用的语言。

    语言(*langue*)：一个"语言社团"共有的语言系统。

    言语(*parole*)：说话人实际说的话语。

2. 查阅至少四本语言学导论的教科书(不是词典)，记下每本书对于语言的定义。仔细比较这些定义，然后写一篇文章讨论这些定义中哪些要点是重复的，解释这些定义中相似与区别的意义。

    所有教材都不应该排除这本教材提及的定义特征。最好还要包括其他定义特征，比如互换性或者说文化传递。但是给出一个关于语言的无可挑剔的定义似乎是不可能的，因为人们想强调的方面很少一致。比较几个定义会使你意识到争论之所在。
3. 你能想出一些英语的拟声词吗？
   Creak：很久没上油的门打开时发出的声音。
   Cuckoo：布谷鸟的叫声。
   Bang：突然发出的大声响。
   Roar：低沉的持续巨响。
   Buzz：嗡嗡的声音。
   Hiss：嘶嘶的声音。
   Neigh：马发出的长而响亮的叫声。
   Mew：海鸥发出的声音。
   Bleat：绵羊、山羊或小牛发出的声音。
4. 你是否认为拟声词表明了形式与意义之间非任意的关系？

   无论你回答"是"还是"不是"，你都不能否认拟声词需要任意性。在我们感到一个词是拟声词之前，我们应该首先知道这个词模仿的是哪种声音。正如第一章所说，要模拟飞蚊的声音有很多选择，比如 murmurous 和 murderous。这两个词跟真正天然的声音都相仿，但是 murmurous 被幸运地选为代表这种声音而 murderous 被选做表示完全不同的意思。跟能指一样都是任意的。

5. Robert Louis Stevenson 写的故事中有这样一句话："As the night fell, the wind rose"。这句话能表达成"As the wind rose, the night fell"吗？如果不能，为什么？这是否表明了词序有一定的非任意性？（Bolinger,1981:15）

   不能，两部分不可交换。是的，该例子说明了词序的非任意性。当句子的前后两部分交换时，该句的焦点和意思就会被迫发生变化，因为以线性顺序排列的从句在没有时间指示词的情况下会被看做与事情实际发生的顺序一致。这样作者的原意被歪曲了，而我们阅读时也可以轻易地感觉到意思被歪曲。这就是为什么系统功能语言学者和美国的功能语言学者认为语言在句法层面不是任意的。

6. 交通灯系统有二层性吗？你能画张简图解释一下吗？

   交通灯没有二层性。很显然交通灯不是双层的系统。符号与意义之间只有一一对应的关系，而意义单元不能进一步分为更小的无意义的成分。因此，交通灯跟动物的叫声一样，只有底层没有上层。

红	→ 停
绿	→ 行
黄	→ 准备

7. 语言的递归性为语言的创造性提供了理论基础。你能按照 1.3.3 节的例子写一个递归的句子吗？

Today I encountered an old friend who was my classmate when I was in elementary school where there was an apple orchard in which we slid to select ripe apples that...

8. 交流有多种形式,如符号、口头言语、身体语言和面部表情等。身体语言和面部表情具有人类语言的哪些独特特征?

　　总的来说,身体语言和面部表情缺乏人类语言大部分的本质特点,如二层性、移位性、创造性等。身体语言体现了一点点任意性。比如,点头对我们来说意思是"行"或"是",但在阿拉伯世界点头等于说"不"。某些面部表情有非任意性,因为它们是本能的,比如新生婴儿的哭和笑。

9. 你是否同意这个观点:没有哪种语言是特别简单的?

　　是的,人类所有的语言都是复杂的交际系统,这是由他们共有的定义特征决定的。

10. 对狗的语言有这种评价:无论一只狗叫得多么起劲,它也不能告诉你它的父母虽然贫穷但是诚实。你如何看待这种观点?你熟悉动物之间或动物与人交流的某种方式吗?

　　比如瞪羚发觉潜在的危险后会逃跑,并以此向附近的瞪羚发出预警信号。狗通过叫来表明它想被许可进入房中,通过露出尖牙表明它可能马上就要咬东西。

11. 你能举几个汉语中典型的寒暄语吗?《语言学教程》第12页有个P夫人和Q夫人的对话。有人使劲打喷嚏时你会说带有寒暄语性质的话吗?你有没有注意到你父母或祖父母在这种场合说特别的话?

　　汉语中的一些典型寒暄语有:吃了吗?家里都好吧?这是去哪里啊?最近都挺好的?如果有人使劲打喷嚏,你父母和祖父母或许会说:"你没事吧?""要看医生吗?""要喝水吗?""要手帕吗?""感冒啦?",或者诸如此类的话来表明他们的关心。

12. 语言中有很多元语言或自省性的表达,即谈论"谈话"和思考"思考",例如 *to be honest, to make a long story short, come to think of it, on second thought*,你能再收集一些这样的例子吗?我们何时最常使用这种表达?

　　这样的例子还有:*To tell the truth, frankly speaking, as a matter of fact, to be precise, in other words, that is to say...*

　　在论证中想用另一种方式详述前文的意思时,我们常用这种表达法。

13. 评论下列规定式规则,你认为这些规则可接受吗?

(1) (A) It is I.　　(B) It is me.

你应该说A而不说B,因为根据拉丁语的规则,be后面应该接主格而不是宾格。

(2) (A) Who did you speak to?　　(B) Whom did you speak to?

你应该说B而不说A。

(3) (A) I haven't done anything.   (B) I haven't done nothing.
B 是错的因为双重否定构成肯定。
(1) 拉丁语的语法规则并不是普世的。英语中,me 是非正式语法而 I 让人觉得非常正式。
(2) whom 用在书面语和正式口语中;who 在非正式口语中更常用。
(3) 语言不必遵循逻辑推理。这里双重否定只是形成了一个更强烈的否定。该句在标准英语中不可接受并不是因为不合逻辑,而是因为语言变化了,现在淘汰了这种用法。

14. 语法规则的规定式做法现在已经转移到了对词语的规定。在英国社会学会发行的"反性别歧视语言指导方针"中,有如下一些指导方针。你认为这些是描写式的还是规定式的?你做何评论?
(1) 不要用 man 泛指人类,使用 person, people, human beings, men and women, humanity, humankind。
(2) colored 这个词在英国被看做过时了,应该避免使用,因为人们普遍认为该词对许多黑人不敬。
(3) civilized 这个词仍然带有源自殖民主义世界观的种族主义色彩,常与社会达尔文主义思想联系在一起,充满了暗含的价值评价,忽略了非工业世界的历史。

这些肯定是描写式的。指导方针不是那些能够决定一句话是否正确的规则。这些方针建议你避免使用那些合乎语法但对某些群体不敬的词语。事实上,这些方针描述了倡导反性别歧视的人说话和写作的方式。

15. 为什么语言能力与语言运用的区分在语言学中很重要?你认为能明确区分两者吗?你如何看待交际能力这一概念?

这一区分是乔姆斯基在他的形式语言学理论中提出的,有时很难做出严格区分。应用语言学的某些研究者认为,与纯粹的理论上区分语言能力和语言运用相比,在语言教学中,语言交际能力或许是个更有启发性的概念。

16. 你认为语言学的哪个分支在中国会迅速发展?为什么?

这要在你读完全书后由你自己决定。目前我们认为语言学的所有分支都有可能繁荣。

17. 下面是句法研究中两个著名的歧义句,你能解歧吗?
(1) *The chicken is too hot to eat.*
(2) *Flying planes can be dangerous.*

句(1)可作两种理解,即(a)鸡肉太烫了,所以现在不能吃;(b)小鸡觉得太热了(或许刚做过剧烈的有氧运动),不能吃东西,需要先冷静下来。

句(2)的歧义来自 flying planes,可以理解为"正在飞行的飞机"或"开飞机"。

18. 造成正常的语言使用者在语言能力和语言运用之间出现差异的原因有很多,你能想出哪些?

　　民族背景、社会经济地位、在国家中所处的地区以及身体状况(比如醉酒、疲劳、走神、生病)等,这些情况都因人而异。

19. 下面两段引文揭示了语言研究中哪些不同的重点或视角?

　　……一种人类语言是一个极其复杂的系统。对于不是特意为懂得人类语言而设计出来的生物来说,懂得一种人类语言是一项非凡的智力成就。一个正常的儿童通过较为有限的接触不经过特别的训练就能获得这种知识,然后他能毫不费力地使用一种具有具体规则和原理的精密结构将自己的思想感情传达给他人,……因此从某种深刻、重要的意义来说,语言是思维的镜像。语言是人类智力的产物,在每个个体中通过超出意志或意识之上的操作被重新创造出来。(乔姆斯基:《关于语言的思考》1975:3—4)

　　很明显,语言是用来满足各种不同的需要,但是直到我们考察语法后才有清楚的理由来按照某种特定方式给语言的使用分类。然而,当我们考察语言本身的意义潜势时,我们发现语言包含的众多选择组成了几个相对独立的"网络";而且这些选择的网络对应语言特定的基本功能。这使我们能够解释语言的不同功能,而这种解释是与语言结构的全面理解相关而不是与任何特定的心理或社会调查相关。(韩礼德,1970:142—143)

　　第一段引文表明,儿童天生有能力获得关于包含具体规则的精密结构的知识。这意味着对语言研究者而言,语言使用者关于规则系统的潜在知识是有价值的研究对象。第二段强调了语言的功能,将语言的使用看做所需功能的选择。语言的意义可以完全包括在几个"网络"中,与语言的基本功能直接相关。该段指出了研究语言功能的必要性。

20. 你可能熟悉下列谚语,根据语言的任意性和常规性两种特征,你如何看待这些谚语:

　　The proof of the pudding is in the eating.
　　Let sleeping dogs lie.
　　You can't make a silk purse out of a sow's ear.
　　Rome was not built in a day.
　　When in Rome, do as the Romans do.
　　All roads lead to Rome.

　　任意性和规约性来自主题的选择。例如,在"The proof of the pudding is in the eating"中,pudding 这个词是任意选取的,我们可以用另一个词如 cheese 替代 pudding 而不会改变这个谚语的联想意义。而另一方面,特定的词和联想意义之间的这种关系一旦建立就成了一种规约性。
21. 通常认为不标准的用法（如 ain't）在某些场合是可接受的,甚至是合适的。请再举一些其他例子。

　　在非常随意的语境中,可以说"gimme that!"而不用说"give me that!"可以说"wachya doin'?"而不用说"what are you doing?"这种例子不胜枚举。

22. 以下是一些语言学著作的书名。你能仅从书名判断著作的研究倾向是历时或共时的吗？
　　(1) *English Examined: Two centuries of Comment on the Mother-Tongue.*
　　(2) *Protean Shape: A Study in Eighteenth-century Vocabulary and Usage.*
　　(3) *Pejorative Sense Development in English.*
　　(4) *The Categories and Types of Present-Day English Word-Formation.*
　　(5) *Language in the Inner City: Studies in the Black English Vernacular.*

　　共时的：(2), (4), (5)
　　历时的：(1), (3)

第二章　语　音

1. 术语解释。

　　语音学(phonetics)：对语音的发生、传递和感知的研究。可以分为三个主要的研究领域：发音语音学、声学语音学和感知(听觉)语音学。

　　发音语音学(articulatory phonetics)：对语音发生的研究,或研究语音是如何产生的。

　　音系学(phonology)：对各种语言的语音模式和语音系统的研究,其目的是发现语言中支配语音组合方式的规律并解释语音中出现的变化。

　　音姿(gesture)：发音时舌与唇的运动(由手势的动作比喻而来)。

　　发音器官(speech organs)：人体参与语音发生的部分。

　　带声性(voicing)：指声带的振动。当声带靠拢(贴近),气流使其产生振动,形成的发音叫"带声音"(浊音)；当声带分离,气流容易通过,发出的音就是"不带声音"(清音)。

　　国际音标(International Phonetic Alphabet, IPA)：1888 年以来由国际语音学会设计的一套表格形式的标准语音符号(国际音标表),经不断修改,反映了新的发现和语音学理论与实践中的变化。最新版国际音标表于 2015 年修订。

　　辅音(consonant)：音段的一个主要分类,由于声道紧闭或声道变窄程度达到气流无法排出,一旦排出就会产生可闻的摩擦,这样产生的音叫"辅音"。

元音(vowel):音段的一个主要分类,发音时不发生声道的阻碍,气流可以相对无阻地从口腔或鼻腔排出。

发音方式(manner of articulation):指完成发音过程的方法:①发音器官暂时或较长时间关闭口腔通道;②发音器官使空间明显变窄;③发音器官互相贴近,改变声道的形状。

发音部位(place of articulation):指发辅音时气流被阻碍的位置。

基本元音(Cardinal Vowels):一套人为确定的、固定不变的元音音质,为实际语言中的元音描写提供一个参照的框架。

半元音(semi-vowel):既非辅音也非元音的音段,如[j]和[w]。

滑元音(vowel glide):发生音质变化的元音,包括二合元音(双元音)和三合元音(三元音),发二合元音时舌运动一次,发三合元音时舌运动两次。

音位(phoneme):明显的语音对立单位。如果一种语言中两个音在不同词中出现对立,它们就是不同的音位。

音位变体(allophone):同一音位的变化形式。如果两个或更多个发音不同的音在意义上没有产生对立,它们就是同音位变体。同音位变体还要满足两个条件:互补分布和发音近似。

互补分布(complementary distribution):在某一语言或言语变体中,两个或两个以上语音从不出现在同一环境中的一种关系。当这些语音具有发音相似性时,就是同一音位的同音位变体。

同化现象(assimilation):一个音获得邻音某些或全部特征的过程。如果后面的音影响前面的音,叫做"逆同化";反之如果前面的音影响后面的音,称为"顺同化"。

剩余位置条件(Elsewhere Condition):较为特殊的规则应用在先。适用于底层形式到表层形式的推导过程中涉及两个以上规则时。

音节(syllable):超音段研究中的一个重要单位。音节必须有一个"节核"或"韵峰",通常由元音来承担,但有时也可以由具有成音节特征的辅音来起节核的作用,通常在节核的前后还可以有辅音丛出现。

最大节首原则(Maximal Onset Principle):当两个元音之间有辅音丛时划分音节的一个原则——当辅音的位置面临选择时,将其归入节首而不是节尾。

响音阶(sonority scale):根据内在音响程度对不同语音类型的排列。一般来说,元音是最强的响音(5),依次下来是通音(4),鼻音(3),擦音(2),塞音(1)。

重音(stress):指在音节发音时所用的力度。音节发音力度增强时更为突显,形成重音节;与之相对的略少突显的音节就是非重音节。

语调(intonation)：重复出现的升降模式，每个模式都应用于一套相对一致的意义，要么以词为单位，要么以各种长度的词群为单位。

声调(tone)：一套影响字词意义的升降模式。

连读变调(tone sandhi)：汉语等声调语言中，在自然说话时，如果两个连续的音节有相同的声调，其中一个音节的声调会发生改变。例如，在普通话中如果两个连续出现的音节(字)都是三声时，前一个音节的声调变为二声，如"你好""洗澡"。

强制曲线原则(Obligatory Contour Principle, OCP)：禁止相邻成分具有相同特征。该规则适应面比较广，覆盖很多音系现象，包括屈折形态学中两个元音之间增加辅音和两个辅音之间增加元音的规则，以及超音段音系学中的连读变调等。

2. 给出下列音标符号的语音描述：

1) [ð]   2) [ʃ]   3) [ŋ]   4) [d]   5) [p]
6) [k]   7) [l]   8) [ɪ]   9) [uː]   10) [ɒ]

1) 带声齿擦音
2) 不带声齿龈后擦音
3) 软腭鼻音
4) 带声齿龈塞音，或带声齿龈破裂音
5) 不带声双唇塞音，或不带声双唇破裂音
6) 不带声软腭塞音，或不带声软腭破裂音
7) (齿龈)边(通)音
8) 高前展唇松元音
9) 高后圆唇紧元音
10) 低后圆唇松元音

3. 根据下列语音描述给出国际音标符号：

1) 不带声唇齿擦音
2) 带声齿龈后擦音
3) 硬腭通音
4) 不带声声门擦音
5) 不带声齿龈塞音
6) 中高前展唇元音
7) 高央圆唇元音
8) 低前圆唇元音
9) 中低后圆唇元音
10) 高后圆唇紧元音

1) [f]   2) [ʒ]   3) [j]   4) [h]   5) [t]
6) [e]   7) [ʉ]   8) [œ]   9) [ɔ]   10) [u]

4. 写出下列音标代表的英语句子：

1) ɒn ə klɪə deɪ jukn siː fə maɪlz
2) səm piːpl θɪŋk ðət fɜːst ɪmpreʃnz kaʊnt fə ə lɒt

1) On a clear day you can see for miles.
2) Some people think that first impressions count for a lot.

5. 下面的链接是国际语音学会的官方网站。请自己浏览网站内容并在课上汇报。

https://www.internationalphoneticassociation.org/

(本题不提供答案)

6. 讨论题：
　　1) 言语发生涉及哪些器官？
　　2) 为什么萧伯纳说 fish 可以拼为 ghoti？
　　3) 对辅音和元音的描述有何不同？
　　4) 语音学和音系学有哪些异同点？
　　5) tell 的发音是[teɫ]，但 teller 的发音是[telə]，为什么音位/l/在这两个词中分别表现为[ɫ]和[l]？

　　　1) 见《语言学教程》第二章2.1.1节。
　　　2) 因为 gh 在 enough 一词中发音为/f/，o 在 women 一词中发音为/ɪ/，ti 在 nation 中发音为/ʃ/。当然萧伯纳意在讽刺英语的发音不规范，现实中人们不会把 ghoti 发成和 fish 一样的音，因为 gh 在元音前不会是/f/音，ti 也只有在-tion 中才发/ʃ/音，而 o 几乎只有在 women 一词中才发/ɪ/。
　　　3) 见《语言学教程》第二章2.2节。
　　　4) 语音学研究语音的发生、传递和感知。假设说话人甲发出语音，传递给受话人乙并被乙所感知，这样语音就经历了一个分为三个步骤的过程：语音的发生，语音的传递，语音的感知。语音的研究也就自然地分成三个主要领域，分别对应这一过程中的三个步骤：发音语音学研究语音的发生，声学语音学研究语音的物质特征，感知语音学或听觉语音学研究语音的感知。音系学研究各种语言的语音模式和语音系统，其目的是发现语言中支配语音组合方式的规律并解释语音中出现的变化。音系学的一般方法是：首先从一门具体语言（如英语）的研究开始，确定其音系结构，即使用了哪些语音单位，这些语音单位如何进行组合，然后把不同语言语音系统的特征进行比较，得出对于某些语言群体语音使用潜在规律的假设，最终得出有关所有语言语音规律的假设。
　　　5) teller 一词由基础词 tell 加后缀-er 构成的新词。我们都熟悉支配音位/l/变体的规则：在元音前发[l]，元音后发[ɫ]。然而，在 teller 中，它的前后各有一个元音，怎样确定它是[l]而不是[ɫ]呢？我们注意到，tell 是单音节词，teller 是双音节词。在多音节词中，要遵循"最大节首原则"进行音节划分，所以/l/必须被划在第二个音节的节首位置，而不是第一个音节的节尾位置。因此，音位/l/的具体表现应该是按第二个音节中在元音前的位置。类似的词还有 telling 和 falling 等，从中我们可以看出，复杂词的音系结构和它的构词结构往往是不同的。也就是说，从构词来说是 tell＋-er，而从音节结构来说是[te＋lə]。

7. 英语词中拼写和发音的关系比较复杂。根据下面的词语，讨论其复杂性（不规则性）并分析其中是否仍具有规则性。必要时可以使用其他例子说明。

　　although, beauty, bomb, ceiling, charisma, choice, cough, exercise, hour, light, phase, quiche, quake, sixteen, thigh, tongue, whose, writhe

英语拼写和发音的复杂性表现在拼写和发音之间缺乏规律性。在上述词语中：

although, light 和 thigh 中的 gh 不发音，但在 cough 中发/f/音，类似的例子还有 laugh, rough, tough 等。字母 c 在 ceiling 和 exercise 中发/s/音，但在 cough 中发/k/音。ch 在 charisma 中发/k/，在 quiche 中发/ʃ/，在 choice 中发/tʃ/音。b 在 bomb 中以及 h 在 hour 中不发音，但 h 在多数单词中（如 hot, hat, honor 等）是发音的。字母 o 的发音比较多：在 bomb 和 choice 中是/ɒ/，在 tongue 中是/ʌ/，在 whose 中是/u:/。字母 i 也是如此：在 ceiling, charisma, choice 和 sixteen 中是/ɪ/，在 quiche 中是/i:/，在 exercise, light, thigh 和 writhe 中是/aɪ/。qu 在 quiche 中是/k/，但在 quake 中是/kw/。/i:/音有时拼写为 ei (ceiling)，有时为 i (quiche)，有时为 ee (sixteen)。

混乱之外也有规则之处。比如，除带有重读标记的外来语（如 cliché）以外，字母 e 在词尾处都是不发音的，在这种情况下其前面的元音通常是发字母本身的音（如 exercise, phase, quake, writhe 等），但即便如此也还是总有例外（如所列词语中的 choice, quiche, tongue, whose 以及这里没有列出的其他词语）。

8. 在英语的一些方言中，下列词有不同的元音（如音标所示）。根据这些数据，回答后面的 6 个问题。

	A		B		C
bite	[bʌɪt]	bide	[baɪd]	tie	[taɪ]
rice	[rʌɪs]	rise	[ɹaɪz]	by	[baɪ]
type	[tʌɪp]	bribe	[bɹaɪb]	sigh	[saɪ]
wife	[wʌɪf]	wives	[waɪvz]	die	[daɪ]
tyke	[tʌɪk]	time	[taɪm]	why	[waɪ]

1) A 栏和 B 栏的词尾发音在分类上有什么不同？
2) C 栏中的词和 A、B 两栏的词有什么不同？
3) [ʌɪ]和[aɪ]是否处于互补分布？为什么？
4) life 和 lives 的语音记音是怎样的？
5) 下列词的语音记音是怎样的？
   (a) trial (b) bike (c) lice (d) fly (e) mine
6) 写出联系上述词音位表达式和语音表达式的规则。

(根据 Fromkin, et al. 2014：268—9)

1) A 栏词的最后一个音都是清辅音（[-voice]），B 栏词的最后一个音都是浊辅音（[+voice]）。
2) C 栏的词都是开音节，即节尾都是元音。
3) 这两个音属于互补分布，因为[ʌɪ]只出现在清辅音之前，而[aɪ]出现在浊辅音之前和开音节中。
4) (a)[lʌɪf] (b)[laɪvz]
5) (a)[traɪ] (b)[bʌɪk] (c)[lʌɪs] (d)[flaɪ] (e)[maɪn]
6) /aɪ/→[ʌɪ] / ____ [一带声]
　　　　[aɪ] 其他位置

9. 以下英语词包含前缀 in- 的不同形式。请按其变体形式把这些词分组，确定哪一组词使用哪个前缀形式，并说明导致这种变化的机制是什么。建立一个规则，然后用没有给出的其他同类词检验你的规则。

irregular	incomprehensible	illiterate
ingenious	inoffensive	inharmonic
impenetrable	illegal	incompetent
irresistible	impossible	irresponsible
immobile	illogical	indifferent
inconsistent	innumerable	inevitable

（根据 Plag, 2003：42）

从拼写来看有四种形式：in-、im-、ir- 和 il-，细致观察可以看出 in- 在软腭辅音前发音为 [ɪŋ]，所以可以将这些词按发音分为五组：

(1) [ɪn]：inharmonic, ingenious, inoffensive, indifferent, inevitable, innumerable

[ɪn] or [ɪŋ]：incomprehensible, incompetent, inconsistent

[ɪm]：impenetrable, impossible, immobile

[ɪl]：illiterate, illegal, illogical

[ɪr]：irresponsible, irresistible, irregular

显然，基础词的首音支配着变体的分布，因为前缀 in- 的发音必须和基础词的首音段发生同化，结果是在双唇辅音 /m/ 和 /p/ 前面是 [ɪm]，边音 /l/ 前面是 [ɪr]，/r/ 前面是 [ɪr]。如果基础词的起首辅音为软腭辅音 /k/，在快速说话时是 [ɪŋ]，在认真说话时是 [ɪn]。遇到所有其他情况都是 [ɪn]。假设底层形式为 /ɪn/，前缀 in- 的规则大体如下（最简单的形式）：

(2) /ɪn/→{[ɪn], [ɪŋ]} / ____ [软腭]
　　　　　[ɪm] / ____ [唇]
　　　　　[ɪl] / ____ [l]
　　　　　[ɪr] / ____ [r]
　　　　　[ɪn] 其他位置

由于 [ɪŋ] 不是必须的，我们可以去掉第一个规则，使这一规则系统得到简化。与其他规则不同的是，这一变体出自快速言语中同化现象的一种更为广泛的机制，是自然发生的。例如，in conference 在快速言语中也常变成

[ɪŋkɒnfərəns]，thank 和 think 中的鼻音也会变成软腭音。我们可以通过考察带有前缀 in-的其他基础词来检验这些规则，比如 correct，moveable，legible，rational 和 adequate，加前缀 in-时分别发音为[ɪn]correct（或[ɪŋ]correct），[ɪm]moveable，[ɪl]legible，[ɪr]rational，以及[ɪn]adequate，支持上述规则。

（根据 Plag，2003：200－201）

10. 在古英语中，擦音/f/、/þ,ð/和/s/各代表两个不同的音：

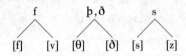

其中带声性可以通过语境预测。学一下这些词，找出其中的规则：

sæt	[sæt]	"坐着"
hūs	[huːs]	"房子"
ēast	[æːəst]	"东方"
cyssan	[kyssɑn]	"接吻"
hlāf	[hlɑːf]	"面包"
cēosan	[tʃeːozɑn]	"选择"
heofon	[hɛovɔn]	"天"
Wuldorfæder	[wʊldərvædɛr]	"上帝"
onstal	[ɔnstɑl]	"提供"
hrōfe	[hroːvɛ]	"屋顶"
eorean	[ɛorðɑn]	"大地"
æfter	[æftɛr]	"之后"
ēeel	[eːðɛl]	"本地君主"
nīt	[niːθ]	"仇恨"
niter	[nɪðɛr]	"向下"
nīeheard	[niːθhæərd]	"大胆"

（根据 Fennell，2001：60－64 和 Mitchell ＆ Robinson，2012：§9）

在古英语中，没有带声擦音（浊擦音）音位，其带声（浊音）变体是不带声擦音（清擦音）的语音变体，只出现在两个浊音之间。该规则可表示为：

擦音→［＋带声］／［＋带声］＿＿＿＿＿［＋带声］
　　　　［－带声］　其他位置

11. 研究题（不提供答案）：

1)"河口英语（EE）"指伦敦及周边地区或泛指英格兰东南部（泰晤士河沿岸和入海口地区）普遍使用的一种或几种口音。下列网站有关于这一英语形式的大量信息，查看这些网站上的资料，看看河口英语有什么特点。

http://www.phon.ucl.ac.uk/home/estuary

http://www.ic.arizona.edu/~lsp/EstuaryEnglish.html

Cruttenden(2014)第7章也有关于英式英语变化的一些讨论。

2) 根据你对中国学生学说英语的观察,讨论他们可能遇到的典型语音和音系上的问题,提出帮助他们解决这些问题的建议。注意要尽量运用本章学习过的知识。

3) 本章对于音系过程和音系规则的讨论都是用英语的例子来说明的,考虑一下汉语中的有关语料,看看是否有同样或类似的现象。

第三章 单词与形态学

1. 术语解释。

  语素(morpheme):就表达和内容之间的关系看,语素是最小的语言单位,不能再进一步分成更小的单位而不破坏或彻底改变词汇意义或语法意义。例如,tourist 这个词包括三个语素,其中一个最小的意义单位为 tour,另一个为-ist,(意思是"做某事的人"),以及一个最小的语言功能单位-s(表示"复数")。同时,从上面的例子我们能进一步把语素按不同的标准分成不同的类型:(a) 自由语素和粘着语素,前者能独自成词单独存在,例如 tourist 中的 tour,后者通常不能单独存在,必须附加在其他形式之上,例如-ist,-s。(b) 词汇语素和功能语素。这两种语素都属于自由语素的范畴,第一种语素是一组普通的名词、形容词和动词,承载了我们要传达的信息的主要内容,例如:house,long 和 follow。第二种语素主要包括语言中的功能词,像连词、介词、冠词和代词。例如 but,above,the 和 it。(c) 派生语素和屈折语素。这两种语素属于"粘着"的范畴。派生语素用来产生语言中的新词并且产生的词往往有着与词干不同的语法范畴。例如形容词 good 加上派生语素-ness 就变成了名词 goodness。相反,屈折语素从不改变词的语法范畴,但表示词的语法功能。例如,old 和 older 都是形容词,屈折变化-er 仅创造了这个形容词的一种不同的形式,表示出是比较级。下面的图表能作为一种有效的方式来帮助记忆语素的不同种类:

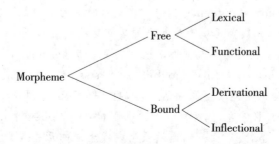

需要指出的是,语素也可以分为词根和词缀,词根是指词去掉所有

的词缀后所剩余的那部分。词根语素可以是粘着的，也可以是自由的，并且语言中词根的数量是无限的。词缀是粘着语素且数量有限。例如,在 try, tries, trying, tried 中,词根是 try,而-s,-ing,-ed 是词缀。

复合词(compound):是指那些由一个以上词汇语素构成的词,或者由两个独立的词连接起来构成新的形式,例如,classroom(教室)、mailbox(邮箱)、fingerprint(指纹)、sunburn(晒黑)。复合词分为名词复合词(如:daybreak 黎明)、动词复合词(如:brainwash 为……洗脑)、形容词复合词(如:dutyfree 免税的)和介词复合词(如:throughout 遍及)。同时,复合词根据其结构组织可以进一步分为向心复合词和离心复合词。名词性向心复合词和形容词性向心复合词的中心成分是从动词派生出来的,并且第一个成员通常是动词过程的参与者。请看下面的例子:self-control(自制)和 virus-sensitive(对病毒敏感的)。离心的名词性复合词由 V+N, V+A 和 V+P 构成,而离心形容词性复合词由 V+N 和 V+A 构成,以下是一些例子。

名词	形容词
scarecrow（稻草人）	takehome（可以带回家的）
playboy（花花公子）	lackluster（无光泽的）
cutthroat（凶手）	breakneck（非常制造的）

屈折(变化)(inflection):通过添加屈折词缀,如数、人称、限定性、体和格等来表示某词语法关系的变化。

词缀(affix):是一个构词成分的集合,它们只能附加于另一个语素之上。语言中词缀的数量总是有限的,根据它们与词根或词干的相对位置,一般可以把词缀分为三小类,即前缀、后缀和中缀。前缀是需要放在词前面的词缀(如:unhappy 中的"un-");后缀是加在词后面的(如 foolish 中的-ish);中缀,作为词缀中的第三种,在英语中并不常见,而在其他语言中是相当普遍的。就像这个术语指出的,中缀是放在一个词中间的词缀,这个规则在一些表达中是可以适用的,偶尔被感情激动的讲英语的人用在偶然的或正恶化的情况下:absolutegoddamlutely! 和 unfuckingbelievable! 事实上,所有的词缀都是粘着语素。

派生(derivation):英语中产生新词的最常见的构词过程。它通过大量的词缀实现并表明词根与词缀之间的关系。例如:mis+represent → misrepresent, joy+ful → joyful, sad+ness → sadness。与屈折词缀不同,派生词可能改变原词的词类,也可能不改变词类,例如,dis+card → discard(丢弃,抛弃)(词类改变了)和 dis+obey → disobey(词类未改变)。值得一提的是,通过派生方式生成的形式其数量是相当多的,而且其潜力是无穷的。如:preamble(导言)、pre-arrange(事前安排)、

precaution(预防,警惕), precede(在……之前), precedent(先例), precept(规则), precinct(区域,范畴), precognition(预知), precondition(前提), precursor(先驱)等。

词根(root):是词的基本形式,不能再做进一步的分析而完全不损失同一性,在 internationalism 这个词中,去掉 inter-、-al 和 -ism 后,剩下的就是词根 nation。很明显,所有的词都包含一个词根语素,词根能被进一步划分为自由词根语素和粘着词根语素,首先,自由词根语素是那些能独立存在且能作为词的基础的形式,例如,black(黑色),blackbird(山鸟类),blackboard(黑板),blacksmith(铁匠)中的 black。语言中的这类语素在数量上的潜力是无限的。其次,英语中的粘着词根语素相对来说数量很少,如 receive(收到),perceive(察觉)和 conceive(构思)中的 -ceive,remit(宽恕),permit(许可),commit(犯(错误))和 submit(使服从)中的 -mit,retain(保持),contain(包含),maintain(维持)中的 -tain,incur(招致),recur(重现),occur(发生)中的 -cur。再次,英语中有些词根既可以是自由的也可以是粘着的,例如:sleep(/sli:p/)和 child (/tʃaɪld/) 都是自由词根语素,然而在 sleep 过去分词 slept- 中的 slep-,child 的复数形式 children 中的 child- 都不能独立存在,因此是粘着的。

语素变体(allomorph):语素是语言的抽象体,就像音位,在不同的语音环境中会表现为特定的语音形式或变体。每个语音形式或变体都是一个语素变体,一个单独的语素在语音上可以由两个或更多语素变体实现。反映某个语素或由某个语素派生出来的不同的语素变体叫做这个语素的语素变体。事实上,有些语素在任何语境中都只有一个形式,如"dog","bark"等,另外一些语素可能有相当多的变体形式,也就是说,一个语素有可选择的形式或语音形式,例如,英语中表达复数的语素可以用轻音 /s/、浊音 /z/、元音—辅音结构 /ɪz/,不规则形式如 /maɪs/ 中的双元音 /aɪ/、/ɒksn̩/ 中的鼻音 /n̩/、/tiː θ/ 中的长元音 /iː/ 和 /ʃiːp/ 中的零形式 /i:/ 等来表示。每一个都可以说是复数语素的语素变体。

词干(stem):是指能加上屈折词缀的语素或语素的组合。例如:friends 中的 friend,friendships 中的 friendship 都是词干,前者表明词干可以和词根同形,而后者表明词干可以包含词根和一个或多个派生词缀。

粘着语素(bound morpheme):指的是不能单独出现,必须和至少一个其他语素共现的语素,例如,单词 distempered 有三个语素,即:dis-、temper 和 -ed,其中 temper 是一个自由语素,dis- 和 -ed 是两个粘着语素,有两类语素属于"粘着"范畴:派生语素和屈折语素。派生语素用来产生语言中的新词,并且这些词常与词干有着不同的语法范畴。例如形容词 good 加上派生语素 -ness 就变成了名词 goodness。相反,屈折语素从不改变词的语法范畴,但表示词的语法功能。例如,old 和 older 都是形容词,屈折变化-er 仅仅创造了这个形容词的一种不同的形式,表明比较级。

自由语素(free morpheme):是指那些可以独立存在或单独构成单词的语素。在英语 cats 中,cat 是自由语素,因为 cat 本身是一个独立的单词。因此自由语素一定可以构成单语素词。所以所有的单语素词都是自由语素。多语素词或复合词完全由自由语素构成,像 aircraft, godfather, housewife 等。自由语素还可以再分为词汇语素和功能语素。前者是指一组能够表达我们所要传达信息内容的普通的名词、形容词和动词,例如 house, long, follow 等。广义上后者包括语言中的功能词,像连词、介词、冠词和代词。例如 but, above, the, it 等。

语法词(grammatical word):是指那些主要用来构建词组、短语、从句、复合句、甚至篇章的词。例如连词、介词、冠词、代词。语法词把不同内容的部分连接在一起,因此也称为功能词。

词汇词(lexical word):是指那些主要用来指代物质、动作和性质的词。例如名词、动词、形容词和副词。词汇词承载着语言中的主要内容,因此词汇词也被称为实义词。

封闭类(closed-class):如果一个单词属于封闭类,那么它的成员数目是固定的或有限的,例如代词、介词、连词、冠词等。我们不能随意地增加或减少它的成员。

开放类(open-class):是指在原则上其成员是不定的或无限的。但新的观点、发明、发现出现时,新的成员持续不断的增加到这类词汇中去。名词、动词、形容词和很多副词都属于开放类。

整合法(blending):是一种相对复杂的混合形式,由两个单词混合而成,一般是把第一个单词的开头部分和第二个单词的最后部分连接起来,或者是把两个单词的开头部分连接起来。

例如:telephone+exchange→telex; transfer+resister→transistor

缩略语(acronym):缩略语是由组织机构名称的首字母构成的,而这个组织机构的名称有多重修饰语。例如,WTO 代表 World Trade Organization。在科学、科技以及其他特殊领域中,也常用这种方法来把很长的单词或词组缩短。例如,Aids—acquired immune deficiency syndrome, COBOL—common business oriented language。

逆构词法(back-formation):是构词法中一种不规则的类型,即删去一个语言中已有的较长单词的想象的词缀,由此造出一个较短的单词。以 *televise* 为例,*television* 比 *televise* 先存在于语言中,*television* 的前面部分被提取出来,分析成词根,尽管实际上英语中并没有这样的词根。

2. 给下列词加上适当的否定前缀
   a. removable   b. formal   c. practicable   d. sensible
   e. tangible   f. logical   g. regular   h. proportionate
   i. effective   j. elastic   k. ductive   l. rational
   m. syllabic   n. normal   o. workable   p. written
   q. usual   r. thinkable   s. human   t. relevant
   u. editable   v. mobile   w. legal   x. discreet

   答案见本书第 20 页。

3. 阅读下面一段话,列出所有能找到的功能词(包括 be 作为功能词的所有形式),并给出这段话中功能词的百分比。

       She was a small woman, old and wrinkled. When she started washing for us, she was already past seventy. Most Jewish women of her age were sickly, weak, broken in body. But this washwoman, small and thin as she was, possessed a strength that came from generations of peasant ancestors. Mother would count out to her a bag of laundry that had accumulated over several weeks. She would lift the heavy bag, load it on her narrow shoulders, and carry it the long way home.

       这段话中的功能词包括:*she*, *was*, *a*, *and*, *when*, *she*, *for*, *she*, *was*, *past*, *of*, *her*, *were*, *in*, *but*, *this*, *and*, *as*, *she*, *a*, *that*, *from*, *of*, *would*, *to*, *her*, *a*, *of*, *that*, *had*, *over*, *she*, *would*, *the*, *it*, *on*, *her*, *and*, *it*, and *the*。在这段话中,共有 85 个词,其中功能词 40 个。所以这段话中功能词的百分比是 40/85≈47%。

4. "完全由两个或更多的较小形式构成的自由形式是短语,不是短语的自由形式是词。那么,词……是最小的自由形式"(Bloomfield, 1935:178)。
   回答下面的问题:
   (a) "词"这个术语是有歧义的,Bloomfield 的定义想要涵盖哪一种词?
   (b) 英语中有没有传统上认为是词(在"词"的适当意义上)却不能满足 Bloomfield 定义的词。
   (c) 词的定义中还用到了哪些其他的标准?
   (a) 在 Bloomfield 看来,words 即在普通意义上作为概念单位的最小自由形式,是指能够独立存在或能够独自构成完整话语的最小单位。那些能独立作为完整话语存在的像 hi, possibly, darling 叫做单词。
   (b) 有。例如,那些不能单独存在或在普遍意义上能独自构成话语的单词,像英语中的 a, the,并不能满足 Bloomfield 的标准,尽管他自己都没有意识到这一点。
   (c) 除了最小自由形式的标准,稳定性和相对的连续性都用来定义单词。除此之外,单词的三种含义,即自然的有界限的单位,支配一组形式的共同因素和语法单位都可以用来定义单词。

5. 找出下列混合词的来源。假如词典中没有提供答案，请根据自己的理解来判断。

  (a) bash   (b) smash   (c) glimmer   (d) flimmer
  (e) clash   (f) flare   (g) brunch   (h) motel
  (i) transistor   (j) medicare   (k) workaholic   (l) spam
  (m) telethon   (n) aerobicise   (o) chunnel   (p) chortle
  (q) bit   (r) modem   (s) guestimate   (t) threepeat

  答案见本书第 22 页。

6. 确定第一栏中词的确切的历史语源，并在第二栏或第三栏中选出正确的解释。

第一栏	第二栏	第三栏
(a) hangnail	aching nail	hanging nail
(b) female	a male's companion	little woman
(c) crayfish	crawling fish	crab
(d) shamefaced	face reflecting shame	bound by shame
(e) Jordan almond	imported almond	garden almond
(f) sparrowgrass	a genus of herbs	bird nesting in grass
(g) belfre	bell tower	bell
(h) bridegroom	a woman is just or about to be married	a man is just, or about to be married
(i) muskrat (Algonquian:musquash)	a large rat-like animal	a large musk deer
(j) woodchuck (Algonquian:otchek)	a north American goat	a north American marmot

  答案见本书第 22 页。

7. 根据下列的逆构词确定其最初的形式。

  (a) asset   (b) burgle   (c) enthuse   (d) greed
  (e) hush   (f) automate   (g) donate   (h) escalate
  (i) homesick   (j) peddle   (k) diagnose   (l) tuit
  (m) amusing   (n) loaf   (o) self-destruct   (p) attrit
  (q) hairdress   (r) emote   (s) drowse   (t) frivol

  答案见本书第 23 页。

8. 确定下列词语的直接语源。（例如，meaning 的直接语源是法语，尽管它更远的来源是拉丁语）

  (a) air   (b) barbecue   (c) bungalow   (d) cola
  (e) gusto   (f) babel   (g) buffalo   (h) cocoa
  (i) costume   (j) ill   (k) mule   (l) decreed

(m) revolution　　(n) benevolent　　(o) lie　　　　(p) topic
(q) subject　　　 (r) theme　　　　(s) wind　　　(t) datum

答案见本书第 23 页。

9. 如果有两个词缀-ly,一个生成形容词,另一个附在形容词后生成副词,那么我们能找到同时包含这两个词缀的词吗?

   * friendlily (frierd-frienly-friendlily *)

   * oilily(oil-oily-oilily *)

10. 列出下列词中后面能加-s 的名词。

Epiphany	foot	hat	house
kitchen	ox	phenomenon	region
sheep	tomato		

　　hat　　house　　kitchen　　region

11. 有没有这样的词缀,能附加在动词后面不会产生或没有很特殊的意义,而且不会改变动词的类别。

　　-ing, He is walking home,进行时
　　-ed, He walked home,一般过去式
　　-s, He walks home,一般现在式

12. 有学者认为汉语是没有形态的语言。你是否赞同此说法?赞同或反对的理由是什么?

　　(以下提供的答案仅供参考。你可以扩展或者推翻这个答案,但需要确保你的答案有语料和严格的逻辑推理支持。)

　　与英语等语言相比,汉语确实在很多情况下没有形态标记。比如说,汉语没有格标记、性标记(现代汉语新出现的"他"和"她"是个例外)和时标记。此外,英语词类转换中常出现的词性标记在汉语中也很少出现。

　　但认为汉语没有形态的说法与事实不符。首先,汉语有复数标记"们"。"们"一般是粘附在指称"人"的名词上,如"学生们"。"们"也可粘附在人称代词上构成复数性人称代词,如"你们"、"我们"和"她/他们"。

　　其次,汉语中有一些特殊的粘附在动词上的小品词,提供"体"信息(如完成体)。动词后的小品词"了"是一个典型的例子。这个小品词粘附在动词上,常常表达动词表达的动作已完成的信息。某种意义上来说,这个小品词类似于英文中的粘着语素(当然学者们会有不同的视角来分析其本质),因为这个小品词无法单独出现,而必须粘附在动词上;此外,这个小品词也缺乏普通汉语词汇的一个特征,即独立的语调。

　　第三,汉语的词类转换有时候在形态上也会有体现。以"化"为例。"化"经常出现在名词/形容词至动词的词类转换过程中。如"石"—"石化"、"美"—"美化"、"丑"—"丑化"。

　　还有更多的语料可以证明汉语确实具备形态特征。对你来说,一个可

行的研究不仅仅是挖掘更多的语料,而是探索汉语和英语(或者其他语言)形态差异的内在原因。

13. 一个类似 blackbird 的英语合成词包含一个形容词和一个名词,而一个名词词组也可以包含这两个成分,比如 black tie。如果不考虑在书写中两个成分之间是否有空格,类似 blackbird 的合成词与类似 black tie 的名词词组之间的区别是什么?

最明显的差异是语义差异:一个包含形容词和名词的名词词组,其语义总是组合性的,因此也是可以预测的。如 black tie 意为"黑色的领带",expensive laptop 意为"昂贵的笔记本电脑"。合成词在语义上具有非组合性,因此也无法通过其包含的词来预测意义。如 blackbird 并不是指黑色的鸟,而只特指某种鸟(乌鸫)。

第二个差异体现在音系层面。blackbird 这样的合成词,重音一般在第一个词,而前面带有修饰语的名词词组,重音一般在名词上。因此,当我们在会话中听到 BLACK 和 BIRD,通过明确重音的位置,我们可以知道对方是在谈论某种鸟类(乌鸫)(BLÁCKbird)还是在讨论黑色的鸟(blackBÍRD)。

第四章 句法:从语词到篇章

1. 术语解释。

句法(syntax):指研究语言中不同成分组合成句子的支配规则,或者是研究句子构造中各个成分之间的相互关系。

共现(co-occurrence):指的是句子中不同部分的各类词允许或要求与另外一个词类的词搭配使用,这样才能组成一个完整的句子或是句子中的某一特定成分。例如,用在名词(dog)前面的通常是限定词或是形容词,而当这个名词作主语时,后面接续的词是谓语(如 bark、bite、run 等)。简言之,共现就是句子构建的环境,在这个环境中一个结构体能够与其他相关成分一起出现,既合乎语法又符合规范。因此,从一定程度上讲共现关系既属于组合关系又属于聚合关系。

结构体(construction):指的是语言中任意一个句子结构。该结构具有一个或多个语法功能,并且包括任何合乎语言规范的成分,该成分对结构中所包含的用法或意义发挥了作用。这个结构体包含外部特点和内部特点。以句子 The boy kicked the ball 为例,从外部特点而言,我们将整个句子看做一个独立小句,而从内部特点角度看,该句子中的名词词组("the boy"),动词词组("kicked")和名词词组("the ball")都分别属于不同的句子成分。

成分(constituent):成分,作为一个术语,指的是用于句子结构分析的一个语言单位,它是一个比其更大的语言单位的一部分。几个成分共同构成一个结构体:例如,在 The boy ate the apple 这个句子中,S(A),the boy (B)，ate the apple(C)，这三个部分分别可以算做一个成分。各个成分可以和其他成分组合构成更大的语言单位。在上面的例子中，如果两个成分 B (the boy)和 C (ate the apple)连接构成了更大的成分 A ("S"，在此表示句子)，那么 B 和 C 就是 A 的直接成分。

向心结构(endocentric)：向心结构是指该结构的分布在功能上相当于它的一个或多个成分，如，一个词或一个词组，在功能方面它们都可作为一个可定义的核心或中心。在短语 two pretty girls 中，girls 是这个短语或词组的核心或中心。

离心结构(exocentric)：离心结构由一组句法上相关的词构成，但其任何成分的功能都不与这个词组作为一个整体时的功能相同，即该词组没有可定义的"核心"或"中心"。离心结构常常可以是一个基本句，一个介词短语，一个谓语结构(动词+宾语)或是一个连接结构（连系动词 be +补语）。句子 The boy smiled 中没有成分可以代替整个结构。

从属关系(subordination)：指将两个语言单位连接起来以使其具有不同句法功能的过程或结果，一个语言单位依赖另外一个，并常常是另外一个的构成成分。因此，从属成分是修饰中心的一组词，可以被称为修饰语。在短语 swimming in the lake 中，swimming 是中心成分，而 in the lake 修饰该中心。

范畴(category)：这个术语在一些方法中指狭义上的类和功能，如名词、动词、主语、谓语、名词短语、动词短语等等。它尤其指以下这些通用单位的本质特征，如名词范畴，包括数、性、格和可数性，动词范畴，包括时、体、语态等。

并列关系(coordination)：在英语和其他语言中有一个常见的句式是通过用连词 and, but, or 等把两个或更多同类型的范畴连接起来构成的。这种现象常被称为并列。在结构 the lady or the tiger 中，两个名词短语 the lady 和 the tiger 句法地位相同，每个都可以单独代表最初结构的功能。

一致关系(agreement)：又叫做协同关系，是指两个或更多处于某种语法关系中的词，要在某些突显的聚合关系的范畴内保持一致的形式。例如，下面对话中"this pen"与"it"的语法关系恰恰体现了这种一致性：
——Whose is this pen? (这是谁的笔?)
——Oh, it's the one I lost. (噢,这正是我丢的那只。)

嵌入(embeding)：指某小句在主从语法关系中附属于另一小句的形式。例如，I saw the man who had visited you last year. (我看见了去年拜访你的那个人。)

递归性(recursiveness)：递归性主要是指一种短语成分被嵌入到（也即被支配）另一种有着相同范畴的成分内部，但递归性已变成一个包罗万象的术语,它涵盖若干重要的语言现象,如并列和从属现象、连接和嵌入现象、主次和并联现象。与语言的"开放性"一样,递归关系是构成语言独创性的核心。例如,"I met a man who had a son whose wife sold cookies that she had baked in her kitchen that was fully equipped with electrical appliances that were new."

语法主语与逻辑主语(grammatical subject & logical subject):语法主语与逻辑主语是被动语态中诠释主语格结构的两种术语。现以"a dog bit John"和"John was bitten by a dog"为例。在被动语态中,核心的宾语名词(例中为"John")往往被置于动词前的空位中,所以其被称做语法主语,因为原先的宾语名词短语占据了动词前的语法空位,而在一般情况下,主语应出现在此位置上;另一方面,核心主语(a dog)现在则成了介词后的宾语(by a dog),被称为逻辑主语,因为从语义上讲,核心主语在句子中仍然扮演着本应由主语承担的角色,即动作的施动者。

衔接(cohesion):以指称、替代、省略、并列和语词搭配等方式实现的语篇连接。比如,下面这个语篇就以"there"回指"the park"取得语篇连接:Smith lives near the park. He often goes there.(史密斯住家近那个公园,他经常上那儿去。)

连贯(coherence):这是概念关联,读者应用此关联与话语提供的线索相适配,建构一个连贯的心智表象。如:There was a loud knock. I opened the door. Two policemen.(有人使劲敲门,我打开门,两个警察。)这个语篇缺乏面上的衔接词,但却是连贯的。

2. 指出下列这些句子每个词的范畴(提示:可以参考本章 4.2.2 节)

(1) The instructor told the students to study.(老师告诉学生们学习。)

(2) The customer requested for a cold beer.(那位顾客要了一杯冰镇啤酒。)

(3) The pilot landed the jet.(那名飞行员驾驶直升机着陆。)

(4) These dead trees must be removed.(必须砍伐清理这些枯死的树木。)

(5) That glass suddenly broke.(那个玻璃杯突然碎了。)

(1) [NP(det.+n.)+V+NP(det.+n.)+inf.]
 [名词词组(限定词+名词)+动词+名词词组(限定词+名词)+动词不定式]

(2) [NP(det.+n.)+V+PP(prep.+det.+adj.+n.)]
 [名词词组(限定词+名词)+动词+介词词组(介词+限定词+形容词+名词)]

(3) [NP(det.+n.)+V+NP(det.+n.)]
 [名词词组(限定词+名词)+动词+名词词组(限定词+名词)]

(4) [NP(det.+adj.+n.)+mv(modal verb)+be(auxiliary verb)+Past

Participle]

[名词词组(限定词+形容词+名词)+情态动词(情态动词)+be(系动词)+动词过去分词]

(5) [NP(det.+n.)+adv.+V]

[名词词组(限定词+名词)+副词+动词]

3. 划分下列句子的直接成分,在划分处用斜线(/)标示。不计括号内的成分。

例如:I rode back/when it was dark.(当天黑的时候/我正骑车回去。)

(a) The boy was crying.(男孩正在哭。)

(b) The pretty little girl in a clean white dress has been talking since she came into the room.(这个俊俏的小女孩穿着一件干净的白色套裙/自从进入房间后一直在谈。)

(c) Shut the door.(关上门)。

(d) Open the door quickly.(快点打开门)

(e) The happy teacher in that class (was beaming away).(在那个班里的那位心情愉快的老师正灿烂微笑着离开。)

(f) (I spoke to) the kindly old lady in the choir who was praying for me. (我跟)那会正为我祈祷的唱班里的那位友善的老妇人(说话了)。

(g) (He) bought an old car with his first pay cheque.(他)用他第一张薪金支票买了一辆旧车。

(a) The boy/ was crying.(男孩/正在哭。)

(b) The pretty little girl/ in a clean white dress/has been talking/since she came/ into the room.(这个俊俏的小女孩/穿着一件干净的白色套裙/自从进入房间后/一直在谈。)

(c) Shut/the door.(关上/门。)

(d) Open/ the door/quickly.(快/开/门。)

(e) The happy teacher/ in that class (was beaming away).(在那个班里的/那位心情愉快的老师/正灿烂微笑着离开。)

(f) (I spoke to) the kindly old lady/ in the choir/who was praying/ for me. ((我跟)那会正为我祈祷的/唱班里的/那位友善的老妇人(说话了)。)

(g) (He) bought/an old car/with his first pay cheque.((他)用他第一张薪金支票/买了/一辆旧车。)

4. 就下列画线的结构体和词组,按照示例回答问题:

(1) 判断画线部分是否有中心词;

(2) 如果有,指出其中心词;

(3) 标出结构体的类别。

例:His son will be keenly competing.

答案:有中心词,中心词为"competing";动词词组

(a) Ducks quack. （鸭子呱呱叫）
(b) The ladder in the shed is long enough. （货棚里的梯子足够长。）
(c) I saw a bridge damaged beyond repair. （我看到了一座无法修葺的大桥。）
(d) Singing hymns is forbidden in some countries. （在某些国家中，唱赞美诗是严令禁止的。）
(e) His handsome face appeared in the magazine. （他帅气的脸庞出现在这本杂志里。）
(f) A lady of great beauty came out. （一位美妙绝伦的女士出现了。）
(g) He enjoys climbing high mountains. （他非常喜欢攀登高山。）
(h) The man nodded patiently. （那个人耐心地点了点头。）
(i) A man roused by the insult drew his sword. （那个人被羞辱激怒，将剑拔出了鞘。）

(a) 没有中心词，独立小句。
(b) 没有中心词，介词短语。
(c) 有中心词，中心词为"damaged"；形容词词组。
(d) 有中心词，中心词为"singing"；动名词短语。
(e) 有中心词，中心词为"face"；名词词组。
(f) 没有中心词，介词短语。
(g) 有中心词，中心词为"climbing"；动名词短语。
(h) 没有中心词；一个整句。
(i) 有中心词，中心词为"roused"；形容词短语。

5. 在下列的每一组句子中，用"N"标注出哪组句子在使用"and"连接时不需要遵循固定的次序。用"Y"标注哪组句子在使用"and"连接时必须遵循固定的次序。根据你的观点你认为除了以下这些例句，哪一类型更相关。

(a) The sun is shining. 阳光明媚。
The wind is blowing. 微风吹拂。
(b) Susie went to sleep. 苏茜睡着了。
She had a dream. 她做了一个梦。
(c) John came in. 约翰进了房间。
He closed the door. 他关上了门。
(d) He came in. 他进了房间。
John closed the door. 约翰关上了门。
(e) She felt embarrassed. 她感到很尴尬。
She blushed. 她脸红了。
(f) The sky is blue. 天空湛蓝。
The grass is green. 草色青青。

(g) He walked away. 他走开了。
　　He got up. 他站了起来。
(h) He enjoyed the meal. 他饱餐了一顿。
　　He loved the pickles. 他喜欢泡菜。
(a) N　　　(b) Y　　　(c) Y　　　(d) Y
(e) Y　　　(f) N　　　(g) Y　　　(h) N

6. 将下列各组句子合并为一句话；并将每组中第二句改为关系从句，然后再将其镶嵌在第一句中。

(1) The comet appears every twenty years. Dr. Okada discovered the comet.
(2) Everyone respected the quarterback. The quarterback refused to give up.
(3) The most valuable experiences were small ones. I had the experiences on my trip to Europe.
(4) Children will probably become abusers of drugs or alcohol. Children's parents abuse alcohol.
(5) Many nations are restricting emissions of noxious gases. The noxious gases threaten the atmosphere.

(1) The comet that Dr. Okada discovered appears every twenty years. （奥卡达博士发现的彗星每隔20年出现一次。）
(2) Everyone respected the quarterback who refused to give up. （人人都非常尊敬那位永不言放弃的四分卫球手。）
(3) The most valuable experiences that I had on my trip to Europe were small ones. （这次欧洲之行过程中最宝贵的经历莫过于那些细节性的事情。）
(4) Children whose parents abuse alcohol will probably become abusers of drugs or alcohol. （父母为酗酒者的孩子很可能成为毒品或酒精滥用者。）
(5) Many nations are restricting emissions of noxious gases which threaten the atmosphere. （许多国家都在限制那些污染大气的有毒气体的排放。）

7. 请用例证阐释拓展句式成分的不同方法。

　　本章中通过介绍递归介绍了拓展句式的几种方法，包括并列与主从、连结与嵌入、主次与并连等等。并列与连结指代同样的语言现象，即用 and, but 或 or 将具有相同功能的句法成分连结起来。例如，句子 A man got into the car 可以被扩展为像"[名词短语 A man, a woman, a boy, a cat... and a dog] got into the car"这样的句子。而主从和嵌入可以被理解为通过将一个或更多个具有不同功能的句式成分嵌入到另外一个成分的拓展句式成分的方法。I saw the man <u>who had visited you last year</u>(我看到了<u>去年拜访过你的那个男人。</u>)是通过将独立小句变为一个从属成分(这里是一个关系从句)后扩展而成的。

然而,主次和并连是描述句间句式关系的两个传统术语。看下面的例子,前者有主次关系,而后者又并连关系。

　　We live near the sea. <u>So</u> we enjoy a healthy climate.
　　He dictated the letter. She wrote it.

8. 请使用分词短语、动名词短语等术语分别标出 4.5.2 节中例 4—37 中各句的画线部分。

(a) The best thing would be <u>to leave early</u>.
(b) It's great <u>for a man to be free</u>.
(c) <u>Having finished their task</u>, they came to help us.
(d) <u>Xiao Li being away</u>, Xiao Wang had to do the work.
(e) <u>Filled with shame</u>, he left the house.
(f) <u>All our savings gone</u>, we started looking for jobs.
(g) It's no use <u>crying over spilt milk</u>.
(h) Do you mind <u>my opening the window</u>?

(a) 不定式短语　　　　　(b) 不定式短语
(c) 过去分词短语　　　　(d) 独立主格短语
(e) 过去分词短语　　　　(f) 独立主格短语
(g) 动名词短语　　　　　(h) 动名词短语

9. 请说说英语中主语的主要特征。

　　主语作为一个语法范畴在不同的语言中具有不同的特点。在英语中,主语一般具有以下几个特点:

　　A. 语序:在陈述句中主语位置通常位于谓语动词的前面。例如:Sally collects stamps. (萨利集邮。)。

　　B. 代词形式:当主语是代词的时候,英语中的第一人称和第三人称代词通常以特定形式出现。当代词出现在句子中的不同位置时不使用充当主语的代词形式。

　　He loves me. 他爱我。
　　I love him. 我爱他。
　　We threw stones at them. 我们朝他们扔石头。
　　They threw stones at us. 他们朝我们扔石头。

　　C. 主谓一致:在一般现在时态中,当主语是第三人称单数时谓语动词后面要添加"s"但是,句子中的宾语或其他成分的人称和数的变化根本不会影响谓语动词的形式,如:

She angers him. 她惹他生气。
They anger him. 他们惹他生气。
She angers them. 她忍怒他们。

D. 内容疑问句:如果主语被一个疑问词(who 或 what)取代,句子的其他成分保持不变,见句(b)。但当句子的其他成分被疑问词取代时,主语前必须出现一个助动词。如果这个基本句子不含有助动词,必须在疑问词的后面紧跟上 did 或 do(es),见句(d)和句(e)。

(a) John stole/would steal Mrs. Thatcher's picture from the British Council.
约翰从英国参议会偷了/愿意偷撒切尔夫人的相片。

(b) Who stole/would steal Mrs. Thatcher's picture from the British council?
谁从英国参议会偷到了/将要偷撒切尔夫人的相片?

(c) What would John steal, if he had the chance?
如果有机会,约翰愿意偷什么?

(d) What did John steal from the British Council?
约翰从英国参议会偷了什么?

(e) Where did John steal Mrs. Thatcher's picture from?
约翰从哪偷了撒切尔夫人的相片?

E. 附加疑问句:一个附加疑问句是用来寻求对一个陈述的确认的。它常含有一个只能指代前面主语而不能指代该句中任何其他成分的人称代词。

John loves Mary, doesn't he?
约翰爱玛丽,不是吗?

第五章 意 义

1. 术语解释。

   概念意义(conceptual meaning):这是 Leech 提出的七种意义类型中的第一种。他把它定义为"逻辑的、认知的、外延的内容"。换言之,这种意义跟指称意义在很大程度上是重合的。但是,Leech 也把 sense(涵义)用作"概念意义"的简称。因此,Leech 的"概念意义"实际上包含"涵义"和"指称"两个方面。

   外延(denotation):按照哲学界的用法,外延涉及语言单位跟非语言实体之间的关系。在这个意义上,它跟指称意义是一样的。例如,"人"这个词的外延是约翰、玛丽这样的任何人。

   内涵(connotation):按照哲学界的用法,内涵跟外延相对,指的是一个词所指称的实体的特性。例如,"人"这个词的内涵就是"双足"、"无毛"、"有理性"等。

指称(reference):指称涉及一个词跟它所指称的实体之间的关系,更一般地说,它涉及的是语言单位跟非语言实体之间的关系。

涵义(sense):跟指称相反,涵义可以被界定为词跟词之间的语义关系,更一般地说,它涉及的是一个语言单位跟另一个语言单位之间的关系,是语言内关系。

同义关系(synonoymy):"同义关系"是一个专门术语,表示语言单位之间的一种相同的涵义关系。

等级反义关系(gradable antonymy):等级反义关系是有程度差别的反义词之间的涵义关系。这种反义词之间有一个中间地带。否定其中的一个不一定等于肯定另一个。一个不"好"的东西不一定就是"坏"的。它可能只是"马马虎虎"或"一般"。

互补反义关系(complementary antonomy):互补反义关系是有互补关系的反义词之间的涵义关系。换言之,这种反义词完全瓜分一个语义场。不仅肯定其中的一个等于否定另一个,否定其中的一个也等于肯定另一个。不仅"他是活的"等于"他不是死的","他不是活的"也等于"他是死的"。

反向反义关系(converse antonymy):反向反义关系是一种特殊的反义关系。两个反义词不构成肯定、否定对立,而是显示两个实体之间的一种反向关系。"X从Y处买了某物"等于"Y把某物卖给了X"。"X是Y的家长"等于"Y是X的孩子"。

关系对立项(relational opposites):"关系对立项"是"逆向反义词"的另一个名称。因为逆向反义关系通常见于两两相对的社会角色、亲属关系、时间关系、空间关系,这种反义词也叫"关系对立项"。

上下义关系(hyponymy):"上下义关系"是个专门术语,表示包容涵义关系。这是一种类属关系。例如,"书桌"的意义包括在"家具"的意义中,"玫瑰"的意义包括在"花"的意义中。

上坐标词(superordinate):上下义关系中的上位词,即类属名称,叫"上坐标词";下位词,即成员名称,叫"下义词"。一个上坐标词通常有好几个下义词。例如,"花"这个上坐标词除了包含"玫瑰"以外,还包含"牡丹"、"茉莉"、"菊花"、"郁金香"、"紫罗兰"、"康乃馨"等。

语义成分(semantic components):语义成分,或"语义特征",是比词的意义更小的意义单位。例如,"男孩"这个词的意义可以被分析成三个成分:人、年轻、男性。

组合性(compositionality):组合性原则的意思是:句子意义由其中词语的意义及组合方式所决定。

命题逻辑(propositional logic):"命题逻辑"又称"命题演算"、"句子演算"。

它研究命题的真值条件:复合命题的真值是如何由其成分命题的真值及相互关系决定的。

命题(proposition):命题是陈述句被用于描述时所表达的意义。

谓词逻辑(predicate logic):"谓词逻辑"又称"谓词演算"。它研究简单命题的内部结构。在这个逻辑系统里,"苏格拉底是人"这样的命题由两部分组成:主目和谓词。主目是一个陈述所讲述的主体,谓词则赋予该主体一种性质,或赋予几个主体一种关系。在"苏格拉底是人"这样的命题中,"苏格拉底"是主目,"人"是谓词。

逻辑连词(logical connective):逻辑连词是把简单命题组合成复合命题的逻辑成分。五个常用的逻辑连词是:否定连词 ∼,合取连词 &,析取连词 ∨,蕴含(或称"条件")连词 →,等值(或称"双条件")连词 ≡。

2. 下面这段话选自 Lewis Carroll 的 Through the Looking Glass,讨论其中的 mean 一词的意义。

"Don't stand chattering to yourself like that," Humpty Dumpty said, looking at her for the first time, "but tell me your name and your business."

"My name is Alice, but—"

"It's a stupid name enough!" Humpty Dumpty interrupted impatiently. "What does it *mean*?"

"Must a name *mean* something?" Alice asked doubtfully.

"Of course it must," Humpty Dumpty said with a short laugh: "my name *means* the shape I am and a handsome shape it is, too. With a name like yours, you might be any shape, almost."

这个 mean 的意思是"指的是"。这是 mean 在指称论中所用的意思。

3. 从语义学角度,特别是从涵义关系角度,分析下面这首诗。

         Coloured

Dear White Fella   You White Fella

Couple things you should know—   When you born, you pink

When I born, I black   When you grow up, you white

When I grow up, I black   When you go in sun, you red

When I go in sun, I black   When you cold, you blue

When I cold, I black   When you scared, you yellow

When I scared, I black   When you sick, you green

When I sick, I black   And when you die you grey

And when I die-I still black   And you have the cheek

                To call me coloured?

这首诗涉及 coloured 一词的意义。作者巧妙地利用了它"不同的颜色"这一意义来反对把黑人称为"有色人种"。这也从另一个角度说明,col-

oured 不是 red, green, yellow 等词的上义词。
4. 按要求做下列练习：
   (a) 写出下列单词的同义词：
      youth; automobile; remember; purchase; vacation; big
   (b) 写出下列单词的反义词，并说明它们在哪个方面意义相反：
      dark, boy, hot, go
   (c) 写出下列单词的两个或更多的相关意义：
      bright, to glare, a deposit, plane

   (a) youth (adolescent)［青少年］; automobile (car)［汽车］; remember (recall)［记得］; purchase (buy)［买］; vacation (holidays)［假期］; big (large)［大］
   (b) dark［暗黑的］(light［明亮的］: with respect to brightness［在亮度方面］); boy［男孩］(girl［女孩］: with respect to sex［在性别方面］); hot［热］(cold［冷］: with respect to temperature［在温度方面］); go［去］(come［来］: with respect to direction［在方向方面］)
   (c) bright (a. shining［发亮的］; b. intelligent［聪明的］); to glare (a. to shine intensely［闪耀］; b. to stare angrily［瞪］); a deposit (a. minerals in the earth［矿藏］; b. money in the bank［储蓄］); plane (a. a flying vehicle［飞机］; b. a flat surface［平面］)

5. 有人认为没有真正的同义词。如果两个单词的意义确实一模一样，其中一个就会被废弃。人们经常引用的例子是 wireless 这个词，它已被 radio 所取代。你同意这种看法吗？当我们说两个词是同义词时，一般指的是在哪种意义类型上同义？

   没有绝对的同义词，这个看法是正确的。所谓的同义词，其意义都是有区别的，不管是文体区别\内涵区别，还是方言区别。当人们说两个词同义时，通常是指它们有相同的概念意义。就 wireless 这个词而言，其"（无线电）收音机"这个意义（英国英语）确实已被废弃多年。但是，随着互联网的普及，wireless 又流行起来了。只是，仅表示"没有电线连接"这个意义。如，"And the market for wireless earpieces depends on people's willingness to look as though they are talking to themselves", "The point of this standard is to make switching between wireless access points fast", "The developer claims that this game has been a top-seller on wireless and on retail platforms" (https://www.bing.com/dict/search? q=wireless & FORM =BDVSP2, 2017 年 2 月 27 日提取)。

6. 课文没有提及 friendly：unfriendly, honest：dishonest, normal：abnormal, frequent：infrequent, logical：illogical, responsible：irresponsible 这样的反义词，它们属于哪种反义关系？

从词源说讲,这些反义词可能都是互补的。两个反义词能完全切分有关的语义场,没有中间地带。肯定一个就是否定另一个,反之亦然。但是,实际上,其中有些现在是用做等级反义词的,特别是 friendly：unfriendly 这对。它们可以受等级副词 very 修饰,可以有比较级、最高级,其中的正面成员 friendly 可以用做覆盖词。

7. 英国语言学家 F. R. Palmer 在他的 *Semantics*(p.97)一书中说,"在[等级反义关系和互补反义关系]之间没有绝对的区分。有时我们可以把 male/female, married/single, alive/dead 看做等级反义词,有人可能 very male 或者 more married,而且当然可能 more dead than alive。"试评论该观点。

　　对语言学初学者讲等级反义词和互补反义词之间的区分是相对的,这一做法不可取。尽管有时候,有的反义词同时具有两类反义词的特性,如 true：false。一般来说,"It is true"表示"It is not false",所以可以说这是一对互补反义词。但是,true 也表现出等级反义词的特性,它可以受 very 修饰,可以作为覆盖词,有真正的比较级 truer、最高级 truest。然而,这样的反义词毕竟是少数。更何况,more dead than alive 这个表达式并不是真正的比较级。

8. 姜望琪(1991:79)认为,"在某种程度上,我们可以说任何两个同词性的词都可以成为反义词,只要这两个词之间的意义差别在该上下文正好是需要强调的这一点。"他用的两个例句如下所示。你怎么看待这一观点?

　　　You have to peel a raw potato but you can skin a boiled one.
　　　He's no statesman, but a mere politician.

　　这一看法是有道理的。如作者在文章里指出的,man 可以是 woman 的反义词。但是在年龄差别很重要的情景中,它也可以是 boy 的反义词。当人跟动物的差别很重要时,man 还可以是 dog 的反义词。当有生命的跟无生命的这个差别很重要时,man 甚至可以是 stone 的反义词。"You have to peel a raw potato but you can skin a boiled one"和"He's no statesman, but a mere politician"这两个句子是一种极端的情况,所谓的同义词用做反义词了。

9. 下列词语的上坐标词是什么?
　　　man, stallion, male, boy, bull, boar
　　　这些词的上坐标词是 male[雄性],它们都属于 male 这个类属。

10. 按照语义成分分析法分析下列单词:
　　　teacher, typewriter, chopsticks
　　　teacher[老师]的语义成分是 human[人], knowledgeable[有知识的], instructive[教育的], respectable[可尊敬的];
　　　typewriter[打字机]的语义成分是 machine[机器], typewriting[打字];

chopsticks[筷子]的语义成分是 pair [成双], eat [吃饭], tool [工具]。

11. 指出下列词语中的二元谓词：

attack (verb), die (verb), between, put, love (verb), in, cat, elephant, forget

下列单词是二元谓词：attack [进攻], between [在……之间], love [爱], in [在……里], forget [忘记]。

12. 把下面的逻辑式翻译成英语，其中 a＝Ann, b＝Bill, c＝Carol, L＝like, M＝mother, x 和 y 是变项，可根据不同的量词译成"someone"、"anyone"或"everyone"。

(a) M (a, b)
(b) L (b, c) & L (c, b)
(c) L (a, b) & ~L (a, c)
(d) ∃x(L (x, b))
(e) ~∀x (L (x, c))
(f) ~∃x (∀y (L (y, x)))

(a) Ann is Bill's mother. [安是比尔的母亲]
(b) Bill loves Carol, and Carol loves Bill. [比尔爱卡罗尔，卡罗尔爱比尔]
(c) Ann loves Bill, but Ann doesn't love Carol. [安爱比尔，但是安不爱卡罗尔]
(d) Someone loves Bill. [有人爱比尔]
(e) Not everyone loves Carol. [不是每个人都爱卡罗尔]
(f) There is no one who is loved by everyone. [没有一个人是每个人都爱的]

第六章 语言与认知

1. 术语解释。

认知(cognition)："认知"一词可适用于多种不同却又相关的学科。在心理学界，"认知"是指个体的心理过程，尤其与人的内部心理状态相关（例如：信念、愿望和意图）；在认知心理学界，特别是当知识、技能和学习共同作用时，"认知"可从信息加工的角度加以理解。在认知语言学中，"认知"则是指对语言结构和模式加以的概念化过程。

心理语言学(psycholinguistics)：心理语言学是研究语言的心理方面的跨学科领域，主要考察与语言行为有关的心理状态和心理活动；心理语言学植根于语言学与认知心理学，与人类学和神经科学有着密切的关系。心理语言学有六大研究主题：语言习得、语言理解、语言产生、语言能力障碍、语言与思维、语言神经认知基础；通常，前三者即习得、理解和产生居于心理语言学领域的核心位置。

认知语言学(cognitive linguistics)：认知语言学是一种语言研究的全新方法，发轫于20世纪70年代。认知语言学是基于人类对世界的经验以及对世界感知和概念化的方式来研究语言的。其基本原则在于语言是象征性的而非自主性的，并且深受使用方式和人的一般认知能力的影响。认知语言学的主要研究领域包括：隐喻和转喻、认知语义学、认知语法和构式语法、认知语用学。

语言习得(language acquisition)：语言习得是心理语言学的中心主题之一，主要考察儿童语言习得过程。每个儿童都可以成功地习得一门语言，这样的习得在短短几年时间内无需正规的教学便可实现。由于语言与人类的核心特征密切相关，儿童语言习得便备受关注。而语言习得领域，学者们把儿童言语的笔记记录作为研究数据，便携式录音机和录像设备常常用于系统地分析儿童的自发言语行为。当前，对儿童自发言语的自然研究可以输入成计算机文件，然后进行自动切分和分析。

单词句阶段(holophrastic stage)：本术语用于指语言习得的第一阶段，在此阶段，婴幼儿用一个词来表示整个句子的意思。在一岁期间，处于语言习得初期的婴幼儿的主要成就是学会控制言语肌肉和敏感地辨别父母的语言中的声音。满一岁时，婴儿开始理解单词，一岁生日前后，婴儿开始产生单个的词，近一半的词是物体和客观实物，如食物（果汁、饼干）、身体部位（如眼睛、鼻子）、衣服（尿布、袜子）、交通工具（小汽车、小船）、玩具（布娃娃、积木）、家居物品（瓶子、灯）、动物（小狗、小猫咪）、人（爸爸、婴孩）等。全世界婴幼儿的第一批词都是类似的，这一单词句阶段可持续的时段为二个月到一年。

双词句阶段(two-word stage)：这一术语适用于语言习得的第二阶段，这一阶段的幼儿使用两个词来代替整个句子，一岁半左右的儿童开始在醒着的一两个小时内不停地学习词语并保持这一学习速度至青春期，在此阶段内，儿童的词汇量激增，以两个词开头的原始句法开始出现，如：all dry, I sit, I shut, no bed, dry pants, 等等。儿童双词组合具有高度的跨文化相似性，全世界的儿童在此行为阶段都一样，当物体出现、隐去、移动时，儿童都可以说出，可以指出物件的特点和主人，可以评说正在做着某件事情的人，可以拒绝和要求实物和活动，并且可以提出谁、什么以及哪里等语言内容。这些序列已经反映出语言已经得到习得，在儿童所说出语言的95%中，可以对词序进行恰当安排。

三词句表达(three-word utterances)：这是一个用来指语言习得第三阶段的术语，在这一阶段，儿童可以用来完整地表达自己的语言行为，儿童的三词表达类似于从更长的表达完整和复杂思想的句子中提取出的样例，在儿童语言发展的这一阶段，他们可以用完整的顺序产生出包含所有句子成分的句子,如:Mother gave John lunch in the kitchen, Give doggie paper, Adam put it box 等等。

联结主义(connectionism):这是心理语言学中的一个假说。该假说认为,读者使用拼写单位和声音单位之间相同的联结系统来生成书面单词,如 tove 的发音通过 stove 的相同发音或是属于这些词的例外的形式如 love 的拼音来通达和提取与之类似的词,在这个假说中,相似性和频率在加工和理解语言中起着重要的作用。因为,对新的语言项目的加工处理是以它们与已知项目的相似度为基础的。

列队模型(cohort model):这是由 Marslen-Wilson 和 Welsh 于 1990 年提出的解释句子理解中单词识别的心理机制模型。这一模型假设,一个口头单词的前几个音位会激活与输入相一致的一列词内候选音位,而这些候选音位互相竞争等待激活,随着更多的声音输入得到分析,不再与输入相一致的那些候选音位便掉队出列。这一过程会持续到只有一个单词候选音位项匹配上输入为止,如果没有一个最清晰的获胜的备选项,那么就会选择一个最合适的词,比如说,对于"pick up the candle"这句指令,听者有时候会首先瞥一下一张有 candy(糖果)的图片,这说明一组以/kæn/开头的单词起初都被激活了,听者也可能会注视一下有 handle 的图片,这说明单词备选项的队列也可能还包括与目标词在韵脚上一致的词。

互动模型(interactive model):这是心理语言学中用来解释单词识别的一个模型,其假设认为,在语言使用者识别一个口语单词时,较高的加工层会对较低的加工层有一个"自上而下"(top-down)的影响,词汇知识会影响对音位的感知和听辨,在词汇对词内更小单位的影响形式中存在着一种互动,在某些情况下,听者的单词知识会导致对某些音位的抑制,在另一些情况下,听者会持续地"听"那些已经从言语信号中移除而被噪音所代替的音位。

竞争模型(race model):这是心理语言学中单词识别的模型,它假设在单词的识别中有两条互相竞争的路径,一种是前词汇路径,它从声音信号中计算音位信息,第二种是词汇路径,是指单词本身得以提取时,与单词有关的音位信息就变为可用;当单词层面的信息要影响较低层面的加工时,词汇路径便赢得竞争。

串行模型(serial model):是关于句子理解的心理语言学模型,该模型认为,句子理解系统持续而有序地以明显的速度遵循着一种语言的语法限制规则,语言处理器可以很快地根据与句子解读有关的有限语法信息构造出一个句子的一种甚或多种表征,然后使用有关的全程信息对这些表征加以解读和评估。

并行模型(parallel model):这是关于句子理解的心理语言学模型,它强调人的句子理解系统容易感知大量的信息,包括语法、词汇和语境信息,以及关于言者/作者的知识和一般的外界世界知识等。并行模型描述了语言处理器是如何运用全部的相关信息从而快速地评估对一个句子的所有可能的解读;人们普遍认为的是,听者和读者会把语法知识和情境知识整合起来理解一个句子。

共振模型(resonance model):这是心理语言学中讨论文本理解的一个模型。文本或语篇连通读者长时记忆中的知识与语篇内先期提到过的材料,从长期记忆中的信息提取检索可能是一个在整个理解过程中自动发生的无调节的过程。在共振模型中,承载着一个大致语义关系的材料呈现时,长时记忆中的信息自动激活,语义细节包括诸如强烈地改变命题真值的否定等也不一定影响共振过程。它强调更为积极和智能的意义搜索,读者据此发现语篇的概念结构。在阅读一个叙事文本的过程中,读者会尝试建立起一个对于文本中因果结构的表征,而这主要是依据目标、行动、反应等对事件进行分析。共振过程作为加工文本中的第一阶段而发挥作用,而阅读目标和文本结构的细节决定一个读者是否会继续读下去并寻找该文本的连贯结构。

识解(construal):作为认知语言学的基本概念,识解意指以交替的方式对同一场景进行构想和描述的能力,它可以通过详略度、心理扫描、指向性、有利位置、图形—背景分离等不同方式加以实现。

识解操作(construal operations):识解操作是认知语言学中关于概念识解的重要术语。对认知语言学家而言,识解操作是人类在语言加工过程中运用到的概念化的过程。或者说,它是人类理解语言表达时所启用的潜在心理过程和心理资源。基本的识解操作包含以下内容:注意力与突显、判断与比较、视角与观察者的位置等。

图形—背景关系(figure-grand alignment):这是一种进行判断/比较的识解操作。作为人类的基本认知能力,也是人类判断之下的认知操作,图形—背景关系似乎可运用于空间研究,背景由介词宾语和表征空间关系结构的介词来充当。这种关系也适用于人类对运动物体的感知,因为运动的物体是典型的突显物。正是因为它的运动,物体成为典型的图形,而余下的刺激则构成背景。例如,"垫子上有只猫","猫"是图形,而"垫子"是背景。

射体(trajector):射体是用于解释判断/比较类识解操作的认知语言学术语。它表示一个事件中运动的图形。例如,"我们穿过了田野","我们"就是射体,因为在此事件中"我们"可以移动。

路标(landmark):路标与射体相关。认知语言学家兰盖克用射体表示运动的图形,用路标表示运动图形的背景,以此来区分静态和动态的图形/背景关系。例如,"他要去伦敦","伦敦"就是路标。

基本层次范畴(basic level category)：在认知语言学中，范畴化是人类基于共性和差异对经验进行分类的过程。范畴分三个层次：基本层次范畴、上义范畴和下义范畴。基本层次范畴是指那些文化上最突出，最能实现我们认知需求的范畴。例如，"狗"的下义范畴各不相同，但它们的共有特征足以区别于猫、鸟、蛇及灵长目动物等。在基本层次范畴，人类可以发现范畴特性的理想化结构，同时它也是最经济的范畴，因为正是在此层次，我们可以找到最相关的信息。

下义层次范畴(subordinate level category)：在认知语言学中，下义范畴的范畴性弱于基本层次范畴，它们的成员与邻近范畴成员的区别性很低。另外，下义层次范畴的信息量比它们直接的上义层次和基本层次范畴相对较少，且通常是多词素的。

意象图式(image schema)：在认知语言学中，意象图示一词定义为在我们感知互动以及动觉程序中反复出现的动态模式，这种模式给我们的经验以连贯性和结构性。意象图式存在于抽象层面，在位于命题结构和具体意象之间的心理组织层面上进行操作；意象图式还可以反复充当无数经验和感知的识别模式，为那些在相关方面结构相似的物体和事件构建意象。

隐喻(metaphor)：认知语言学里，隐喻通常涉及两个概念之间的对比，即通过一个概念去识解另一个概念。隐喻存在于目标域和源域的建构中。目标域是隐喻所描述的经验，源域是人们用来描述经验的工具。例如，"我们在此浪费时间"，此句基于"时间是金钱"隐喻，其目标域"时间"是依照源域"金钱"得以概念化的。在认知语言学里，隐喻可用一个简单的公式表达："X是Y"，X是目标域，Y是源域。

转喻(metonymy)：在认知语言学里，转喻被建构为理想化的认知模型。转喻是人类的基本思维方式之一，在此我们用一个实体去替代另一个实体，它同时也是一种认知过程，在这个过程中，一个更为突显的概念实体为识解另一个概念实体提供心理通道。同域实体和异域实体的相关性使得各种理想化认知模型和转喻成为可能。

实体隐喻(ontological metaphors)：实体隐喻是指人类以对物体的经验为基础，把事件、活动、情感、思想等抽象概念视做实体和物质。实体隐喻可以给不太清晰可分的实体(山、篱笆、街角)有界的平面，并把事件、行为和状态概念化归为具体物质。在实体隐喻中，人们正是基于与客观的、有界的物体的互动经验，才可将事件、活动和想法等视为实体和物质。以涨价经验为例，这种经验可以通过名词"通货膨胀"来隐喻为实体。"通货膨胀"被视为实体可以使人们对其进行指称、量化、辨别、个案对待、采取行动，甚至相信我们理解它。

结构隐喻(structural metaphors)：在认知语言学中，结构隐喻暗指一个概念是如何以另一个概念域的结构为基础来构建隐喻的,并使得根据一个概念建构另一概念成为可能。例如,"争论是战争"隐喻可以产生诸如"他向我争论里的每个弱点发起进攻。"之类的英语表达。显然,我们不仅以战争指称争论。事实上我们会赢得或输掉一场争论。我们还会把与我们争论的人视为对手。我们向他的观点发起进攻,固守自己的观点。我们赢得或失去阵地。我们谋划并使用策略。如果我们发现观点守不住了,我们会放弃,选取新的进攻路线。我们在争论中所做的很多事情都是由战争概念部分建构而来。

类属空间(generic space):语言学家Fauconnier和Turner提出并详尽说明了概念整合理论,其中类属空间建立在两个输入空间基础之上,可为新空间的生成与产生,即合成空间,提供映射源。类属空间也是在类比过程中建立的额外空间,可与每一个输入空间(输入空间I_1和I_2)形成映射。因此,它可以反映输入空间I_1和I_2所共享的一些抽象结构与组织。一般而言,类属空间定义了输入空间I_1和I_2的跨空间映射的核心内容。

合成空间(blend space):在认知语言学领域,Fauconnier和Turner提出并详尽说明了概念整合理论,其中合成空间接收的所有背景知识、结构模式和认知模型来自于输入空间I_1和I_2及类属空间相关的领域。最后,输入空间I_1和I_2部分地投射到第四空间,即合成空间,新的认知由此生成并获得。

理想化认知模型(ICMs):在认知语言学中,ICMs是由一连串单词"理想化认知模型"的首字母缩略而成,其下的替代关系就是我们所指的转喻模型。我们可将实体域分为三类:"概念"世界、"形式"世界和有关"事物"与"事件"的世界。这些域对应着三种实体,即思想、符号和所指,它们共同构成了著名的符号三角。同域实体和异域实体的相关性使得各种理想化认知模型和转喻成为可能。因此,在实体域内共有三种理想化认知模型:符号ICMs,指代ICMs和概念ICMs。

2. 心理语言学研究什么?其研究主题是什么?

心理语言学是研究语言的心理方面的学科,它通常研究与语言使用有关的心理状态和心理活动。心理语言学中的大多数问题都较为具体,包括语言习得,尤其是儿童语言习得研究,以及成年人产生和理解话语和句子的语言行为的研究等,心理语言学的一个重要的聚焦点是语法规则的无意识应用,即它可以使得人们产生和理解可理解的句子。心理语言学家考察和研究语言与思维之间的关系,而这是一个反反复复争论的主题,即到底是语言是思维的机能还是思维是语言使用的机能。心理语言学还关注语言是如何学得的以及语言在人们思维中所起的作用。心理语言学领域的学者和专家用实验调查下列问题,如短时记忆和长时记忆、感知策略、以语言模型为基础的言语感知、语言使用过程中所涉及的大脑活动、大脑损伤所导致的语言障碍、认知与语言等。

  通常,我们把心理语言学的研究划分为六大主题:1)习得:儿童是如何习得语言技能的(一语习得)以及他们是如何扩展到其他的语言的(二语/外语习得)? 2)理解:声学或视觉信号是如何由听者或读者以语言的方式而解读的? 3)产生:一个人意欲传递的信息是如何被转换为声波或书写符号的? 4)障碍:导致言语和语言加工系统出现瞬时或永久性失调的原因是什么? 5)语言和思维:人类语言在思维中起着什么作用? 不同语言对于我们如何思维会产生什么差异? 6)神经认知:语言的认知结构在大脑中是什么样的以及语言处理如何在人脑中实现? 也就是说,人类的语言官能的大脑皮层—机能构造是什么? 这里,我们一般主要集中在前三大主题上,即习得、理解和产生。

3. 请描述第一语言习得的阶段。

  语言习得是心理语言学的核心话题之一,掌握语言是人类的典型特质,学会一种第一语言是每个儿童在短短几年间无需正规课程都能成功而做到的事情。儿童语言习得已备受关注,第一语言习得通常有4个阶段。

  1)单词句阶段:语言习得起始于人生活的很早时期,主要是始于对语言声音模式的习得。在一岁期间,处于语言习得初期的婴幼儿的主要成就是学会控制言语肌肉和敏感地辨别父母的语言中的声音。满一岁时,婴儿开始理解单词,一岁生日前后,婴儿开始产生单个的词,近一半的词是物体和客观实物,如食物(果汁、饼干)、身体部位(如眼睛、鼻子)、衣服(尿布、袜子)、交通工具(小汽车、小船)、玩具(布娃娃、积木)、家居物品(瓶子、灯)、动物(小狗、小猫咪)、人(爸爸、婴孩)等,还有一些表示行动、移动和路径的词,如 up, off, open, eat 和 go 等,也有修饰词,如 hot, all gone, more, dirty 和 cold。最后,是一些用于社会交往与互动的常规性词汇,如 yes, no, want, bye-bye 和 hi ,其中有些表达感觉像是以后的词块,如 look at that and what is that ,尽管这些词不是成人用的单个词。

  2)双词句阶段:一岁半左右,儿童语言以两种方式剧变,词汇量激增,儿童开始在醒着的一两个小时内不停地学习词语并保持这一学习速度至青春期。一些原始的含有类似下列两个词的句法如 All dry, All messy, All wet, I sit, I shut , No bed, Our car, Papa away, Dry pants 等等开始出现。

  3)三词句表达:在这一阶段,儿童可以用来完整地表达自己的语言行为了,儿童的三词表达类似于从更长的表达完整和复杂思想的句子中提取出来的样例,在儿童语言发展的这一阶段,他们可以用完整的顺序产生出包含所有句子成分的句子,如 Tractor go floor, Adam put it box 等句子开始涌现。

  4)流利语法会话阶段:在双词句后期和三词句中期之间,儿童的语言迅速发展成为流利的语法会话,句长平稳增加。由于语法是一种组合型系统,句法类型以指数方式增加,每个月翻倍增加,在三周岁之前达到数以万计的句子数量,尽管他们所经历的阶段通常是一样的,无论这些阶段是如何延伸或压缩的,正常的儿童在其语言发展的速度上会有一年或一年多一点儿的差别,但许多儿童在两岁时都会用复杂的句子说话了。

在语法激增的过程中,儿童的句子不仅变得更长而且更为复杂,他们会把一个句子成分嵌套进另一个句子成分之中,之前,他们可能会说 Give doggie paper(一个三个分支的动词短语)和 Big doggie(一个两个分支的名词短语),而现在他们能说 Give big doggie paper 这样的把两个分支的名词短语嵌套进三个分支的动词短语中的句子了,之前的句子类似于电报,漏掉非重音的虚词如 of、the、on 及 does,也会漏掉屈折变化如 -ed、-ing 以及 -s 等,到了 3 岁时,儿童能够较之前更多地在需要虚词的 90% 的句子中使用这些虚词,所有的句子类型都繁盛迅猛地发展出来,如含 who、what 和 where 的问句、关系从句、比较级、否定句、补足语、连词、被动句等等,这些句子构式似乎展示了大多数甚至是全部用来解释成人语法的语法运转机制。

4. 请阐释用于解释单词识别过程的模型。

单词由于其在传递意义中极为重要角色而在语言理解中居于核心位置,单词识别可从口语词和印刷词的识别上来看待。

列队模型:这是由 Marslen-Wilson 和 Welsh 于 1990 年提出的解释句子理解中单词识别的心理机制的模型。这一模型假设,一个口头单词的前几个音位会激活与输入相一致的一列词内候选音位,而这些候选音位互相竞争等待激活,随着更多的声音输入得到分析,不再与输入相一致的那些候选音位便掉队出列,这一过程会持续到只有一个单词候选音位项匹配上输入为止,如果没有一个最清晰的获胜的备选项,那么久会选择一个最合适的词,比如说,对于"pick up the candle"这句指令,听者有时候会首先瞥一下一张有 candy(糖果)的图片,这说明一组以/kæn/开头的单词起初都被激活了,听者也可能会注视一下有 handle 的图片,这说明单词备选项的队列也可能还包括与目标在韵脚上一致的词。

互动模型:它假设较高的加工层会对较低的加工层有一个"自上而下"(top-down)的影响,词汇知识会影响对音位的感知和听辨,在词汇对词内更小单位的影响形式中存在着一种互动。在某些情况下,听者的单词知识会导致对某些音位的抑制;在另一些情况下,听者会持续地"听"那些已经从言语信号中移除而被噪音所代替的音位。

竞争模型:该模型不同意"自上而下"效应,它假设在单词的识别中有两条互相竞争的路径,一种是前词汇路径,它从声音信号中计算音位信息,另一种是词汇路径,是指单词本身得以提取时,与单词有关的音位信息就变为可用;当单词层面的信息要影响较低层面的加工时,词汇路径赢得竞争。

听者的语言知识以及对语言模式的知识会以某些方式促进单词的辨识,比如,听者会用如起始音/tl/在英语中是不合法的这样的音位配列学信息帮助自己去识别音位和单词边界,听者也会用关于英语单词常常在第一个音节上读重音这样的知识去解析言语信号进而整合为单词,这类知识帮助我们解决我们所知道的语言中的切分问题。

印刷是语言结构的展现,读者会在阅读印刷好的单词时使用含有正字法中的形态结构线索,比如,他们会知道前缀 re- 可以加在自由语素如 print 和 do 之前产生出 reprint 和 redo 这样的双语素词,遇到 vive 时,阅读过程会由于它与 revive 具有密切关系从而把它判断为一个词。音位和其他的语言结构的方面会在阅读中得到检索和提取,在印刷词的识别中,有与格问题,这就是语言结构是如何从印刷体中派生出来的,一种观点认为,有两种不同的过程可用于把正字法表征转化为音位表征中,一是词汇路径,用于寻找心理词汇中的已知单词的音位形式,这一程序产生对于例外词如 love 的正确读音,而是非词汇路径,用于解释阅读过程的能产性:它根据更小单位生成规则词(如 stove)及异常字母串(如 tove)的读音;后一个路径会给出例外词的错误读音。因此,在快速单词命名实验任务中这些词会被读得极慢或被读错(如,把 love 读成 /lʌv/)。联结论认为,一组正字法与音位学的联结可以解释规则词和非规则例外词上的语言行为。

关于正字法—音位学转译的另外一个问题是精细程度,英语是单词辨识和识别中的主要研究对象,而英语有极不规则的书写系统,比如,ea 对应于 bead 中的 /i/ 但又对应于 dead 中的 /ɛ/,c 在 cat 中读 /k/ 而在 city 中读 /s/,这样的不规则特性特别体现在元音上面,然而,定量分析表明,考虑元音所后接的辅音会规定该元音的读音,比如,ea 的读音 /ɛ/ 更多的是处在 d 而不是 m 的前面,这样的考虑促使人们提出一个假设,即英语读者会在拼写—语音转译过程中使用对应于音节 rime 的字母组来进行书写和拼读之间的转译。

5. 影响句子理解的因素是哪些?

心理语言学家从不同的方式讨论句子理解的现象,普遍认可听者和读者会把语法和情境知识整合在一起来理解一个句子。

句子理解中的结构因素:心理语言学家提出了解释与语法限制因素有关的句子理解的原则,其中,最普遍的原则是"最简连接",该原则限定了"结构更简",认为结构上的简洁性指导着句子理解中的所有最初的分析。根据这一观点,句子处理器构建起句子的单一分析并尝试解释它,首先要求语法规则的最少应用用于每一个正在输入的单词进而输入到正在建构的结构中,如句子"The second wife will claim the inheritance belongs to her"中,当 inheritance 首次出现时,将会被解读为既是 claim 的直接宾语也是 belongs 的主语,研究者会观察到读者眼睛注视 belongs 的时间会长于通常,而这正是在为句子消解歧义。他们解释说,这一结果意味着读者首先将 inheritance 解读成了是一个直接宾语,当读者必须修正这一初步解读使其成为 inheritance 是 belong 的主语时,他们就中断了起初的解析。心理语言学家认为读者是被引入一个花园小径中了,因为直接宾语的分析在结构上比之其他可能的分析要更为简洁。

句子理解中的词汇因素:心理语言学家提出,人类的句子处理器主要受关于储存于词库中的具体单词的信息所指引,比如,在 The salesman glanced at a/the customer with suspicion/ripped jeans 这个句子中,借此短语 with suspicion 或 with ripped jeans 既可以修饰动词 glance 也可以修饰名词 customer,但这只对行为动词才行,而对像 glance at 这样的感知动词是不行的,因为人们注意到,只有当名词有一个不定冠词 a 时,才会出现用于名词短语修饰成分的表示实际偏好的成分。

6. 请解释语言产生的各个方面。

语言产生过程的诸多方面如言语过程中的概念化和线性化、语法即音位编码、自我监控、自我修复以及手势示意等等,均是语言产生过程的主题。

1) 单词通达:单词在几个步骤中得到计划和设计,每一个步骤生成一个具体的表征类型,信息通过激活的扩散在表征之间进行传送。第一个加工步骤称为概念化,即决定所要表达的概念,在做出这样的选择中,说话者会考虑各种各样的事情,包括某个人是否在前面已经提及并且听者是否可能知道他的专名等。下面一个步骤是选择一个与已经选定的概念相对应的单词,说话者会首先选定一个规定单词的句法类型及额外句法信息的句法词单元,一旦该单元的激活水平超过所有其他竞争单元的总激活量则该单元即被选定,核查机制会保证该选定单元的确能映现到意向概念上。接下来的加工步骤是形态一音位编码,即开始检索和提取对应于已选单词的语素,有时候,形态上相关的词项会比语义上或音系上相关的词项对目标词的产生具有更为不同的效应,一般而言,根据其在话语中的顺序,语素是依据顺序获得通达和提取的。

2) 句子生成:在生成句子的过程中,第一个步骤也还是概念准备——决定要说的内容。句子生成的理论假设说话者是以递增的方式来准备自己的话语的,也就是说,说话者在说出一段话时或在话语的部分过渡时,一旦选定最初的几个词汇概念并准备稍后的词汇概念,便会立即启动语言规划和设计。说话者可能会选择不同大小的概念计划单位,但是适用于许多情境的典型单位似乎只是大致对应于从句,当说话者计划句子时,他们也会检索和提取单词,说话者还必须把句法知识用来生成句子。两组截然不同的过程包含于生成句法结构的过程中,第一组常称为功能计划过程,用来指派和选定语法功能词,如主语、动词、直接宾语等,第二组常称为定位编码,即使用已经得到检索和提取的词汇—语法单元及已为它们指定的功能去生成能够承载句子成分及其顺序中依存关系的句法结构。从功能层到定位层的映现通常相当直接,即主语通常置于动词之前,然后是直接宾语和间接宾语。

3) 书面语产生:书面语产生中的步骤类似于口头语产生中的步骤,一个主要区别是必须要检索和产生的是正字形式而不是音位形式,音位学在这一过程中起着极为重要的作用,这类似于它在阅读中从印刷文字中派生出意义的过程中所起的作用。写作不同于说话之处在于作者常常有更多的时间来进行概念准备和计划,而且,由于意向读者常常在时空上远离作者,他们也更需要这样做。同样,监控和修改在写作中比在口语中常常起着更大的作用,由于这些原因,大多数关于写作的研究都更为关注构思和修改过程而不是句子生成和词汇通达过程,后者是口语产生所关注的焦点。

7. 请问认知语言学的定义为何?

认知语言学是一种语言研究的全新方法,发轫于20世纪70年代,是对当时盛行的生成范式的反叛,该范式追求的是语言的自足性。认知语言学是基于人类对世界的经验以及对世界感知和概念化的方式来研究语言的。其基本原则在于语言是象征性的而非自发性的,并且深受使用方式和人的一般认知能力的影响。语言的发展并非依靠"普遍语法",相反语言是需要习得的。认知语言学的国际性学术组织是国际认知语言学协会(ICLA),该协会成立于1989年,每两年召开一次国际认知语言学会议。针对认知语言学圈内学者的学术刊物是《认知语言学》和《认知语言学评论年刊》。

8. 请描述三类概念隐喻。

隐喻涉及两个概念之间的对比,即通过一个概念去识解另一个概念。它通常按照目标域和源域来描写。在认知语言学里,隐喻可表达为一个基本公式:"X是Y",X是目标域,Y是源域。Lakoff和Johnson把隐喻分为三类:实体隐喻、结构隐喻和方位隐喻。

实体隐喻:实体隐喻是指人类以对物体的经验为基础,把事件、活动、情感、思想等抽象概念视做实体和物质。实体隐喻可以给不太清晰可分的实体(山、篱笆、街角)有界的平面,并把事件、行为和状态概念化归为具体物质。在实体隐喻中,人们正是基于与客观的、有界的物体的互动经验,才可将事件、活动和想法等视做实体和物质。例如,涨价的经验可以通过名词"通货膨胀"来隐喻为实体,即"通货膨胀是实体"。这为我们理解类似"通货膨胀正在降低我们的生活标准"。这样的经验提供了一条路径。在这个例子中,将"通货膨胀"视为实体可以使人们对其进行指称、量化、辨别、个案对待、采取行动,甚至相信我们理解它。实体隐喻在处理人类经验时必不可少。

结构隐喻:结构隐喻为我们依循一个概念架构另一个概念提供可能性。

结构隐喻暗指一个概念是如何以另一个概念域的结构为基础来构建隐喻的。例如,"争论是战争"隐喻可以产生诸如"他向我争论里的每个弱点发起进攻。"之类的英语表达。显然,我们不仅以战争指称争论。事实上我们会赢得或输掉一场争论。我们还会把与我们争论的人视为对手。我们向他的观点发起进攻,固守自己的观点。我们赢得或失去阵地。我们谋划并使用策略。如果我们发现观点守不住了,我们会放弃,选取新的进攻路线。我们在争论中会做的很多事情都是由战争概念部分架构而来。

方位隐喻:方位隐喻赋予概念以空间方位,并以共现经验为特征。方位隐喻建立在连接隐喻两部分的经验之上。作为隐喻句的一部分,连系动词"is"应被视为两种不同的共现经验间的连接。例如,"多是向上"。这句隐喻就是基于同时发生的两种不同经验:物质数量的增加和物质水平的可见增长。还有"高兴为上;悲伤为下"的隐喻,例如:"我感到高兴。"和"我感到情绪低落。"从上述句子不难看出,低垂的姿态明显与悲伤和沮丧的情感相联系,而直立的姿态多与积极向上的状态相关。

9. 请阐述概念整合理论的模型。

Fauconnier 和 Turner 提出并详尽说明了概念整合理论。在此理论下,整合在两个输入心理空间中进行操作从而产生第三个空间,即合成空间。合成空间部分地继承了两个输入空间的结构,并且形成了自己的层创结构。两个输入空间 I_1 和 I_2 的合成需要满足 4 个条件,用到 4 种空间。

1) 跨空间映射:这是合成的第一步,在此过程中,输入空间 I_1 和 I_2 会有选择地投射或映射到第三个空间,即有层创结构的合成空间。投射或映射是以跨空间映射的方式来运行。

2) 类属空间:类属空间建立于两个输入空间基础之上,它是在类比过程中建立的额外空间,可与每一个输入空间(输入空间 I_1 和 I_2)形成映射。所以,类属空间可以反映输入空间 I_1 和 I_2 所共享的一些抽象结构与组织。类属空间定义了输入空间 I_1 和 I_2 的跨空间映射的核心内容。

3) 合成空间:合成空间接收并采用的所有背景知识、结构模式和认知模型来自于输入空间 I_1 和 I_2 还有类属空间相关的领域。最后,输入空间 I_1 和 I_2 部分地投射到第四空间,即合成空间,新认知由此生成并获得。

4) 层创结构:层创结构存在于合成空间中并呈现出一个更为简洁的结构。它可视为整个合成网络中的一个动态结构而非合成空间自身。它帮助建立的是一个简单却最为有效的合成空间,使之能利用现存的,可取的结构。在合成网络中,层创结构可以把所有的心理空间连接并联系起来。

10. 请用意象图示分析以下段落。

你从睡梦中醒来,从被窝里向外窥视着屋内。你慢慢地从昏昏沉沉中清醒一点后,从被窝里爬出来,穿上睡袍,伸展一下四肢,在恍惚的状态中走出卧室,走进洗澡间,朝镜子里看了一眼,看到镜子里的那张脸也在向外看着你,你把手伸进牙具箱,拿出牙膏,挤出一些,把牙刷放进嘴里,匆忙地刷起牙来,然后把漱口水吐出。早餐时你表现出一副主人的姿态,不断进进出出——倒出咖啡,摆开盘子,把面包片放入烤箱里烤一烤,在面包上不停地涂抹开果酱。一旦你更加清醒,你或许会沉浸于读报,或许会进入交谈状态,而这会让你对某个话题滔滔不绝。

这里 in 和 out 的一些意义涉及明确的空间物理定向而其他意义则涉及的是更加抽象的非空间关系,例如:"走在恍惚中"、"匆忙刷起牙"、"沉浸于读报"、"进入交谈状态"、"对某个话题滔滔不绝"。然而,它们皆需要在实在的或者抽象的实体或事件活动中,建立起某些关系。

第七章 语言 文化 社会

1. 术语解释。

人类语言学(Anthropological Study of Linguistics):是关于某一群体中,语言与文化关系的研究。具体来说,人类语言学家试图通过特定群体成员的语言使用、文化传统、信念体系、社会行为的研究,达到进一步了解这个话语群体的目的。

交际(Communication):指发生在至少两个人或两个群体的信息交流过程。

交际能力(Communicative Competence):是社会语言学家 Dell Hymes 提出的一种理论,同理论语言学中的"语言能力"概念形成了鲜明的对比。

语境理论(Context of Situation):为英国伦敦学派创始人 Firth 提出,首次以比较完善的方式,阐述了说话人、语言形式、语言环境等因素相互之间的关系,开创了语言学研究中的"语境学说"。语境之说,包括下列具体内容(Firth, 1950:43—44[Palmer, 1981:53—54]):

    A. 参与者的相关特征:个人与个性:
        (i) 参与者的言语行为;
        (ii) 参与者的非言语行为;
    B. 相关的话题内容;
    C. 言语行为所产生的效果。

文化表现类型(Nida's Classification of Culture):为 Nida 提出,Nida(1964)认为,作为一个翻译家,如果想出色完成跨文化交际的任务,有必要在具体的翻译工作中,注重以下 5 种文化的表现:1)生态文化;2)语言文化;3)宗教文化;4)物质文化,以及 5)社会文化。

交际民族学(Ethnography of Communication):包括三个方面的核心内容:1)言语社团;2)场景、事件和行为,以及 3)交际民族学模式。判定说话人是否属于同一个言语社团,不但要看成员之间是否共享一套话语规则,还要看他们是否至少共享一种语言变体形式。

广义语言能力(FLB):是理论语言学的新观点。乔姆斯基认为,在语言学研究中,有必要区分"广义语言能力"和"狭义语言能力"之间的异同。"广义语言能力"包括感觉运动系统、概念意念系统,以及递归运算机制三个方面的研究内容,为我们提供了从有限元素组群生成无限表达方式的可能。

狭义语言能力(FLN):能同广义语言能力形成互补对立,其内容主要是递归特征,构成了人类语言独特的语言能力。

语言性别差异(Gender Difference):指的是在具体的语言使用过程中,由于说话人性别的差异而引发的各种语言差异现象。

语言决定论(Linguistic Determinism):是美国语言学家 Sapir 提出的一种观点,是"萨丕尔—沃尔夫假设"的主要内容。这种观点认为,语言影响着我们的思维,不同的语言有可能导致不同的思维模式。

语言相对论(Linguistic Relativity):是德国民族学家洪堡特提出的一种观点,同美国语言学家萨丕尔和沃尔夫的"萨丕尔—沃尔夫假设",有异曲同工之处,可以相互换用。这种观点认为,语言影响着我们的思维,不同的语言有可能导致不同的思维模式。

语言性别歧视(Linguistic Sexism):是指语言使用过程中,一种性别形成了对于另外一种性别的歧视现象。一般而言,这种歧视现象反映出一种"大男子沙文主义"倾向。

六种人称代词形式(Six-Person System):是从类型学的角度,对于语言代词系统的一种归纳表述。这种归纳可以用下面这种列表形式表现:

Six-Person System

singular	plural
I	we
thou	you
he	they

话语群体(Speech Community):正如 Dell Hymes 指出的那样,指的是一个群体,群体成员不但共享一套话语规则,而且至少共享一种语言变体形式。

交际民族学研究(SPEAKING):是交际民族学采用的一种研究模式,有八个方面的内容:场景(Situation)、参与者(Participant)、目的(Ends)、相关形式与内容(Act sequence)、语气(Key)、语式(Instrumentality)、准则(Norms),以及体裁(Genres)。为了记忆上的方便,取八大要素的首字母,合成了 The SPEAKING mnemonic 的说法。

萨丕尔—沃尔夫假设(Sapir-Whorf Hypothesis):该假设认为不同的语言有助于形成人们对于世界的不同看法。不过,现在很少有人全盘接受这一理论的初始观点。事实上，随着时间的流变，这一假说从原来的初始形式中，逐渐衍生出了"强式"和"弱式"两种理论模式。强式之说，指的是这一理论的初始假说，即强调语言在塑造人类思维方式过程中所起的决定性作用；弱式之说，则是对于初始假说的修正，认为语言、文化和思维之间有相关性，但是思维方式的跨文化差异是相对的，不是绝对的。

社会语言学(Sociolinguistics of Language)：它的研究目的是：了解语言变体现象，提供语言功能说明。换言之，这是一种微观层面上的社会语言学研究。在这个层面上，可以研究的问题有：结构变化、称谓形式、性别差异、话语分析、洋泾浜语现象、克里奥尔语机制等等。

语言社会学(Sociolinguistics of Society)：主要考察社会成员的语言行为，达到了解社会的目的。换言之，这是一种宏观层面上的社会语言学研究。在这个层面上，可以讨论的内容有：双语问题、多语现象、语言态度、语言选择、语言保持、语言流变、语言规划、语言标准、语言政策等等。

三大交际原则(Tripartite Model for Successful Communication)：为美国心理学家罗杰斯提出，可以简约归纳为：1)学会从对方的角度看待事物；2)学会从对方的角度感受事物，以及 3)学会从对方的角度了解世界。

语言变体研究(Variationist Linguistics)：主要研究的是，在不同社会语境、不同地理区域，因为受到经济、教育、阶层、性别、文体差异方面的影响，产生的语言变化现象以及语言变体的使用情况。

女子英语文体(Women Register)：为美国社会语言学家莱考夫首先提出。她认为，美国文化里有一种独特的女子英语文体形式，其具体表现可以大致概括为：委婉文雅；含蓄客气；语气游移；内容琐细。细究起来，女子英语文体可以归纳为以下六个方面的特征：

1) 在词语的选择，特别是色彩词语的使用上，男女不同；
2) 女性喜用含义空泛、语义虚指的形容词形式；
3) 女性善用反意疑问句，以及陈述句作为一般问句的用法；
4) 女性常用表示语气游移不定的语气词语；
5) so 作为强势语的用法为女性所偏爱；
6) 女子英语中出现更多礼貌客气的表现手法，以及矫枉过正的语言形式。

2. 社会语言学对语言研究有何重要贡献？

社会语言学对语言学的贡献至少有三个方面：1)传统语言学强调对语言的形式分析，社会语言学着重多层面分析，因此使得研究框架更为平衡；2)传统语言学更多侧重研究语言结构，而社会语言学则强调功能的研究，因而使得对语言问题的全方位研究成为可能；3)传统语言学尝试解释语言内部因素,而社会语言学则是关注语言的外部因素,进而使得人们对语言和社会以及说话者之间的关系得到一个更好了解。
3. 语言教学为何需要文化学习?

  总体而言,就外语学习而言,文化知识的学习,至少有三个方面的作用:
  1) 有助于学生了解文化差异;
  2) 有助于语言学习者跳出自身文化的圈子,从目标文化的角度考虑问题;
  3) 有助于通过各种课堂练习,强调语言与文化不可分离性的理解,促进外语学习。

4. 作为语言学专业的学生,如何理解功能与形式之间的关系?

  语言功能与语言形式,是语言这块"硬币"两个不同的表现方面;功能研究与形式研究,同样也构成了语言学研究的两个研究焦点。社会结构呈现出一种多元化的趋势,话语群体中普遍存在的语言变体现象,是这种多元化现象在社会成员言语行为方面的具体反映,单一的形式化分析,不足以满足这一要求。因此,语言学研究有必要采用一种形式与功能互补的观察视野,建构整体论意义上的语言学观。

5. 过去的20年里,大量新词新语涌入我国人民的日常生活。列举若干新词新语,考察使用语境,说明其快速增长的原因。

  词汇是反映社会变化的晴雨表,通过观察这个晴雨表,即可了解语言与社会的动态变化关系;语言是社会之镜,透过这面镜子,可以更好地展示社会生活的五彩斑斓;社会是语言之根,置身社会语境,可以切身感受到语言使用的方方面面。改革开放以来,我国人民的生活有了天翻地覆的巨变,大量新词新语的产生和使用,正好说明了这一点。例如,新事物的层出不穷,就有了"动漫"(动画漫画)、"网游"(网络游戏)、"拇指文化"(又称"手机文化")这样一些新词新语,极大地丰富了我们的概念表达。

6. 略

7. 你对跨文化研究中的"萝卜青菜各有所爱"现象有何评论?

  一种语言形式,在不同的语境中可能获得完全不同的社会含义。面对这种困惑,在跨文化交际中,首先,有必要遵循一条社会语言学的定律,弄清楚"什么人对什么人,为了什么目的,什么时候,说什么"的问题。其次,为了保证有效的跨文化交流,我们还必须懂得"萝卜青菜各有所爱"的道理,不能简单地用自己的文化传统、价值观念、社会习俗,去理解、判断、评价异文化中的文化表达、话语行为、语言表现。否则,轻则容易产生跨文化误读现象,重则引发文化冲突。

8. 语言教师为何应当关注社会语言学?

  1) 社会语言学促进了语言教学内容与重点的改变;
  2) 社会语言学有助于教材内容和教学活动的创新;
  3) 社会语言学为卓有成效的教学研究提供了广阔天地;

4) 社会语言学为研究语言使用与语言发展提供了一种新视野。

9. 对于新世纪的语言学研究而言,广义语言能力与狭义语言能力的划分,有何意义?

  语言学最新研究表明:语言学研究有必要采用多学科、进化论的视角,才能产生新的理论贡献;在语言学研究中,有必要区分"广义语言能力"和"狭义语言能力"之间的异同。"广义语言能力"包括感觉运动系统、概念意念系统,以及递归运算机制三个方面的研究内容,为我们提供了从有限元素组群生成无限表达方式的可能;"狭义语言能力"仅含递归特征,构成了人类语言独特的语言能力。有理由认为,"广义语言能力"可能来自于语言之外的进化动因。

  因此,语言学研究必须采用跨学科比较的视野,通过与生物学、心理学,以及人类学联袂的方法,才有可能产生新的理论假设,找出形成语言能力配置的进化推力。面向新世纪的语言学研究,应当体现这种观点。

10. 众所周知,相对于词汇的剧烈变化而言,语言的称谓形式比较稳定。汉语的称谓系统里,近来却发生了一个新变化:"亲"和"亲们"用作称谓语。从社会语言学的角度,应当怎么看待这一现象?

  实际上,这一新变化是受到电商的推动而快速传播开来的。所以,这种用法又被称之为"淘宝体"。从社会语言学的角度来看,这种变化有下列几个方面的特点。

  从形态上来看,"亲"是源于"亲爱的"这一固定说法的。虽然后者本身没有什么特别之处,但是这种缩略说法却很新奇。从语义上来说,即便作为一种称谓语,"亲爱的"也仅限于夫妻、恋人、家人、好友之间,基本上不用于陌生人之间。基于这种分析,"亲"作为一种新兴的称谓用法,确实有其可圈可点之处。首先,能够从"亲爱的"结构中分离出来,自立门户,就很不易。其次,从原来仅指"亲密关系",到现在"泛指他人"的语义变化,也堪称奇。最后,还能以复数"亲们"、"众亲",甚至"众亲们"的形式呈现,则更为新奇了。仅此一例,即可看出语言与社会共变的道理来。

第八章 语言的使用

1. 术语解释。

  施为句(performative):施为句是"I name this ship the Queen Elizabeth"(我命名这艘船为"伊丽莎白"号)这样的句子。它们不描写事物,没有真假。说出这样的句子就是,至少部分是,实施一种行为。像 name 这样的动词叫"施为动词"。

  叙事句(constative):叙事句跟施为句相对。"I pour some liquid into the tube"(我往试管里倒一些液体)这样的句子是对说话人正在做的事的描写。说话人不可能通过说这几个字往试管里倒任何东西,他必须同时真的实施倒东西的动作,否则我们可以说他撒谎。

发话行为(locutionary act):发话行为是我们说话时的普通行为,即,移动发音器官,发出按一定方式排列的声音,并且有一定的意义。例如,当有人说了"Morning!"(早晨好),我们可以说他发出了一个声音,一个词,或一句话——"Morning!"。

行事行为(illocutionary act):行事行为是在实施发话行为同时实施的一种行为。我们说话时,不仅要发出具有一定意义的某些语言单位,而且要说清楚自己的意图,希望自己的话被怎么理解,或者用 Austin 的说法,我们的话有一定的"语力"。在"Morning!"那个例子里,我们可以说,这句话有问候的语力,它应该被理解成问候。

取效行为(perlocutionary act):取效行为涉及一句话对听话人的影响。通过告诉听话人某事,说话人可以改变听话人的有关看法,可以误导他,惊吓他,或诱惑他去做某事,等等。不管这些效果是不是符合说话人的意图,它们都可以被看做说话人所实施的行为的一部分。

合作原则(cooperative principle):这是 Grice 提出的关于会话规律的原则。全文是"使你所说的话,在其所发生的阶段,符合你所参与的交谈的公认目标或方向"。合作原则下面有四条准则:数量准则、质量准则、关系准则、方式准则。

会话含义(conversational implicature):这是一种暗含意义,可以在合作原则及其准则的指导下,在词语的常规意义基础上,联系语境推导出来。在这个意义上,会话含义跟言语行为理论中的行事语力是一样的。它们都涉及语境意义,或汉语所谓的"言外之意"。

衍推(entailment):衍推涉及的是两个句子之间的这样一种逻辑关系:第一个句子为真,第二个句子就一定为真;第二个句子为假,第一个句子就一定为假。例如,当"I saw a boy"为真时,"I saw a child"必真;当"I saw a child"为假时,"I saw a boy"也必假。

明示交际(ostensive communication):"明示交际",或"推理交际",是"明示—推理交际"的简称。换言之,交际不只是简单的编码和解码的过程,它也涉及听话人的推理和说话人的明示(一种表明自身说话意图的行为)。

交际关联原则(communicative principle of relevance):这是 Sperber 和 Wilson 在 1986 年首先提出的原则。全文是"每一个明示交际行动都传递一种假定:该行动本身具备最佳关联性。"

(作为相对概念的)关联性(relevance (as a comparative notion)):Sperber 和 Wilson 从三个角度界定了关联性这个概念。他们认为关联性也是一个相对概念,因此他们又有如下的附带"程度条件"的关联性定义:

程度条件 1:如果一个设想在一个语境中的语境效应大,那么这个设想在这个语境中就具有关联性。

程度条件2：如果一个设想在一个语境中所需的处理努力小,那么这个设想在这个语境中就具有关联性。

(Horn 的)Q 原则(Horn's)Q-principle：Q 原则(基于听话人)：

你的话语要充分(参照数量准则第一条次则)

说得尽可能多(在符合 R 原则的前提下)

R 原则(R-principle)：R 原则(基于说话人)：

你的话语应是必要的(参照关系准则、数量准则第二条次则和方式准则)

只说必须说的(在符合 Q 原则的前提下)

语用劳动分工(division of pragmatic labor)：Horn 注意到,Q 原则和 R 原则常常直接冲突,并提出解决它们之间冲突的办法就是如下的语用分工:"在可以使用相应的无标记的(简单而'省力'的)表达式时,使用有标记的(相对复杂而且/或者冗长的)表达式,往往被解释成要传递有标记的信息(无标记表达式不会或不能传递的信息)。"

Levinson 的三条探索法(Levinson's three heuristics)：莱文森在 2000 年把他的三条原则改称为"探索法",并且把内容简化如下:

探索法 1 没有说的,就是不想说的。

探索法 2 简单描述的是用通常方式举例说明的。

探索法 3 用不正常方式表达的,就是不正常的;或者说,有标记信息表示有标记情形。

2. 分析下面这个父亲和女儿之间的对话,说明每句话的行事行为。

   [女儿到厨房里拿了些爆米花]

   Father: I thought you were practicing your violin.（我以为你在练小提琴呢）

   Daughter: I need to get the [violin] stand.（我要拿琴谱架）

   Father: Is it under the popcorn?（它在爆米花下面吗?）

   "I thought you were practicing your violin"(我以为你在练小提琴呢)这句话的行事语力是批评女儿没有在练小提琴。女儿的回答是在为自己辩护——我正要去练小提琴。而父亲的反问揭穿了女儿的托词。

3. 如果你问某人"Can you open the door?"(你能开开门吗?),他回答"Yes"(能),却不去开门,你会有什么反应? 为什么? 请用言语行为理论加以说明。

   我会很生气。"Can you open the door?"(你能开开门吗?)通常是请求听话人做某事,而不是询问他的能力。他回答"Yes"(能),实际上却不去开门,说明他拒绝了我的请求。

4. 谣传美国当选总统比尔·克林顿要背弃他在竞选时许下的一些诺言,1993年1月14日克林顿就此答记者问。当被一些记者穷追不舍,逼入窘境时,他说了下面这段话:

> 我认为如果美国总统,任何一个美国总统,不能因环境改变而改变政策,那将是愚蠢的。就我所知,每一个美国总统,尤其是那些做出杰出贡献的总统,都知道如何应对环境的变化。如果一个美国总统不这么做,那显然是愚蠢的。

有些语言学家认为,竞选演讲,就像所有的政治演讲,都是合作原则及其准则被中止的典型场合,你同意吗?你能否指出其他类似的场合?

是的,这是合作原则及其准则被中止的场合。Grice 在提出他的合作原则时,用了"normally"(通常)、"characteristically"(典型情况下)、"ceteris paribus"(其余情况相同时)等字眼。也就是说,合作原则及其准则并不是在任何情况下都会得到遵守的。或者说,"说话人相信他自己说的话"这样的假设只是会话含义。在有迹象显示相反情况时,这些含义就会被取消。类似的情形还有葬礼上的悼词、诗歌创作、开玩笑等。

5. "车棒"(The Club)是一种阻塞汽车方向盘的装置,能使其免遭偷窃。下面是它的一个广告:

THE CLUB!(车棒)

Anti-theft device for cars(反盗车装置)

POLICE SAY:(警察说)

'USE IT'("用它")

OR LOSE IT(还是丢失它)

按照格赖斯理论,这里利用了什么准则?请找出两个同样的汉语广告。

这个广告主要利用了方式准则中的"避免歧义"这一条次则。其中的两个 it(它)指的不是同一个东西。类似的汉语广告是"买一送一";"要想皮肤好,早晚用大宝"。

6. A 正在看报纸,B 问他"What's on television tonight?"(今晚有什么电视节目?)他回答"Nothing."(什么也没有。)一般情况下,A 是什么意思?找出两种情况,使"Nothing"的这种含义能被取消。

这里的"Nothing"一般表示"Nothing interesting"(没什么有意思的节目)。如果 A 接着说"The workers are on strike"(工人正在罢工)或"There's going to be a blackout tonight"(今天晚上要停电),那么"Nothing interesting"这个解读就会被取消。

7. 在下列句子中,各组的 A 句都衍推 B 句吗?

(1) A. John is a bachelor.

   B. John is a man.

(2) A. Janet plays the fiddle.

   B. Someone plays a musical instrument.

(3) A. I've done my homework.

   B. I haven't brushed my teeth.

(4) A. Some of the students came to my party.

   B. Not all of the students came to my party.

(5) A. Mary owns three canaries.

   B. Mary owns a canary.

(6) A. John picked a tulip.

   B. John didn't pick a rose.

（1）Yes. （2）Yes. （3）No. （4）No. （5）Yes. （6）No.

8. 下列对话多少都有点问题，请问在多大程度上，这些问题能用格赖斯的合作原则及其准则加以解释？

(1) A：Have you seen Peter today?

   B：Well, if I didn't deny seeing him I wouldn't be telling a lie.

(2) A：Are you there?

   B：No, I'm here.

(3) A：Thank you for your help, you've been most kind.

   B：Yes, I have.

(4) A：Can you tell me where Mr Smith's office is?

   B：Yes, not here.

(5) A：Would you like some coffee?

   B：Mary's a beautiful dancer.

(6) A：Has the postman been?

   B：He leant his bicycle against the fence, opened the gate, strode briskly down the path, stopped to stroke the cat, reached into his bag, pulled out a bundle of letters and pushed them through our letter box.

在没有合适上下文的情况下，这些对话可以被看成是在利用格赖斯的合作原则及其准则开玩笑。

在第一个对话里，说话人B用一个冗长、烦琐的方式表达了"Yes, I have"（是的，我看见他了）的意思。他违反了"要简练（避免冗长）"这条方式准则。

在第二个对话里，说话人B利用了质量准则，表面上看起来他是在说实话，实际上他故意曲解了A的"there"的意思。

第三个对话里的(3B)是另一个利用质量准则的例子。从逻辑上讲，说话人B可能真的对A做出了很大的帮助，但是我们一般不这样回应别人的感谢。

从一个角度说,(4B)又是一个利用质量准则的例子。斯密斯先生的办公室真的"not here"(不在这里)。但是,从另一个角度说,说话人B违反了数量准则,他没有提供足够充分的信息量。说话人A需要的不仅仅是"not here",他需要更具体的信息。

(5B)是对说话人A的提议的一种间接拒绝。从格赖斯准则的角度说,说话人B违反了"要有关联"这个准则。

在最后一个对话里,说话人B用了一个冗长、烦琐的方式表达了一个简单的意思——"Yes, he has"(是的,他来过了),因而违反了"要简练(避免冗长)"这条方式准则。

第九章 语言与文学

1. 术语解释:

    第三人称叙述者(third-person narrator):如果叙述者不是虚拟世界中的角色,他或她常常被称为"第三人称叙述者",因为当故事虚构世界中的所有人物被提及时,用的都是第三人称代词"他、她、它或他们、它们"。这种类型的叙述者,据认为是占主导地位的叙述类型。

    第一人称叙述者(I-narrator):讲述故事的人也可以是故事虚构世界中的一个角色,在事件发生后讲述故事。在这种情形下,评论家们称叙述者为"第一人称叙述者"或"我—叙述者",因为叙述者在故事里提到他或她自己的时候,总是用第一人称代词"我"。第一人称叙述者常常被认为"有局限性",因为他们并不了解所有事实;或者被认为"不可靠",因为他们通过有保留地讲述信息或说谎来欺骗读者。此类情形常出现在凶杀和疑案推理小说中。

    自由间接引语(free indirect speech):自由间接引语的形式乍一看好像是间接引语,但又有直接引语的特征。明显的例子就是下面句子的后半句:"……并且希望他好多了"。该句的前半句"孩子问他怎样了……"明显是间接引语,传达了原句表达的内容,但没用原句中的词语。

    直接思维(direct thought):直接思维倾向于被用来表达意识中慎重的思想。比如:

    "他要迟到了",她想。

    意识流写作(stream of consciousness writing):"意识流"这一术语最早是由哲学家William James创造的。他在《心理学原理》(1890)一书中用该词描述头脑中观念与印象的自由联系。该词后来在20世纪初被威廉•福克纳、詹姆斯•乔伊斯、弗吉尼亚•沃尔夫等作家应用于小说写作,试验展现思维的自由流动。然而,应注意的是:小说中多数情况的思想表达并非意识流写作。本章我们讨论过的例子也不是意识流写作,因为他们太有序了，无法形成观念的自由联系。或许最著名的使用意识流手法的段落是乔伊斯的作品《尤利西斯》中描写 Leopold Bloom 的一段。文中，他在一家餐厅里思考着牡蛎：

> 脏兮兮的壳。撬开也麻烦得很。是谁发现的？垃圾、污水是它们的饲料。香槟就红岸牡蛎。对于性有效果。春……今天上午他在红岸餐厅。他会不会是桌上老牡蛎床上新鲜肉也许他不对六月没有 R 不吃牡蛎。① 可是有人就是喜欢吃不太新鲜的东西。变质的野味。坛子兔肉。首先你得逮住兔子呀。中国人存了五十年的鸭蛋，都变成蓝的绿的了。一顿饭三十道菜。每道菜都没有害处，吃下去却会混合起来的。用这个主意，可以设计一篇下毒疑案小说。（金堤译《尤利西斯》第 267 页）

这个曲折的认知过程全部是通过直接思想以最自由的形式来表达的。其另一特征是句子结构高度省略，尽最大可能将语法词都省略掉，使读者只能推断当时事态的发展。语言不太衔接，并且违反了格莱斯的数量准则和方式准则。但是我们必须假设：明显违背常理的写作行为是与相应的作者意图相联系的。这个假设就是：虽然 Joyce 显然使我们的阅读变得困难，但实际上他是在更深的层次上与我们合作。由此我们得出结论：他试图促使读者随他一起驰骋想象。

文本风格(text style)：文本风格紧密关注的是，语言选择如何帮助建构文本意义。正如可以说作者有风格一样，我们也可以说文本有风格。批评家们可以像讨论乔治·艾略特的风格一样，去讨论小说《米德尔马契》的风格，或者甚至讨论该小说某些部分的风格。观察文本或文本节选的风格时，同上面讨论过的作者风格的世界观模式相比，我们甚至更把关注焦点集中于意义。因此，当我们考察文本风格时，需要考察那些与意义有内在联系、并对读者产生影响的语言层面的选择。我们在本书中谈到的所有方面，都与其特定文本的意义及其风格相关：比如词汇方面和语法模式方面。甚至一些似乎不重要的东西的位置，如逗号的位置，有时对文本风格的解释非常重要。

2. 下面是 George Herbert（1593—1633）的诗《复活节翅膀》中的第一节，你能找出几种不同的语音模式？

> Lord, who createdst man in wealth and store,
> Though foolishly he lost the same,
> Decaying more and more,
> Till he became
> Most poore:
> With thee

---

① 西方谚语：在没有 R 的月份不宜吃牡蛎。六月的字母（June）中没有 R。

第九章　语言与文学　·147·

O let me rise
As larks, harmoniously,
And sing this day thy victories:
Then shall the fall further the flight in me.

　　头韵： store/same； Lord/lost； this/thy/then/the； fall/further/flight； more/me

　　准押韵：Lord/store/fall； Though/most； same/decaying

　　辅音韵：man/in

　　押韵： more/poore/store； became/same； thee/me/harmoniously

　　半押韵：rise/victories

　　反复：more/more； me/me

（Thornborrow and Wareing 1998/2000：218）

3. 找出下列例句中采用的比喻手法。
  1) 这个男孩像狐狸一样狡猾。
  2) ……天真的睡眠，……每天生命的死亡，……（莎士比亚）
  3) 白金汉宫已被告知，铁路系统私有化后，皇家专列可能会被砍掉。(《每日镜报》1993年2月2日)
  4) 特德·德克斯特昨天晚上说，英国队又进入了正确轨道，在盘算着今年冬天怎么击败印度队。(《每日镜报》1993年2月2日)
  1) 明喻　　2) 暗喻　　3) 转喻　　4) 提喻
4. 选择一个戏剧场景，仿照本章描述的步骤对其进行分析。这个场景可以是看过或读过的，可以是在电台广播中听到的(广播剧合集印刷版可以找到)，也可以是你正在研究的。
  1) 对场景进行解释；
  2) 对同一场景进行评论；
  3) 选取一个前面讨论过的话语特征，分析所选戏剧场景是如何使用该特征的，该特征又是如何作用于你的解释的。
  （自由答案）
5. 讨论同练习4第3个步骤相关的问题。你对该场景所做的话语分析是否改变了你对其进行的解释或评论？如果是，改变在何处？如何改变的？
  （自由答案）
6. 你对英国诗人 Philip Larkin 有所了解吗？
  菲利普·拉金(1922—1985)擅长表现流行于20世纪50年代的英语诗歌中含混的反浪漫主义的情愫，他是此类诗歌创作最具代表性的人物，备受时人推崇。他曾就读于牛津大学。(《梅里亚姆—韦伯斯特文学百科全书》1995年版)
7. 你如何看待文学研究中的认知分析？
  文学研究中的语言学分析和认知分析是互补的。认知分析有助于提高

语言学分析的质量,加强语言学分析的深度,提升语言学分析的价值。(Burke, 2005)

第十章 语言和计算机

1. 术语解释。

计算机语言学(computer linguistics):计算机语言学可以看做应用语言学的分支,即通过计算机处理人类语言。计算机语言学包括:对语言数据的分析;人工言语的电子生成(言语合成)和人类语言的自动识别;不同自然语言之间的自动翻译和语篇处理;人与计算机的交流。

计算机操作能力(computer literacy):对计算机硬件和软件的使用具有熟练的知识和技能。

言语合成(speech synthesis):电子生成人工言语。

计算机辅助语言学习(computer-assisted language learning, CALL):在第二语言或外语教学中使用计算机。

程序教学(programmed instruction):基于对语言材料进行分析后按学习者不同语法规则的顺序或某些特定项目的出现频率进行的教学。

局域网(LOCAL AREA NETWORKS, LAN):在教室、实验室或其他建筑里,通过光缆把计算机连接在一起,为教师和学生创造更多的活动,对目标语言提供更多的时间和经验。某些 LAN 设置允许学生和教师通过计算机互相通信,或指导学生用目标语言合作写作和对话。

光盘只读内存(COMPACT DISK-READ ONLY MEMORY, CD-ROM):可储存大量信息的磁盘,以便快速获取信息。近年来,许多外语计算机程序已经放在光盘上,淘汰了对过多软盘的需求。

机器翻译(MACHINE TRANSLATION, MT):指使用机器(通常为计算机)将语篇从一个自然语言翻译至另一个自然语言。机器翻译可以分为两类:不需帮助的和需要帮助的。

共现索引(Concordance):指数据分类的一种方式,如通过计算机,按字母顺序将出现在紧接着某个词的上下文里的词进行分类。

电子邮件(electronic mail, e-mail):同过互联网发送邮件、文件和图片。电子信箱,通过"电子邮件转发系统"(listserv 或 majodomo),可以帮助用户参与学术活动,或向一个电子论坛、学会或杂志订购书刊。

博客(weblog, blog):具有各种链接点和帖子的网络杂志,按逆年代顺序编排,最新的帖子出现在网页的上端。

谈话室(chatroom):一个网络论坛,人们可以在那里进行网络谈话(如与同一论坛的人们进行实时的谈话)。有时这些网址受到剪辑,或对谁讲话可加以限制(不常见),或由剪辑人员在该网址巡游,提防破坏性的或不受欢迎的行为。

互联网浏览器(Internet Explorer，IE)：微软公司推出的一款用于浏览网页的工具软件。

FYI(for your information)：供你参考

语料库(corpus)：在语言学和词典编纂学上，指语篇、语句或其他样本的集合，通常作为一个电子数据库储存。

计算机介入的信息交流(computer-mediated communication，CMC)：使用语篇分析的方法研究语言在计算机网络环境中使用的关系。以语篇为基础的 CMC 有多种形式，如电子邮件、讨论组、实时聊天、虚拟现实的角色扮演游戏等。

操练(drill and practice)：一种重点放在词汇和离散的语法点的教学方法。

慕课(MOOC)：大型开放式网络课程。

2. 在教育理念方面，计算机辅助教学(CAI)和计算机辅助学习(CAL)有何不同？

  计算机辅助教学是从教师的视角看教学问题的，而计算机辅助学习强调在教与学两方面使用计算机，目的是帮助学习者通过他们自己的推理和实践达到教学目标，这反映了最近发展的自主学习的理念。

3. 计算机辅助语言学习发展的 4 个阶段是什么？

  阶段 I. 第 1 阶段的计算机都是研究单位中的大型计算机。所存储的程序只能在一些大学的终端中接触到。

  阶段 II. 小型便携式计算机开始出现，价格降低。这使新一代程序的开发成为可能，并存储在磁盘和软盘上。

  阶段 III. 这一阶段的学习基于解决问题的认知技术，和小组中学生之间的互动，如采用角色扮演的活动。

  阶段 IV. 学生能在计算机上以非永久的形式编写和创作。这阶段使用了多媒体技术。这导致智能计算机辅助语言学习(intelligent CALL，ICALL)的发展。

4. 语言学方法在机器翻译研究中是否成功？为什么？

  不太成功。这涉及多个理论。人们也发现这些新理论初期阶段在小样本中是成功的，最后却问题很多。

5. 你对基于知识的方法有何看法？

  为改进机器翻译系统需要 3 种类型的知识，即不依赖语境的语言学知识(语义学)，有关语境的语言学知识(语用学)，和有关世界的常识(非语言学的)。前两个方面关系到语言，但包含双语词典和语法知识不能保证产生优质的翻译。更有甚者，计算机缺乏真实世界的语言使研究者困扰不已。计算机不懂得事物彼此之间的关系或相互契合。

6. 你对于机器翻译和人工翻译之间的关系有何看法？

  如果翻译要达到"可出版"的质量，人工翻译和机器翻译都要发挥作用。

人工翻译对非重复的语言学上复杂的语篇(如文学和法律),甚至特定的高度专业化的技术专题的一次性语篇来说,现在和将来都不能被胜出。对那些翻译质量不很重要的语篇,机器翻译是理想的方法。

7. 从下面各组选择项中选取正确的答案。
   a. 在识别资料中的歧义时,定性分析是没有用的。
      错误
   b. 语料库 A 的 350,000 个词有 615 个"get"的实例,语料库 B 的 20,000 个词中有 35 个"get"的实例,哪个语料库有最大比例的"get"?
      语料库 B
   c. 根据下面的数据进行词频分析时,哪个词具有最大频率?
      bat 16   bats 2   batting 1
      batty 4   can 22   clock 16
      locked 4   dark 7   darkening 11
      gave 11   give 6   given 3
      gives 1
      bat/can/clock/dark/give

8. 如何看待乔姆斯基对语料库语言学的批评和语料库语言学的重新兴起?
   乔姆斯基认为语料库从来不是语言学家的有用工具,因为语言学家必须寻找理想的语言能力,而不是语言行为。其次,解释一个语言的语法的唯一方法是描写它的规则,而不是枚举它的句子。第三,语言不是有限的构建。在实践中,乔姆斯基尚未找到理想的模式。计算机的奇迹宣告了语料库语言学的新生。计算机有能力在语篇中查找某个词,一连串的词,甚至某段言语。计算机也可以检索某个词的所有实例,通常是有语境的,这对语言学家帮助很大。计算机也可统计该词的出现频率,从而采集到有关该词词频的信息。我们还可整理这些数据,例如在上下文中按字母排序。

9. 博客(blog)和谈话室(chatroom)有何不同?
   有的人认为博客具有评论功能,与谈话室一样;但有些人认为博客不是谈话室,因为除此以外,博客是以帖子为中心按年代排列的;任何具有网络联系条件者都可以发行自己的网络博客;网络博客一般都利用链接,使读者能按有关主题的条目之间的链接跟踪网络博客之间的会话。

10. 为什么谈话室有时会受到监听?
    网民虽然可以自由进入谈话室,并能自由发表自己的任何观点,有些谈话室还是要监听,以杜绝那些不能接受的、冒犯的、种族歧视的、暴力的,以至色情的内容。

11. cMOOC 和 xMOOC 有何区别?
    cMOOC 中的字母 c 指"连接主义者"(connectivist)。连接型慕课强调连接主义哲学,同行评议和集体合作。学习材料是凑合的而不是预先制定的，从新融合，从新说理，为将来做准备。对比之下，字母 x 指"扩展的"（extended），扩展型慕课代表比较传统的课程，有清楚的特定的教学大纲，包括预先录制的讲课录音和自测的问题。讲师是专家型的知识提供者，学生的活动限于寻求帮助和在难点上互相提示。

12. 微信为何比谈话室和脸书更为先进？

    微信能提供文字信息，说话信息，一人对多人的信息，视频会议，视频游戏，图片和电视，不受地域限制。照片可以润饰，有机器翻译服务。

13. 下面的字首组合词（acronyms）和数字代表什么？

    | AND | AISI | B4 |
    | CU | DIY | EOD |
    | F/F | FYA | G2G |
    | GA | HAGD | HLM |
    | IDC | IHU | JAM |
    | JK | KIT | LHM |
    | LMA | NM | PM |
    | Q4Y | SYS | TA |
    | TTUL | U2 | VBS |
    | W8 | WB | Y |
    | YATB | WW4U | |

    答案见本书第 72 页。

14. 你能猜到下面的表情符号或"笑眯眯"的意义吗？

    | :-* | :{ }: | :< | (-: | :-() |
    | :OI | XD | :) | :-D | \|-I |

    | :-* | 笑眯眯地吻 | :{}: | 两人谈话 |
    | :< | 非常哀伤的笑眯眯 | (-: | 左撇子笑眯眯 |
    | :-() | 吼叫 | :OI | 嘴巴塞满东西 |
    | XD | 极其滑稽的大笑 | :) | 懒汉的标准笑眯眯 |
    | :-D | 大笑 | \|-I | 睡着了 |

第十一章　二语教学与外语教学

1. 为什么语言教师要学习一些语言学知识？

    对于语言教师而言，掌握一些语言学的知识不仅有助于他们进一步领悟语言本质，也有助于他们深入理解教学方法。语言学理论直接或间接地影响着语言教学的途径和方法。为了使教学活动更加行之有效，教师们有必要学习一种（或者多种）语言学理论；他们至少应该了解自己教的那门语言都有哪些规则。要发现真实的语言并且对他们有所理解，语言教师也需要一些语言学知识。很多语言学习理论是基于语言学理论建立的。事实上,如果要了解语言学习者们能够学到什么,怎样学习,和最终能够到达什么水平,我们最根本地还是要学习一些语言本身的知识。因此,语言学在语言习得和语言学习领域内扮演着十分重要的角色。

2. 什么是 FOCUS ON FORM?

　　FOCUS ON FORM 的要点是认为虽然语言学习总体上应以关注意义为中心,为交流服务,我们偶尔关注语言形式仍然是有益并且是必要的。"关注语言形式"的做法是在理解或语言输出遇到问题时,教师和/或一个或多个学生暂时将注意力转移到某个语法规则上。

3. 什么是输入假设(Input Hypothesis)?

　　根据 Krashen (1985) 的输入假设,学习者们习得语言是理解输入的结果。Krashen 提出 i+1 原则,也就是说学习者们接触到的语言应该稍高于他们的现有水平,这样他们既可以理解大部分的语言又可以面对一定的挑战从而取得更大的进步。输入既不能难度过大让人望而生畏,也不能过于接近学习者现有的水平,而不具有任何挑战性。

4. 什么是中介语(interlanguage)? 你能举例说明么?

　　正在学习过程中的第二语言或者外语学习者构建的语言通常被称为中介语。中介语通常被理解为是介于目标语和学习者母语之间的语言。跟目标语相比它还不够完美,但它也不只是学习者母语的简单翻译。然而,我们也不应该把中介语看成是母语和目标语的过渡阶段或者是简单的混合,中介语是一个动态语言系统,它不断地从初级水平向母语水准发展。因此,中介语的"中"实际上表示的是在开始阶段和最终阶段之间。中介语的例子有很多,例如 I no have a book. I like read books.

5. 基于语篇的语言教学观是什么?

　　以语篇为基础的语言观最重要的一点是把语言看做存在于语境中的语段。词汇、从句和句子一向是传统语言学研究的关注对象,而语篇语言学认为语言超越了这些单位(McCarthy & Carter, 1994)。以语篇为基础的语言观研究的是口头和书面的完整语篇以及这些语篇存在的社会和文化语境。相应地,以语篇为基础的语言教学目的在于培养学习者的语篇能力。

6. 真实任务和教学任务分别是什么? 你能否给出例子?

　　真实任务与我们在日常生活或工作中要开展的活动非常接近。例如,学生以小组的形式讨论他们学校的运动器材怎样得到改进(例如,买一些新的器材),并且他们要给校长提出一些建议。这类的活动属于真实世界的活动,因为在生活中我们会遇到这样的问题。教学任务是那些学生只是在教室中开展,在生活中不会发生的活动。例如,学生两人一组,各自拿到一张图片,图片上的大部分内容是相同的,但是还有一些不同之处。活动要求双方通过各自向对方描述自己的图片来找出这些不同。在这个活动中,学习者运用语言来做具体的事情,也就是找出两幅图片的不同。在完成这个活动的过程中,学习者主要关注的是语言的意义而不是形式,因为活动并不是要求他们练习某些特定的语言片段。我们把这种活动定义为教学任务,因为在真实世界中我们不会遇到这种情况。这类活动是专门为教学所设计,目的是来帮助学习者们学习或者复习某些语言知识或者技能。但是这里并不是说真实情况的活动就没有任何教学上的用途。

7. 对于教学大纲设计者而言,最重要的任务是什么?

外语教学中大纲设计过程主要包括选择和排列教学内容。对所学的内容进行选择是不可避免的,因为学习语言的整个体系既不现实也没有必要。选择的过程包括两个步骤:首先,把语言限定在某个特定的方言和语域内。第二,根据一定的标准,例如出现的频率、难易度,或者课堂需求等从所选语域中进一步选择要学习的语言。整个的过程应该在语言的所有层次上进行,例如语音、语法、词汇、语境(语义的或者文化的)。在选择了一系列的语言点后,下一个步骤就是要按照实际的教学目的合理地安排教学的先后顺序。

8. 什么是结构教学大纲?

受到结构主义语言学的影响,结构主义大纲主要以语法教学为导向,以语言结构为基础。大纲编写者参考出现频率、复杂程度和有用程度等因素精心安排大纲中出现的词汇和语法规则在教学中的先后顺序。大纲是根据语法规则的难易度来建构的。这类大纲每一单位课时介绍一个语言点,并且要求在学习下一个语言点之前要完全掌握前面的知识点。

9. 结构教学大纲常受到人们的批判。你认为结构大纲是否也有其可取之处?

结构教学大纲主要的不足在于它只关注语法结构和单个词语的意义,而认为长句的意义是显而易见所以不用讲解的,而且不考虑语境的因素。学生没有学会在真实的语境下去地道地使用语言。结果是,被结构大纲教出来的学生们往往缺少实际交际的能力。但是,结构大纲也有一些优点。例如,许多学生通过学习语法来学习语言会感到很舒服。在许多环境下,老师和学生都希望在大纲和教材中看到语法。此外,系统的语法为大纲设计提供了便利的指导。

10. 任务型大纲中所定义的任务都有哪些特点?

(1) 任务要目的明确;
(2) 任务要与真实事件有某种程度的相似;
(3) 任务要涉及信息搜寻、加工和传递;
(4) 任务要使学生以一定的方式做事情;
(5) 任务要集中在表达意义上;
(6) 任务结束后要有明确的结果。

11. 什么是非语言结果?

(1) 情感态度的培养,如自信心、动机、兴趣;

(2) 学习策略、思维技巧、人际交往能力等；

(3) 文化意识。

12. 什么是对比分析(Contrastive Analysis)？

　　对比分析是通过对比不同语言(如第一语言和第二语言)来确定潜在错误的方法，从而把第二语言学习环境下必须学习的和不必学习的东西最终区分开来。对比分析的目的是为了预测哪些领域容易学得，哪些领域不易学得。对比分析早期与行为主义和结构主义相关。

13. 错误和失误有何区别？你能指出下列句子中的错误和失误吗？

　　1. I bought in Japan.
　　2. These dog are big.
　　3. He was arrived early.
　　4. Joe doesn't likes it.
　　5. Why didn't you came to school.
　　6. I doesn't know how.
　　7. She has been smoking less, isn't it?
　　8. I falled from the bike.
　　9. I no have it.
　　10. Why they look at each other?
　　11. I know what is that.
　　12. Although he was ill, but he still came.
　　13. I go to the university yesterday.
　　14. Teacher said he is right.

　　语误通常是由于学习者知识不足所致，说明能力不足。换言之，学习者不知道正确的形式或者不能正确地使用语言。当学习者没有发挥出自己的能力时就会出现差错，也就是说，学习者已经学会了某种知识或技能，但是由于不注意或者其他因素的影响而没能正确地使用语言。

14. 什么是语料库？你能否举例说明语料库对语言教学有何作用？

　　语料库是输入到计算机中一大批语料的结集。语料库为教材编写人员选择真实、自然、典型的语言提供了可能。语料库中两个最重要的因素是所选材料的长度和类型。一般来说，对语料库的使用决定了语料库中材料的数量和类型。参见11.6.2节的讨论。

第十二章　现代语言学理论与流派

1. 为什么索绪尔被尊为现代语言学之父？

　　索绪尔第一个注意到语言的复杂性。他认为语言是一个符号系统。为了交流思想，符号必须是整个符号系统的一部分，即"惯例"。他指出符号是形式(能指)和意义(所指)的结合，是语言的核心事实。

通过回答与语言多方面相关的问题，索绪尔明确了语言作为一门科学所要研究的对象。他关于符号的任意性和语言单位的相关性的思想，以及对"语言"和"言语"、"历时"和"共时"的区分等等，把语言学推进到一个崭新的阶段。

2. 布拉格学派的三个重要观点是什么？

布拉格学派提出三个特别重要的观点。第一，它强调对语言的共时研究是完全正确的，因为共时研究可以利用全面的、可控制的语言材料；第二，布拉格学派强调语言的系统性，指出任何语言的任何成分都不可能在孤立状态下得到令人满意的分析或评价。换言之，语言成分之间有功能性的对照或对立；第三，布拉格学派把语言视为语言社团用来完成一系列基本功能或任务的工具。

3. 布拉格学派最著名的学说是什么？

布拉格学派最闻名的功绩在于它对音韵学的贡献，以及对语音学和音位学的区分。继索绪尔区分"语言"和"言语"之后，Trubetzkoy 依提出语音学属于"言语"，而音位学属于"语言"。在此基础上，他提出"音位"的概念，即语音系统的抽象单位，区别于实际发出的声音。

为了对音位的区别性特征进行分类，Trubetzkoy 提出三条标准：(1) 它们与整个对立系统的关系；(2) 对立成分之间的关系；(3) 区别力的大小。这些对立可归纳为：a) 双边对立；b) 多边对立；c) 均衡对立；d) 孤立对立；e) 否定对立；f) 分级对立；g) 等价对立；h) 中和对立；i) 永恒对立。

4. 功能句子观的本质是什么？

句子功能观是指对话语或文本所包含的信息进行语言学分析的理论。其原则是，话语中各部分的作用取决于该部分对全句意义的贡献。一些捷克斯洛伐克语言学家从功能的角度出发，认为一个句子总是包含一个"出发点"和一个"语篇目标"。出发点对说话人和听话人来说都是存在的——这是把他们的结合点——交会的地方——叫做"主位"。语篇目标是要传送给听话人的信息，叫做"述位"。从主位到述位的运动，揭示了大脑自身的运动。不同的语言可能采用不同的句法结构，但是表达思想的次序基本相同。基于这些观察，布拉格语言学家提出了"功能句子观"(FSP)这个概念，用以描述信息是如何在句子里分布的。功能句子观特别阐释了语篇中已知信息和新信息分布的效果。已知信息是指那些对于读者或听话者来说并非新的信息，而新信息是指那些将要传送给读者或听话者的信息。

5. 伦敦学派的传统是什么？

伦敦学派具有强调语言功能的传统，并且重视语言环境和语言的系统性。正是因为这些特征，伦敦学派的思想被视做系统语言学和功能语言学。他们认为不同类型的语言学描写适合于不同的目的，这是伦敦学派传统中一个重要而且很宝贵的思想。

6. Malinowski 与 Firth 对情景语境的看法有何不同？

　　Malinowski 区分了三种情景语境：言语与当时身体活动相关的情景，叙述情景和寒暄情景。而 Firth 对情景语境的定义包括言语的整个文化背景和参与者的个人历史，而不仅仅是人类活动进行之时的情景。Firth 发现句子的变化是无穷的，于是他提出了"典型情景语境"的概念，即社会环境决定了人们必须扮演的社会角色。因为典型情景语境的总数是有限的，所以社会角色也是有限的。他还提出，在分析典型情景语境时，应该同时考虑话语的情景环境和语言环境。

7. Firth 的韵律分析法有什么重要性？

　　韵律分析法，或称韵律音位学，是 Firth 对语言学的第二个重大贡献。人的话语是一个连续的语流，由至少一个音节组成，不能被切分为若干独立的单位。音位描写仅仅描写聚合关系，而没有考虑组合关系。Firth 指出，在实际言语中构成聚合关系的不是音位，而是准音位单位。准音位单位的特征比音位少，因为有些特征是一个音节或短语（甚至句子）的音位所共有的。这些共有特征被纳入组合关系中，统称为韵律单位，包括重音、音长、鼻化、硬腭化和送气等特征。在任何情况下，这些特征不会单独存在在于一个准韵律单位中。

8. 系统语法与功能语法是什么关系？

　　系统语法和功能语法是系统功能语法理论这一完整框架中不可分离的两个部分。系统语法的目标是把语言当做一个系统网络或是"意义潜势"来解释其内部关系。这个网络包含语言使用者做出选择的各种子系统。功能语法的目标是要揭示语言是社会交流的手段，其思想基础是，语言的系统和形式是不可避免地被它们的使用者或语言所发挥的功能所决定。系统语法中有一个功能性的成分，功能语法后面的理论是系统性的。

9. 系统功能语言学的特殊之处是什么？

　　系统功能语言学的目标是为句子提供一套分类法，为特殊的句子描述性分类提供方法。尽管系统功能语法在世界某些地方似乎不如乔姆斯基的转换生成语法理论影响巨大，但它更贴近研究语言的不同人群的需要。

　　韩礼德认为语言之所以成为语言，在于语言必须完成一定的功能。换言之，语言的社会需求帮助语言形成了自身的结构。

　　系统功能语言学建立在以下两个事实之上：(1)语言的使用者实际上是在一个由多个系统形成的系统中不断地进行选择，并试图在社会交际过程中实现不同的语义功能；(2)语言与人类的社会活动不可分割。因此，它把语言的实际运用当作研究对象。这一点与乔姆斯基把理想化的讲话人的语言能力当做研究对象恰恰相反。

10. 分析下列句子,先确定其主语和谓语,然后确定其主位和述位。
    (1) Mary gave her daughter a birth day gift.
        主语　　　谓语
        主位　　　述位
    (2) A birthday present was given to Jenny.
        主语　　　　　　　谓语
        主位　　　　　　　述位
        (3) The play was written by William Shakespeare.
            主语　　　谓语
            主位　　　述位
        (4) Do have another drink.
            谓语
            主位　　　述位

11. 根据韩礼德的系统和精密度概念,用图解法表示以下词条。
    (1) she　　(2) we　　(3) always　　(4) 识别过程　　(5) 动作过程
    (1) she(人称:第三人称;单数)
    (2) we(人称:第一人称;复数)
    (3) always(情态:频率)
    (4) 识别过程(及物性:心理过程:内化过程)
    (5) 行动过程(及物性:物质过程)

12. 根据形式和类型,分析下列关系过程句子。
    (1) Linguistics is a difficult course.
    (2) This laptop is Professor Huang's.
    (1) 类型:内包式;形式:归属
    (2) 类型:所有式;形式:识别

13. 从两个层次分析以下句子。在第　层面确定主语、限定成分、谓语和附加语,在第二层面确定语气和剩余成分。如果两个分析层面有所不同,请给出解释。
    (1) Mr Hu made a speech at a conference yesterday.
    (2) The university present has been awarded an international prize.
    (3) Three days ago, an honorary title was given to a professor from Yale.

Mr Hu		made		a speech at the conference yesterday.
主语	限定成分	谓语		附属语
语气		剩余成分		

The university president		has		been awarded	an international prize.
主语		限定成分		谓语	附属语
语气				剩余成分	

Three days ago,	an honorary title was		given	to a professor from Yale.
附属语	主语	限定成分	谓语	附属语
剩余成分	语气			剩余成分

14. 从元功能的三个层面分析下列句子。
(1) John likes linguistics.
(2) The paper was handed in three days later.

概念意义 心理过程:反应	John	likes	linguistics
	感觉者	过程:心理:反应	现象
人际意义 陈述	语气		剩余成分
	主语	谓语	附属语
语篇意义 无标记主位	主位	述位	
	已知信息	新信息	

概念意义 物质过程:动作/被动	The paper	was handed in	three days later
	目标/被动	过程:物质:动作	
人际意义 陈述	语气		剩余成分
	主语	谓语	附属语
语篇意义 无标记主位	主位	述位	
	已知信息	新信息	

15. 什么是"适用语言学"?

"适用语言学"不同于"应用语言学",以韩礼德2006年3月在香港城市大学的演讲为标志。韩礼德认为,语言理论以消费者为基本导向。他在2008年出版的《语言的互补》一书中讨论了词汇与语法的互补、作为系统的语言、作为语篇的语言、说与写等,旨在建立一个具有"适用性"的连贯语言解释,并不是要构建某种强大的理论机制。2010年出版的论文集《适用语言学》和2014年上海交大成立的马丁适用语言学研究中心,支持了韩礼德的主张。

适用语言学研究语言理论的发展和评价,主要包括几个原则:理论与实践的一体性;语言即意义,意义即选择;社会理据;多模态研究。系统功能语言学理论的研究对象和应用在不断发展和完善,旨在迎接新的挑战并解决新的问题。"适用性"概念要求理论与实践要顺应新的形势。适用语言学不是系统功能语言学的一家之言,而是对所有语言学流派有用的理论。适用语言学也不限于语言学领域,对符号学和其他相关学科也有适用价值。

16. 美国结构主义的特征是什么？

　　美国结构主义是共时语言学的一支，但其发展风格与欧洲完全不同。欧洲的语言学始于两千多年前，而美国的语言学却始于19世纪末。传统语法在欧洲大陆占据统治地位，而在美国的影响却微乎其微。欧洲许多语言都有自己的历史传统和文化，而在美国居统治地位的只有英语，因此美国没有欧洲那样的传统。此外，美国的先驱学者面临着一个极为紧迫的任务——记录那些正在迅速消亡的土著美国印第安人的语言，因为这些语言没有书面记录。然而，这些语言之奇特、多样性之大、差异之明显是世界上其他地方不多见的。为了记录和描写这些奇异的语言，也许最好对语言的普遍特征不要有先入为主的假设。这就可以解释为什么这一时期的语言学在理论上没有大的发展，而关于语言描写程序的讨论却又如此之多。

　　结构主义基于以下假设：语法范畴应该通过分布而非意义来定义，并且描写任何一种语言的结构都不应该涉及诸如时态、语气和词性等所谓的普遍性。第一，结构主义语法只描写语言中所发现的一切，而不是制定规则。然而，它的目标被局限于对语言进行描写，而没有解释为什么语言按照自己的方式运作。第二，结构主义语法是经验主义的，非常注重客观性，认为所有的定义和表述要么是可证实的，要么是可证伪的。然后，结构主义语法几乎没有产生一部完整的、能与传统语法书比美的语法书。第三，结构主义语法考察所有的语言，认可并且公正对待每种语言的独特性，但却没有充分对待意义。第四，结构主义语法不仅描写了语言的特殊用法，甚至还阐述了语言结构或语言现象后面存在的最小差别。

17. 行为主义心理学与语言学有何关系？

　　在布龙菲尔德看来，语言学是心理学的一个分支，特别是实证主义心理学即"行为主义"的一个分支。行为主义是一种科学研究方法，建立在如下认识之上：人类无法知道他们所未经历之事。语言学的行为主义认为儿童通过一连串的"刺激—反应—强化"来学习语言，而成年人对语言的使用也是一个"刺激—反应"的过程。当行为主义的方法论经由布龙菲尔德的著作进入语言学研究以后，语言学研究的普遍做法就是接受一个本族语者的话语本身，而舍弃他对自己语言的评论。这是由于当时认为，只有基于说话人自然话语的语言描述才是可靠的；反之，如果分析者通过询问说话人诸如"你的语言能否说……？"之类的问题，他做出的语言描述则是不可靠的。

18. 哈里斯对语言学最重要的贡献是什么？

　　哈里斯的《结构语言学的方法》(1951)标志着美国描写语言学的成熟，因为他以最为完整而有趣的笔触描述了以精确分析程序和高度形式化为特征的"发现程序"。他以分布关系的逻辑作为结构分析的基础，构建了一套严格的描写程序。这种方法极大地影响了美国描写语言学，哈里斯因此被誉为后布龙菲尔德时期最杰出的语言学家之一。

19. 法位学的理论重要性是什么？

　　法位学是由继承结构主义传统最重要的学者 Pike 提出的语言分析技术的一个专有名称。Pike 认为，语言具有独立于意义之外的等级系统。不仅语言存在等级，世间万物都是有等级的，其系统由从小到大、从底层到顶层、从简单到复杂、从部分到整体的各种层级构成。法位学的最终目的在于提供一套整合词汇、语法和语音信息的理论。这个理论基于以下假设，即在语言中存在各种关系，而且这些关系能被分解为不同的单位。然而，为了相信语言是人类行为的一部分，人们必须认识到语言是不能被严格地形式化的。既然没有表达系统能够解释所有与语言相关的事实，那么法位学便采用不同的表达模式为不同的目的服务，并且不再坚持世上只有唯一正确的语法或语言理论。

20. 层次语法的主要特征是什么？

　　Lamb 的层次语法由三个层级构成：音位、词素和词素音位。由于它假设尽管关系系统不能直接观测但却可以进行概括，因此便将语言中的复杂关系视为相互连接的层状系统。在层次语法中，概念与语音没有直接关系，而且不同层级构成了大量层次系统。其中主要的四个：从上到下依次是语义系统、词汇系统、词素系统和音位系统。

21. 乔姆斯基的转换生成语法经历了几个发展阶段？

　　乔姆斯基的转换生成语法经历了五个发展阶段：古典理论旨在使语言学成为一门科学。标准理论论述如何在语言学理论中研究语义学。扩展的标准理论集中讨论语言的普遍性和普遍语法。修正的扩展标准理论（或称管约理论）主要讨论管辖和约束。最近一个阶段即最简方案，是对以前理论的进一步修正。

　　转换生成语法的发展可被视为不断简化理论和控制生成能力的过程。尽管转换生成语法经历了提出、修改和抛弃很多具体规则、假说、机制和理论模型的过程，它的目的和意图却始终如一，即探索人类语言的本质、起源和有关语言知识的运用。

22. 乔姆斯基所说的语言习得机制是什么？

　　乔姆斯基认为语言是某种天赋，儿童天生就具有一种独一无二的、适合语言学习的知识，即"语言习得机制"(LAD)。他指出，儿童生来就拥有独特的天赋才能——不仅是普遍的潜力，而且还有关于世界本质的知识，尤其是关于语言本质的知识。根据这种观点，儿童生来便具备基本语法关系和范畴的知识，而且这种知识是人类共有的。这些语法范畴和关系存在于一切人类语言，有助于揭示人脑的本质。

　　乔姆斯基认为，人类大脑中基本的语言组织使得儿童可以不用家人或朋友的指导而获得极为复杂的语言能力。乔姆斯基还指出语言习得机制可能包含三个要素：假说机制、语言普遍性和评价程序。

23. 画出以下句子的树形图。
   (1) The police attacked the suspect.
   (2) The Children cannot understand her painting.

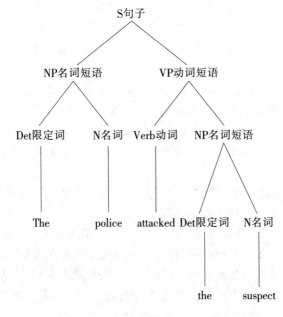

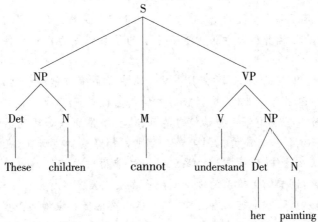

24. 请解释为什么生成语法能够生成正确的句子(如"玛丽读书")而不能生成不合格的句子(如 *"书读玛丽")。
    标准理论有选择性的限制来排除这种不合格的句子。它能确保在主动语态中有生命的名词，而无生命的名词出现在动词之后。

25. 为什么"约翰杀死约翰"这样的句子能够被转换成"约翰杀死自己"?
    反身规则(Reflexive Rule)规定：在简单句中一个名词出现两次，那么第二次必须使用反身形式。所以在"约翰杀死约翰"中，第二个"约翰"变成了"(他)自己"。

26. 转换生成语法的特殊之处是什么?

　　乔姆斯基转换生成语法的出发点在于天赋假设。这一假设建立在他对一些其他方式无法充分解释的重要现象的观察之上。

　　乔姆斯基的转换生成语法具备如下特征:第一,乔姆斯基将语言定义为一套规则或规律。第二,乔姆斯基认为语言学的目的在于建立一套能够捕获本族语人默认知识的生成语法。这就涉及学习理论和语言普遍性的问题。第三,乔姆斯基和他的追随者对任何能够揭示本族语人默认知识的资料都极感兴趣。他们很少使用本族语人实际的话语,而是依赖自己的直觉。第四,乔姆斯基的研究方法是假说—演绎,他将这种方法运用在两个层面上:(a)语言学家提出关于语言结构的假设——语言的普遍理论,由个别语言的语法加以验证;(b)每一个个别语法又是关于语言普遍理论的假设。第四,乔姆斯基继承了哲学上的理性主义和心理学上的心灵主义。

27. 乔姆斯基的语言学理论有什么最新发展?

　　乔姆斯基的《最简方案》(1995)一书标志着生成语法理论进入一个崭新阶段。最简方案产生的动因,涉及两个相互联系的问题:(1)人类语言官能应该满足的普遍条件是什么?(2)如果不考虑普遍条件以外的特殊结构,语言官能在多大程度上受这些普遍条件支配?这一新理论有几个显著变化。首先,它抛弃了以前管约理论中一些分离式的分析模型和两个分析层面。其次,抛弃了一个重要概念"管辖",用几个修正的概念代替了管辖理论解释的语言事实,因此管辖理论由普遍语法的子系统变为输出条件的解释性制约。

　　20 世纪 90 年代末,乔姆斯基重新考虑了最简方案的动因,以做出更加明确的解释。他认为,人类语言的初始状态相同,而获得不同语言的状态却不同。普遍语法是研究初始状态的理论,而个别语法是研究具体语言获得状态的理论。语言能力机制包含一个可以储存诸如声音、意义和结构之类信息的认知系统,而语言运用系统调取并使用这些信息。他提出了一个深奥的问题:语言能力机制的设计到底有多么完美?他想象了一个实例,一种灵长类动物,除了没有语言官能,与人类没有两样。假如某个事件重组了其大脑,使它具有语言能力机制。这一新机制要能顺利运行,必须满足"可理解条件",且它的大脑其他系统必须能够理解这一新机制生成的表达式。另一方面,新机制发出的指令要能被大脑的其他系统识别和接受。因此,乔姆斯基提出了彻底的最简方案理论:语言能力机制是解决可理解条件问题的最佳办法。

　　21 世纪初,乔姆斯基的重心转移到了跨学科视角和语言官能的生物学问题。2002 年,他与两位心理学家一道指出,理解语言能力机制需要大量的跨学科协作,语言学完全可以与进化生物学、人类学、心理学和神经科学的研究结合。在2007年发表的论文里,他追溯了生物语言学的发展历程,从其最早的哲学渊源到20世纪50年代的认知革命,勾画了生物语言学研究在这幅图景里的地位。他认为,人的语言发展依赖于三个因素:基因因素、经验和一般原则。他说道,我们对人类思维的进化和大脑了解得太少,迈出研究的第一步都异常艰难。尽管需要做大量工作才能搞清楚"大脑的组织结构"和"语言的创造性与连贯的日常使用"等相关问题,但只要我们明确设定合理的目标并一步步做出有理有据的解释,就会更清楚地弄清语言的普遍性。

转换生成语法理论的发展其实是一个不断简化理论和控制生成力的过程,最简方案和最简探索正是这一过程中符合逻辑的发展步骤。尽管转换生成语法提出、修正并取消了许多具体规则、假设、机制及理论模式,但他的目标和总之始终没有变化,即探索人类语言知识的本质、来源及使用。

28. 格语法是什么?

格语法是生成语言学的一个方法,着重研究句子成分之间关系。在这一语法体系中,动词被视为句子中最重要的部分,它与不同名词短语之间的关系被定义为"格"。

菲尔墨的论点之假设是,句法在确定格的时候起关键作用,而且隐性的范畴很重要。格在简单句子中出现的不同方式,决定了一种语言中的句子类型和动词类型。

格语法表明了一些概念之间的语义关联,如施事、原因、地点、利益等等。这些概念在语言中极易辨认,而且许多心理学家认为它们在儿童语言习得中发挥着重要作用。

29. 生成语义学是什么?

生成语义学的形成是对乔姆斯基以句法为基础的转换生成语法的反叛。这一理论认为所有句子都由语义结构生成。持有这一理论的语言学家认为在句法过程和语义过程之间没有原则性的区别。这一观点还有一些辅助性的假说作为补充。第一,乔姆斯基于1965年提出的纯句法的深层结构这一层面并不存在;第二,在各种语言中,对派生的最初描述与其逻辑描述是相同的;第三,意义的各个方面都可以用短语标记形式来描述。换言之,句子的派生是从语义学到表层结构的直接转换映射。

尽管生成语义学已不再被视为一个可行的语法模型,但它在许多方面有重要的意义。首先,正是生成语义学家率先对转换规则所不能形式化的句法现象进行深入探讨。其次,生成语义学家最初争论的许多提议后来出现在解释主义的文献中。最后,生成语义学家在各种话题上的重大开创性研究越来越受到人们重视。

30. 为什么要学习语言学理论及流派?

学习任何理论或流派都涉及历史。现代语言学其实始于18世纪。与人类知识和学术的其他领域一样,语言学有历史也有未来,它是历史的产物,也是未来的基础。一门科学的历史,其重要性在于它有助于让我们看清现在并展望未来。了解历史,就会发现语言学家要质疑(如果不全盘抛弃)的许多观点本来就是有问题的。历史知识不仅能让我们学会质疑传统学说,而且能让我们发展和重整这些学说。在学习语言学理论的过程中,我们不仅看到过去几十年的巨大进步,也能看到自古至今语言学史的连续发展。学习语言学理论与流派,可以开阔我们的视野。语言学是在世界上许多不同的地方发展起来的。不同的语言学家所处的学术环境不同,受到的影响不同,因此对待语言的理论和研究方法也不同。每一种理论都有其哲学、历史、社会文化传统。出于许多原因,在许多情况下,不同学派所关注的问题不一样。不了解某一个理论,这不是大问题;但如果只守着一个理论,那则是大问题。赛福生在《语言学流派》里写道:做学术(也许尤其是语言学)的最大危险不是一个人可能没掌握一个思想流派,而是一个流派掌握了人的思想。

《语言学教程》(第五版)练习册

尊敬的老师：

　　您好！

　　为了方便您更好地使用本教材，获得最佳教学效果，我们特向使用该书作为教材的教师赠送本教材配套课件资料。如有需要，请完整填写"教师联系表"并加盖所在单位系(院)公章，免费向出版社索取。

北京大学出版社

教 师 联 系 表

教材名称	《语言学教程》(第五版)练习册			
姓名：	性别：	职务：		职称：
E-mail：	联系电话：		邮政编码：	
供职学校：		所在院系：		（章）
学校地址：				
教学科目与年级：		班级人数：		
通信地址：				

　　填写完毕后，请将此表邮寄给我们，我们将为您免费寄送本教材配套资料，谢谢！

北京市海淀区成府路205号
北京大学出版社外语编辑部　刘文静　外语编辑部电话：010-62754382
邮政编码：100871　　　　　　　　　　邮 购 部 电 话：010-62534449
电子邮箱：liuwenjing008@163.com　市场营销部电话：010-62750672